P9-DFI-977

*Human Rights
Treaties and the
Senate*

NATALIE HEVENER KAUFMAN

Human Rights Treaties and the Senate

A History of Opposition

The University
of North
Carolina Press

Chapel Hill
and London

The paper in this book meets the guidelines for per-
manence and durability of the Committee on Production Guidelines for Book Longevity of the Council on
Library Resources.

94 93 92 91 90   5 4 3 2 1

Library of Congress Cataloging-in-Publication Data

Kaufman, Natalie Hevener.
    Human rights treaties and the Senate : a history
of opposition / by Natalie Hevener Kaufman.
        p.   cm.
    Includes bibliographical references.
    ISBN 0-8078-1922-0 (alk. paper)
    1. Human rights—History.   2. Human rights—
United States—History.   3. Treaties—Reservations—
History.   I. Title.
K3240.4.K36   1990
342.73'085—dc20
[347.30285]   90-50010
                                        CIP

TO DAVID

CONTENTS

ACKNOWLEDGMENTS

The research for this project has been supported with funds from a number of sources at the University of South Carolina: the Department of Government and International Studies, the College of the Humanities and Social Sciences, the Institute of International Studies, and the University Research and Productive Scholarship Fund. I especially want to thank Earl Black, current chair of the Department of Government and International Studies, and the other members of the departmental committee which supported my work by providing me with release time to complete the manuscript.

In the preparation of the manuscript I was given important help by Sandra Hall, Lori Joye, and Becky Deaton. I would like to thank Paul Betz of the University of North Carolina Press for his encouragement and advice and Ron Maner for his expert assistance. Over the years, essential help has been provided, with an enthusiasm and conscientiousness which I appreciate, by my research assistants: Steven Mosher, Ken Menkhaus, Carl Young, Tanja Bruestle, David Carroll, and especially John Creed, who has learned, to my benefit, more about human rights treaties than he ever wanted to know. Special thanks also to Pat Langelier of the University of North Carolina Library for her assistance in locating the many documents consulted in the research for this study.

I am greatly indebted to Sen. Joseph Biden and his exceedingly competent staff, especially Leah Jenkins, who helped me throughout the research project, obtaining documents, arranging interviews, and generally steering me through the maze of senatorial politics. I am also grateful to the anonymous Committee and Member staff who carved time out of their demanding schedules to explain, and occasionally muse with me about, the politics of the Foreign Relations and Judiciary committees. Thanks, too, are due the members of the American Bar Association who were willing to discuss the organization with me—its past and their efforts to change the formal position of the association and to work for ratification of human rights treaties.

My professional colleagues have enriched my knowledge and understanding of my subject through comments on papers and articles, responses at professional meetings, and stimulating private discussions. In particular I have benefited from the work and suggestions of Nicholas Onuf, Richard Falk, Louis Sohn, Lawrence LeBlanc, David

Forsythe, David Weissbrodt, Clifton Wilson, Margaret Galey, and Bert Lockwood. I am also grateful to Ferdinand Schoeman, Jerel Rosati, Moss Blachman, Paul Kattenburg, Glenn Abernathy, Morse Peckham, and Martin Donougho, colleagues at the University of South Carolina who have shared their intelligence and expertise.

My women friends and colleagues continue to support and encourage me with the gift of their time, energy, and sensitivity. Those I work with have transformed the quality of my daily life: Laura Woliver, Jan Love, Ann Bowman, Sue Rosser, Joan Gero, Joan Altekruse, Marjorie Goodwin, and Nancy Lane. Outside the University, Sarah Fox, Robyn Newkumet, Sarah Schechter-Schoeman, Claudia Brinson, and Anita Floyd have been wise and caring friends. I am grateful for the intelligence and good sense of my family, all of whom maintain an improbable optimism while working for change in our highly resistant society. My parents, Helen and Manny Kaufman, continue to infuse the world with their wisdom, humor, and goodwill. My sister Helene Kaufman and my brother, Ted Kaufman, foster my efforts with their critical insights, expertise, and affection. I am deeply indebted to my sister Susan Kaufman for her abiding confidence in me and all my dreams. I am grateful to my daughter Carrollee for her creative and stimulating companionship and for appreciating the importance of my work and hers; my daughter Athey I thank for putting up with the creation of a book without pictures. I dedicate this book to my friend and partner, David Whiteman.

Human Rights
Treaties and the
Senate

My purpose in offering this resolution is to bury the so-called covenant on human rights so deep that no one holding high public office will ever dare to attempt its resurrection.
—Senator John Bricker,
Congressional Record, 1951

As we consider the status of human rights treaties in the United States today, the ghost of Senator John Bricker (R.-Ohio) must be smiling at the fulfillment of his wish. Thirty years after the defeat of the Bricker Amendment, most major human rights treaties have yet to receive Senate approval. These treaties have, however, been ratified by more than eighty-five other nations, including sixteen Western democracies. The United States has long been considered the leading protector of human rights. Many Americans consider the Declaration of Independence and its references to "inalienable rights" to be the source for the reintroduction of basic human rights into the modern political scene. Most Americans also believe that the United States has the best record on human rights of any country in the world. Yet if these treaties appear to reflect the highest ideals of the American people, and if our allies and other democracies have been able to reconcile their political and legal systems with the obligations of the treaties, why has the United States government continually resisted ratification?

The explanation for this situation has little to do with the executive branch, which has generally supported human rights treaties. The U.S. representatives at the United Nations have consistently played an active role in proposing and drafting international human rights treaties. Presidents have approved, signed, and transmitted most major human rights treaties to the United States Senate. Therefore, in exploring the failure of the United States to ratify these treaties, the analysis that follows will focus on the final phase of the ratification process—Senate consideration.

The major argument of this book is that current opposition to human rights treaties is a legacy of the 1950s. What is this legacy? First, it is the basic notion that the treaties are controversial, a notion that grew out of the 1950s opposition. This is apparent today in the senatorial trepidation about the very consideration of human rights treaties that almost completely excludes them from the Senate agenda. Second, it is the continuing assumption during debates over human rights treaties that the treaties threaten the American form of government. This assumption places the burden of persuasion on those favoring rather than those opposing ratification. Third, it is the persistence of a legalistic framework of debate which emphasizes technical legal argumentation. The highly political nature of the opposition and the essential congruence between the treaties and the United States Constitution are lost in the continuing legalism of the debate. Fourth, it is the stability over time of the actual arguments against the treaties, arguments that were developed and refined during the early Senate hearings. Although the current political, social, legal, and economic environment differs significantly from that of the 1950s, the articulated opposition to human rights treaties in the United States Senate has changed very little. This study explores in a systematic fashion both the original development of arguments in opposition to human rights treaties and the residual strength of those arguments in contemporary deliberations. The findings are based on legal analysis, legislative histories, content analysis of congressional hearings, and interviews with congressional staff members.

Part I of the book is devoted to a study of the political development of the opposition to human rights treaties in the late 1940s and early 1950s. The sources and strategy of the opposition are explained, and a typology of the arguments against the treaties is developed and applied.

Chapter 1 explores the political environment during the initial consideration of postwar human rights treaties, an environment dominated by the Cold War and the civil rights movement. Conservative fears commonly held in the 1950s were successfully grafted onto human rights treaties: erosion of individual rights, abridgment of states' rights, expansion of the United Nations toward world government, and enhancement of Communist influence at home and abroad. The grafting process was begun by a small group of lawyers within the American Bar Association (ABA) who viewed the drafting of human rights treaties as central to a strategy to destroy the American way of life. These men persuaded a sufficiently large majority of the ABA that the organization ought to go on record as opposing these treaties, and with official organizational support behind them, they took their case to the United States Senate. The debates of the 1950s over human rights treaties and the proposed constitutional amendment they evoked structured Senate consideration of human rights treaties and left behind a legacy for the decades that followed.

Chapter 2 discusses the Genocide Convention, a treaty widely hailed as an important international response to Nazi atrocities. The Genocide Convention was strongly supported by the U.S. executive branch during the drafting process and immediately signed by the president after its approval by the United Nations General Assembly. It also drew praise from a vast number of domestic groups along a wide political spectrum during the 1949 hearings in the Senate, but the Senate failed to approve it for thirty-five years. As the first postwar human rights treaty, the Genocide Convention took on a special significance. For the opposition, it represented the first in a series of treaties aimed, some claimed, at undermining American ideals. Thus, in large measure, debate on the Genocide Convention involved discussion of other human rights documents as well. The surprising success of the opposition in persuading the Senate not to ratify the Genocide Convention was the first crucial step in establishing the institution's skepticism about human rights treaties generally.

Chapter 3 examines the Human Rights Covenants, which became the focal point of the opposition movement. These two treaties were designed to incorporate into binding treaty law the principles of the Universal Declaration of Human Rights, a nonbinding U.N. resolution. The covenants included economic and social rights as well as traditional Western political and civil rights. These treaties quickly became the center of an intensive anti-Communist and anti-internationalist drive in the ABA and in the Senate. The Truman administration played a leading role in the drafting of these documents, which emerged from the United Nations Human Rights Commission at a time when this body was headed by Eleanor Roosevelt, the U.S. representative. Chapter 3 documents the strong executive branch commitment to these treaties and the extensive success the United States experienced in shaping the treaties to reflect essentially Western and particularly U.S. constitutional values.

The development of the Human Rights Covenants was the immediate reason cited by Senator Bricker for the need to adopt a constitutional amendment to safeguard the United States against the loss of individual rights to communism, world government, and the federal government. The fears of Bricker and others who shared his beliefs were so effectively articulated and convincingly argued that the Senate came exceedingly close to approving an amendment to the United States Constitution designed to eliminate the perceived threat. The Senate debates over the so-called Bricker Amendment, the subject of Chapter 4, included detailed discussion of human rights treaties. It was during these deliberations that the opposition arguments were refined and formalized. The Bricker Amendment hearings also established beyond question the controversial nature of human rights treaties, a key factor that continues to dominate their congressional consideration.

Part II explores the linkage between the 1950s opposition and the current absence of human rights treaties from the Senate agenda. It traces developments from the first reconsideration of human rights treaties, during the Kennedy administration, through the 1986 ratification of the Genocide Convention.

Chapter 5 carefully examines the exceptional circumstances surrounding two treaties that have passed the Senate, the Supplementary Slavery Convention and the Convention on the Political Rights of Women, in an effort to understand how special conditions can occasionally lead to ratification. The controversy normally attached to human rights treaties was not apparent in the final hearings on these two treaties, and both were unanimously accepted without reservations.

A consistent feature of the opposition has been its overwhelmingly legal cast. Chapter 6 investigates the history and validity of this legal framework. The early and vocal opposition of the American Bar Association moved the debate to legal and constitutional ground, where a particular group of lawyers asserted superior legal knowledge and expertise. The normal procedure for dealing with objectionable elements of otherwise acceptable treaties is the attachment of formal reservations, which have the effect of limiting the operation of the treaties' terms in some specific way. Chapter 6 argues that the opposition to the treaties is basically political rather than legal, and that the offering of reservations has become a legalistic strategy in an essentially political game. Using the reservations proposed by the Carter administration for the United Nations covenants, this chapter presents an assessment of this "reservations game" and questions the general notion that the provisions of most human rights treaties raise serious legal challenges to our constitutional system.

The concluding chapter discusses contemporary events, including the 1979 hearings on the U.N. covenants and the 1980s hearings on the Genocide Convention. The reappearance of the same basic opposition arguments reveals the consistency of the opposition in spite of the changing internal and external political environment. This chapter also explains why the 1986 ratification of the Genocide Convention does not portend any significant change in the reception of human rights treaties in the United States Senate.

PART ONE

Politics
of Fear

ONE

History and Background

By and through treaty law-making the federal government can be transformed into a completely socialistic and centralized state. It only requires that the present provisions of the Declaration on Human Rights be incorporated into a treaty . . . to change the relationship between the states and the federal government and to change even our Constitution and our form of government. . . . It is not an overstatement to say that the republic is threatened to its very foundations.—Frank Holman, "Treaty Law-Making," 1950

The first postwar human rights treaties were drafted in the late 1940s and early 1950s. The environment into which they were introduced in the United States was characterized by a particular configuration of national and international forces that was not conducive to favorable consideration. Conservatives, fearing communism from abroad and desegregation at home, viewed the human rights treaties as tools of the enemy. The circumstances that inspired American conservatives to interpret these treaties as a serious threat also created the conditions for a successful attack on the treaties by linking them to widely shared fears.

One nationally prominent conservative, Frank Holman, conducted a personal mission to alert the American public to the dangers of human rights treaties. He and a small group of like-minded conservative lawyers formed the vanguard of the opposition. They adopted a highly effective strategy for defeating the treaties—energetically and consistently working to win over to the opposition cause the leading national association of lawyers, the American Bar Association. Working through a special ABA committee appointed by the organization's president, they successfully argued against all international legal activity on human rights. The organ of the ABA that normally addressed international legal issues was outmaneuvered and outvoted. Victory within the ABA infused a special authority and legitimation into the opposition testimony before the United States Senate, and these men were able to change the very terms of debate on the treaties.

The story of Holman's crusade and the conversion of the ABA is the subject of this chapter. First, the political environment of the initial debate over human rights treaties is described—an environment in which emotions engendered by the Cold War and the civil rights movement combined to create a conservative politics of fear. Second, the Holman crusade is analyzed and shown to have clearly articulated the connections between this politics of fear and the opposition to human rights treaties. The final section of the chapter recounts the struggle within the ABA about how the organization should respond to human rights treaties. Later chapters will show that the general framework and specific arguments that emerged in the 1950s during discussions about human rights treaties within the ABA and in the Senate persisted throughout the decades that followed.

The Political Environment

In the context of the 1950s political environment, hostility toward human rights treaties was certainly understandable, if not entirely predictable. The hostility was due largely to two major developments in the political environment—the civil rights movement and the Cold War—which together would go on to shape the context for much of the debate on the treaties. Political realities born of these two developments, one internally oriented and one externally focused, colored treaty deliberations and eventually became inextricably bound to the treaties themselves.

The Civil Rights Movement

Within 1950s America, human rights had become a major political issue with the reevaluation of domestic racial segregation. The initial integration of American troops abroad during the war and the establishment of a wartime Fair Employment Practices Commission (FEPC) were small steps signaling to some the clear possibility of impending federal action to eliminate racial discrimination. The 1947 report of the Truman Committee on Civil Rights documented lynchings, police brutality, unfair administration of justice, conditions comparable to involuntary servitude, abridgment of the right to vote, and widespread discrimination in employment.[1] The report recommended federal action to address and remedy the country's racial problems. Legislation was introduced in Congress to make lynchings a federal offense, to eliminate the poll tax, and to establish a peacetime FEPC. Although Congress failed to pass these bills and related legislation and, in fact, failed even to pass legislation desegregating the nation's capital, the effort itself was a sign of change. Plans designed to address civil rights abuses through federal action were on occasion publicly supported by a large number of Senate and House members, many of whom knew that these programs would be blocked, either through filibuster or straight votes.

By 1950, the judiciary was also being drawn into civil rights issues. The doctrine of separate but equal, established in *Plessy v. Ferguson*, was brought under scrutiny by the Supreme Court. The Court had ruled against state enforcement of restrictive covenants in *Shelley v. Kraemer* in 1948. Then in 1950, in *McLaurin v. Oklahoma State Regents*, the Supreme Court decided that maintaining separate classrooms, libraries, and cafeterias for black students at a previously all-white graduate school was unacceptable because it impaired the educational opportunities of the blacks. In the same year, the Supreme Court implied that separate was unequal in *Sweatt v. Painter*, ruling that a separately created black law school was not a viable alternative for blacks denied admission to a far superior all-white state law school. Far more threatening, of course, was the decision of the National Association for the Advancement of Colored People (NAACP) to test the separate but equal doctrine in elementary and secondary public schools, which would have a direct impact on large numbers of blacks not in a position to apply to or attend graduate school. In December 1952 the Justice Department submitted an *amicus curiae* brief challenging separate but equal schools, in what became the *Brown v. Board of Education* case. Interestingly enough, even at this point, the Truman administration linked its decision to another major force within the political environment, the Cold War:

> Racial discrimination furnishes grist for the Communist propaganda mills and it raises doubts even among friendly nations as to the intensity of our devotion to the democratic faith.[2]

But while civil rights proponents of the 1950s were skeptical that these measures would bring about actual change, talk of federal action to dismantle segregation within the states was taken very seriously by conservatives. States' rights were ardently defended and often presented as the only bulwark against an expansive federal government that would use its powers to impose a host of liberal programs on states and local communities, programs such as the elimination of racial restrictions on property ownership, marriage, and education.

The Cold War

If the civil rights struggle was the domestic dimension of the political environment most relevant to treaty consideration, the Cold War was the major international dimension. To conservatives of the time, the essence of America was clearly threatened by Communists. McCarthyism was one extreme manifestation of the concern that a worldwide Communist movement, directed from Moscow, was taking power on a global scale and that the United States was the only country with the capability and potential will to halt the menace.

Certain major events contributed to these fears. With the explosion of a Soviet nuclear device on 29 September 1950, the atomic monopoly of the United States disappeared, and the force of any implied or explicit U.S. nuclear threat was greatly diminished. The entire Korean operation, including the effective North Korean resistance to U.S. objectives there, heightened fears of Communist power and the inability of the United States to confront and resist it. The defeat of Chiang Kai-shek and ascendance of the Communist Party in China, when joined with an assumption of Sino-Soviet friendship and cooperation, was interpreted by conservatives as seriously damaging to U.S. interests, influence, and security. The conservative reaction to all of these events was to view them as evidence of the demise of the United States as the preeminent power in the world.

The Cold War rhetoric of the Truman administration contributed to conservative fears and legitimized them in the minds of the public. Richard Freeland argues that the Cold War consensus was established before the important political events cited above took place and that the atmosphere was created by the propaganda effort the administration launched in order to get approval for the Marshall Plan. To win over conservatives who were reluctant to have the United States make economic and military commitments abroad, the administration created a framework for interpreting foreign affairs that stressed the Soviet threat. Thus, the breakdown of the wartime alliance was the result of "Soviet betrayal and aggression," and the economic recovery in Europe was blocked by "Soviet obstructionism and communist subversion."[3] This rhetoric and the political environment it produced had repercussions the Truman White House did not predict and could not control.

> The campaign implanted the idea in the public mind that the United States was imminently threatened by a massive, ideologically based assault upon everything Americans valued. This exaggerated representation of the dangers of international and domestic communism created the emotional and conceptual context within which America reacted to the Soviet explosion of the atomic bomb, the fall of China, the outbreak of the Korean War, and conviction of Alger Hiss.[4]

These are also the emotional themes that were raised by opponents of the human rights treaties. Robert Griffith holds the Truman administration responsible for the environment in which McCarthyism thrived. "The Truman Administration itself couched its policies in a rhetoric of crusading anti-Communism, which stressed American innocence, Soviet depravity, and the necessity for confrontation."[5]

These fears of communism required conservatives to shift away from their traditional rhetorical position favoring demobilization, withdrawal from international affairs, reduction in military involvement, and a return to isolationism. The right, in fact, became so fixated on the Communist threat that they abandoned their insistence on a limited federal government. No less a conservative than William F. Buckley was among those citing the threat of communism as a rationale for governmental expansion, arguing that "we must accept Big Government for the duration—for neither an offensive nor a defensive war can be waged . . . except through the instrument of a totalitarian bureaucracy within our shores."[6] He explained that Republicans "will have to support large armies and air forces, atomic energy, central intelligence, war production boards, and the attendant centralization of power in Washington—even with Truman at the reins of it all."[7] Griffith points out that the conservatives paid a very high price for their ardent anticommunism in the form of a state dependent on federal spending and deficit financing. Their position on human rights treaties was only one result of their dogmatic stance on domestic and foreign policies.

> Their strident polemics helped to create an anti-Communist politics that limited the arena of permissible debate, shifted the focus of political discussion toward the right, and narrowed the range

of options open to policymakers. The resulting cold-war consensus informed American politics at home and abroad for nearly two decades thereafter.[8]

And, even when the Cold War abated to some degree, this conservative dogma never really died but rather lay dormant. The persistence of the deeply felt repulsion toward the human rights treaties was nurtured by at least a segment of the conservative faction as a part of their program. Their success lay in keeping their anti-Communist, anti-international fervor alive and influential in mainstream American political thinking.

Linking the Cold War and the Civil Rights Movement

The issues of domestic civil rights action and anticommunism were linked by some who argued that the American system would be easier to "sell" abroad if we improved our record on civil rights at home. Truman, in fact, warmed to the civil rights demands partly out of political concern for the black vote and partly as a result of the increased intensity of the Cold War. As he argued to Congress, "If we wish to inspire the peoples of the world . . . who have already lost their civil liberties, . . . we must correct the remaining imperfections in our practice of democracy."[9] Some felt that legal segregation in the South opened us up to criticism in international forums and limited our ability to credibly criticize the Soviet Union's rights violations. The NAACP went to the United Nations with complaints about segregation in the United States, and, although the Human Rights Commission rejected the Soviet proposal to investigate the charge, the specter was raised of the United States' being criticized before the world. At a minimum, the increased publicity about domestic human rights violations tarnished the belief that the United States was the leading champion of civil rights. As a 1948 *New York Times* article noted:

> Now that the war is over, this nation finds itself the most powerful spokesman for the democratic way of life, as opposed to the principles of a totalitarian state. It is unpleasant to have the Russians publicize our continued lynchings, our Jim Crow statutes and customs, our anti-Semitic discriminations, and our witchhunts; but is it undeserved? We cannot deny the truth of the charges; we are becoming aware that we do not practice the civil liberty we preach.[10]

Some at the time contended that this factor should lead us to ratify human rights treaties. One writer suggested that our failure to accept the Genocide Convention would be taken

> as an indication that we have some kind of pogrom in mind for our Negro minority. [Non-Americans] will listen eagerly when Russia [says] that ratification was blocked by southern senators who feared it might lead to a federal antilynching law . . . and who were unwilling to make the mass extermination of racial, religious or national groups a crime under international law for fear that the lynching of a Negro might be considered an act of genocide.[11]

For others, awareness of our vulnerability to criticism on civil rights made the notion of an international commitment on this subject in-auspicious. Communists, it was suggested, would turn this commit-ment to their own ends by using the treaties to falsely accuse us and exaggerate our civil rights problems. Efforts to respond to these Com-munist accusations and implement the treaty commitments would lead to abrogation of domestic jurisdiction and federal intrusions into states' rights.

The Truman Committee on Civil Rights was accused of yielding to Communist influence. As one writer stated it, "A singular fact about the President's committee is that half of its members had records of collaboration with Communist enterprise." The same author argued that the program recommended in *To Secure These Rights*, as the com-mittee's report was entitled, would "rescind vital constitutional guar-antees of civil liberty," under the authority of a human rights treaty.[12]

The civil rights movement and the Cold War and the fears that they engendered were clearly intertwined. U.S. civil rights violations marred the democratic-capitalist model being offered as an alternative to communism. But to conservatives, no problem at home, including the increasingly public and well-documented abuse of black civil rights, was as serious as the overwhelming need to stop communism. Conservative leaders called on the country to unite in order to effec-tively meet the threat. Enlarging the powers of the federal govern-ment was justifiable to address the Communist menace; it was not justifiable to address the menace of racial injustice. For conservatives, the human rights treaties represented instruments legitimizing inter-national review of U.S. domestic affairs, including the treatment of blacks; internationalization of a human rights standard that included Communist ideas; and federal action at the state and local level to remedy racial injustice. Sanctioning these actions would represent a victory for Communists in and out of the country and further their plans for replacing the American system with one of their own.

One Conservative's Crusade

The foundations of these conservative fears and the rationale behind them were most elaborately developed and articulated by Frank Holman, president of the American Bar Association in 1948–49. Holman was a distinguished lawyer from the state of Washington; he had been a Rhodes Scholar at Oxford University and dean of the University of Utah Law School. In the years following World War II, he was active on issues of international law within his state, serving as co-convenor of the Seattle Regional Conference on the World Court (1946) and the Seattle Regional Conference on Progressive Development of International Law (1947). Holman served on the Advisory Board of the *American Bar Association Journal*, was an original member of the ABA Special Committee on Peace and Law Through United Nations, and became the first and leading spokesperson on the need "to protect American rights against the dangers of 'treaty-law.' "[13] He considered his vocal opposition to the treaties a "crusade"[14] and believed, probably correctly, that his work against human rights treaties led directly to the introduction of an amendment to alter the treaty-making provisions of the United States Constitution and to the halting of the ratification of human rights treaties by the United States.

Over the course of several years, Holman wrote numerous articles, editorials, and letters to the editor and delivered speeches across the entire country aimed at alerting Americans to the dangers posed by the human rights treaties. He focused on the U.N. treaties as central to a Communist plan for destroying the American way of life. He was awarded the Gold Certificate Award of Merit from the Freedom Foundation (1951) and Gold Medal of Merit from the Veterans of Foreign Wars (1953) for his campaign against the human rights treaties.[15] His conception of the overall threat of the treaties is succinctly revealed in two statements; the first of these was made in September 1950,

> This accumulating body of treaty law can result in changing our form of government from a republic to a socialistic and central-

ized state—with such increase in the power of the Federal Government at the expense of the states that the doctrine of states' rights and local self-government can become as non-existent in the United States as in the highly centralized governments of Europe and Asia.[16]

and the second dates from November 1955,

The Internationalists in this country and elsewhere really proposed to use the United Nations and the treaty process as a law-making process to change the domestic laws and even the Government of the United States and to establish a World Government along socialistic lines.[17]

As these quotes demonstrate, three themes are interwoven in the opposition arguments against the treaties, namely the warnings that these treaties would result in (1) violation of domestic jurisdiction resulting in loss of sovereignty and curtailing of rights, (2) expansion of the powers of the federal government in violation of states' rights, and (3) enhancement of Communist influence and the transformation of the American system to socialism.

According to Holman, the United Nations was drafting human rights treaties with the specific intention of invading national jurisdiction and taking over state sovereignty. He viewed these actions as part of a conspiracy, referring to the Universal Declaration as a "device" to "soften up the American people" and the Genocide Convention as a "false mask for other international purposes."[18] These treaties were the first step, according to Holman, whereby American "internal rights under our own Constitution and Bill of Rights are to be undermined step by step and will continue to be undermined."[19] Our entire domestic system would be assailed. "We would give the super-government absolute control of business, industry, prices, wages and every detail of American social and economic life."[20] One particular objective of the United Nations, according to Holman, was to attain legal jurisdiction within member states. He warned that "the acts of our citizens, our courts, and our public officials will be amenable to examination and condemnation and eventual control by the United Nations."[21] The specter of a constantly harassing U.N. police force is also raised as one of the inevitable horrors of the human rights treaties.

A second dimension of the threat Holman feared was the intrusion of the federal government into states' rights. A special connection was drawn here between the treaties and various civil rights programs. The federal government, it was suggested, would use acquired powers under the treaties to enact laws in violation of states' rights. They would use treaty-making authority to make domestic or local law for the people of the various states.

> No action by the Congress might be necessary to put the whole of the civil rights program into operation. . . . The Supreme Court [may] declare any controversial element of the present civil rights program a part of racial equality . . . and thus, judicially impose the civil rights program upon the states without action by the Congress.[22]

Holman was fond of predicting the extent to which actions normally under local jurisdiction would be changed by the human rights treaties. One of his favorite stories appealed to the racial concerns of his audience:

> I pointed out that if, in driving me from the airport, [someone] had unfortunately run over a Negro child running out into the street in front of him, what would have been a local offense under a charge of gross negligence or involuntary manslaughter would, under the Genocide Convention, because of the racial differential, not be a local crime but an international crime and that [he] could be transplanted someplace overseas for trial.[23]

The treaties would also affect immigration policy and change restrictions on property sales and could even lead to the clearly frightening possibility of "nullifying statutes against mixed marriages."[24] In addition to objecting generally to reduction of the rights of states, Holman feared that the Communists would exploit federal actions based on the treaties which afforded enhanced rights to new groups of Americans. "It leaves Russia or Communist China free to furnish their nationals with funds to buy strategic property up and down our Pacific Coast wherever they can find a willing seller."[25]

For Holman the third great danger posed by human rights treaties was the Communist threat. In 1946, in an article in the *ABA Journal*, Holman warned of the dangers of "boring from within." He claimed that any world government

> would be taken over by Communists who with the zeal of true believers, would in a world federation go on working to insure the . . . universal imposition of their . . . economic, social and

political tyranny. The insistence on submission and subservience to their ideology has taken place again and again in American Labor unions.[26]

Holman was a devoted McCarthyite. He explained in his autobiography that

in my opinion, many of our ordinarily sound citizens who became emotional in castigating and ultimately destroying Senator McCarthy were, themselves, the unknowing tools of the left-wing element in our society and, in many instances, of a Communist conspiracy against the Senator.[27]

As early as February 1949, Holman was warning America of the Communist threat. In a speech that he called "Communist Activities" he said:

A nation-wide housecleaning is urgently needed to rout out the Reds in Government who are burrowing through our structures of government like prairie dogs. Too many Communists today hide behind the star-spangled cloak of Americanism.

He went on to cite a survey of Los Angeles local government employees which he claimed revealed that 20 percent of the employees belonged to "communist front" organizations, "many of which had the prefix 'American' in their titles."[28] The human rights treaties were at the heart of the effort to radically change the American system. The Communist conspiracy was working on several fronts, according to Holman, and on all of them the Communist cause was being forwarded by the human rights treaties. The deception of the treaties was possible because "we have . . . tolerated Communists and fellow travelers in high places."[29] He warned that resistance to ratification was necessary or "you would have by a few pages of treaty language transformed the government of the United States into a socialistic state."[30] The Universal Declaration was described as "a blueprint for State Socialism" to be implemented through further treaties creating a "socialist utopia."[31]

The Special Role of the American Bar Association

Holman's stature as president of the ABA made him an even more effective spokesperson against the treaties. His position placed him in a key role for mobilizing the association itself against the treaties. Holman's fears were shared initially by a small group within the ABA, and the history of ABA consideration of human rights treaties is the story of this group's dedicated commitment to a conservative victory in preventing U.S. ratification.

Throughout the public debate over the human rights treaties, the American Bar Association was the single interest group that consistently held an important place.[32] As the leading organization of the nation's lawyers, the ABA had tremendous influence on public opinion, but, more significantly, it had a powerful impact on Congress. A very large number of senators were, in fact, lawyers (in 1953, 61 percent[33]) and would have had a professional response to ABA recommendations. An understanding of the ABA rationale for opposing human rights treaties, then, took on special importance given the high regard in which the organization was held by the members of the United States Senate. The determination within the ABA that these treaties posed a threat to Americans' basic rights and to their system of government was crucial to the rejection of the Genocide Convention and to the popularity of the Bricker proposal to amend the Constitution. In introducing the amendment, aimed at preventing the dangers of the human rights treaties, Senator Bricker said:

> I should like to pay tribute to the magnificent work of the American Bar Association and its Committee on Peace and Law through United Nations in alerting the American people to the dangers inherent in the treaty-making power.[34]

Serious dissension existed within the ABA about the proper role of international law and organization in U.S. foreign policy. This dissension was institutionalized in a manner that provided important structural power to those who came to oppose human rights treaties. Normally, international issues such as treaties were referred to the Section on International and Comparative Law, composed of ABA members with expertise and interest in international law. However, on 29 February 1944 the ABA House of Delegates approved the appointment of a special committee of seven members, to be designated by the president, to study and report "recommendations as to what proposals the Association should support as America plans for the post-war organization of the nations for peace and the rule of law."[35] The Committee on Peace and Law Through United Nations[36] was chaired by William L. Ransom, who became a strong opponent of the treaties and one of the first proponents of a constitutional amendment to defend American rights. Frank Holman was a member.[37] The committee was approved only after serious and heated debate. Thomas B. Gay, speaking on behalf of the section, questioned former judge Thompson, presenting the Board of Governors' recommendations, about the need for or correctness of a new special committee.

> Would you mind telling the House, Judge, what consideration led the Board of Governors to believe that the President, acting in his wisdom, could select a committee of seven who are more qualified to consider and make recommendations upon the subject matter of these resolutions than the Section of [*sic*] International Law, which is composed, as I understand it, of a group of lawyers of our Association who are technically trained in a subject in respect to which admittedly most of us know very little, and who have given in most instances their entire professional lives in dealing with this question? . . . What possible agency could be set up through a committee of seven which is more capable of conducting that study than the Section on International Law?[38]

Judge Thompson's answer to this question indicated one source of significant division which later became apparent in the debate over human rights treaties.

> The people in the Section on International Law are international lawyers, and this subject has many phases which are not merely international law. We should have the viewpoint and experience also of those who do not know so much about international law and who will think of this subject from the standpoint of the United States of America as a premise and then follow into the field of international law.[39]

Clearly the committee was to monitor U.S. participation in international law and organization using a more narrowly defined concept of national interest than that of the section, which might adopt an international or even global perspective. The repeated victories of the committee iterate the victory of the conservative view that human rights treaties conflict with important national interests, domestic and foreign.

The ongoing dissension between the section and the committee emerged in 1948 as a disagreement about human rights treaties and lasted throughout the years of debate over the treaties. The disagreements within the ABA reflect very much the same controversy that was raging within Congress, although the dissent must be gleaned from the committee and section reports and debates since the points of dispute are not mentioned in the approved ABA resolutions. It was easy to conclude from the resolutions of the House of Delegates, the chief parliamentary decision-making body within the ABA, that the organization was monolithic in its opposition to the treaties; but those who dissented registered serious political and legal objections to the adopted ABA positions.

The differences between the two groups surfaced at the 1948 meeting of the House of Delegates with the initial debate over the first tentative drafts of the Universal Declaration and the Human Rights Covenant. The delegates did not pass judgment on the drafts but did express disapproval of the major provisions of the proposed Measures of Implementation.[40] The Committee on Peace and Law offered resolutions that opposed the creation of a human rights court, limited the right of complaint to parties to the treaty, opposed a committee to handle complaints under the treaty, and opposed the right of individual petition.[41] The Section on International Law suffered its first clear defeat in the battle over human rights treaties when, after it strongly opposed all of these resolutions on the grounds that the proposals being rejected had merit and were, as yet, only in draft form, the resolutions were approved by the House of Delegates.[42] The makeup of the committee was already moving away from diversity of opinion; five members of the now-enlarged nine-person committee were men who were strongly, and publicly, opposed to human rights treaties.[43]

At another meeting later that same year, the committee reported that the State Department had "heeded to a substantial extent"[44] the earlier recommendations of the House of Delegates, but the committee continued to express serious concern about the declaration and covenant drafts. A subcommittee, chaired by Frank Holman, had studied these documents and determined that they were not acceptable.[45] Particular concern was expressed about the declaration because, according to the committee, it was to be approved by the executive branch without reference to the Senate. The committee discussed the declaration as if it would create binding legal obligations that "would leave the door open to Supreme Court decisions and Executive actions that would give the declaration unforeseeable, and perhaps highly objectionable, implications and effects."[46] As a resolution of the General Assembly, the Universal Declaration would not create immediately binding law. Rather, the accompanying covenant, as a treaty, was expected to authoritatively codify the Universal Declaration and create a set of binding obligations. In a report from the committee, the members' confusion over this point is apparent.[47]

> [The] Draft Declaration of Human Rights is to be submitted to the member nations as a recommendation of the General Assembly, to be an 'authoritative interpretation' of the covenant and the charter provisions on the subject.[48]

At this time the House of Delegates approved a recommendation that in part provided,

> That the American Bar Association is of the opinion that any Declaration on Human Rights should not be in any manner approved, accepted or promulgated by or in behalf of the Government of the United States except upon and after the submission of such document, and the approval of it by, the Congress of the United States.[49]

As a sign of the continuing conflict between committee and section, a member of the section moved to abolish the special committee, arguing that a group dealing with issues of international law would function far better as a committee of the section. After a "lively debate," the committee prevailed as the motion was defeated.[50]

In an article in the November 1948 issue of the *ABA Journal* entitled "An 'International Bill of Rights': Proposals Have Dangerous Implications for U.S.," Frank Holman presented the declaration and covenant as a Communist threat. The strength of anti-Communist sentiment within the ABA was also apparent in a series of resolutions passed at the 1948 annual meeting. These resolutions required that lawyers who provided aid to Communists, as party members or not, would be expelled from the organization as "unworthy of our profession," as would any lawyer who refused to answer "before a duly constituted inquiry, as to whether he is or was a Communist."[51]

During the following year, the Committee on Peace and Law held sixteen seminars around the United States on the issues raised by human rights treaties, including the Genocide Convention. The first seminar produced general agreement among the participants on the need to guard against loss of states' rights, increase of federal power, self-executing provisions, and invasion of domestic jurisdiction. Protection against these challenges could, according to the committee, be achieved "through reservations attached by the Senate to its consent to ratification, and possibly through amendment of the Constitution of the United States."[52] This committee report was the first association reference to a constitutional amendment to protect American rights and made clear that the perceived need for such an amendment arose directly from the threat posed by human rights treaties.

The committee continued its attack on the human rights treaties at the 1949 annual meeting, stressing two problems: (1) that the treaties would "take precedence" over existing domestic law and (2) that they would diminish states' rights. The committee expressed its belief that attaching reservations to the treaties would not "adequately protect the Constitutional interests of the United States"[53] and therefore proposed that the ABA recommend to the Senate that it not ratify the Convention on Genocide. The Section on International Law proposed an alternative resolution: ratification of the convention with specific reservations.[54] After serious and strong debate, the section's resolution was defeated and a resolution rejecting the Genocide Convention was adopted. The adopted resolution also provided that the resolutions and comments of both the committee and the section be sent to the Senate and House; thus, the committee's detailed and complete review of the provisions of the Genocide Convention that were considered controversial or that it considered controversial was sent to Congress. The success of the committee during this debate foreshadowed developments in the congressional debate. The basic assumption became the unacceptability of the treaty; the basic question was what to do about it. The section, with a majority of treaty supporters, conceded the fundamental issue by accepting that the treaty was seriously flawed and argued that some very significant reservations would make it acceptable; the committee claimed that the flaws were so severe as to be beyond salvaging through reinterpretation and restriction.

The draft covenant continued to be an object of concern. The ABA adopted a resolution[55] authorizing both the section and committee to respond to the State Department's request for comments on the draft covenant. Committee members provided a complete report on their general and specific objections to the draft and reiterated their fears that reservations would not be sufficient to protect the U.S. system from the dangers of this treaty. They included recommendations to alter the drafts and suggested guidelines for Senate consideration of human rights treaties that specifically referred to protection of states' rights. At this point, the committee began to discuss seriously the possibility of a constitutional amendment to prevent ratification of human rights treaties or to limit their internal effect if ratified. Holman believed that the groundwork was laid at the ABA's 1949 annual meeting for "getting the historic resolution from the House of Delegates favoring a Constitutional Amendment to protect Americans and the American form of government."[56]

At the same time that the ABA was passing resolutions in opposition to human rights treaties, the organization was being criticized from within on grounds that its own admissions procedures discriminated against blacks. Such criticism might easily have been viewed as an example of the kind of problem fueled by U.S. participation in efforts to create by treaty international responsibilities guaranteeing the elimination of racial discrimination. Although the ABA had no policy prohibiting black membership,[57] a 1949 study revealed that of 41,000 members only 13 were "Negro."[58] A report in the *New York Times* of 5 September 1949 described an expected "fight to liberalize the policy covering Negroes" at the ABA meeting in St. Louis that week due to the denial of membership in the ABA to eight New Jersey blacks, all members of the state bar association.[59] The fight took place, and the ABA turned down proposals by Adrian M. Unger, chair of the junior bar conference in New Jersey, which would have made it more likely that blacks would be admitted to the ABA in the future. These proposals would have given state bar associations the ability to determine membership in the national organization and would have eliminated race indicators from the application form itself.[60] In December of the same year, the New Jersey Bar Association strongly criticized the national association for failing to admit blacks, and it adopted proposals similar to those made by Unger at the national meeting.[61]

Unger continued his campaign, and in partial response to demands made in 1951, the organization established the Special Committee on Membership Applications. This committee submitted its report in 1952, completely vindicating the organization's procedures. The report emphasized that the "American Bar Association is a voluntary membership Association, with its membership being selective, and that no person, however eligible, is automatically entitled to membership therein."[62] The authors of the report upheld the desirability of retaining the existing membership form which asked for the applicant's race and sex and also whether the individual had ever been a member of the Communist Party. The committee concluded, "In our judgment Negro applicants are not being rejected by the Board of Governors because of their color," and it held that the procedure for consideration of membership was both democratic and proper.[63] Seven years later complaints continued to be voiced as a group of black lawyers again raised the issue of race discrimination and specifically the matter of the race question on the ABA application. The Harlem Lawyers Association called this question a "criterion of exclusion" and called on black lawyers not to apply for ABA membership.[64] The raising and dismissing of charges of racial discrimination within the organization paralleled civil rights action outside the organization, described earlier in this chapter. It is not difficult to imagine that charges of this sort brought close to home the "threat" posed by human rights treaties like the proposed U.N. covenants, which specifically prohibited discrimination based on race.

Divergent political action continued outside the ABA by both the Committee on Peace and Law and the Section on International Law. Members of the committee met with State Department representatives in connection with the Genocide Convention and draft covenant and appeared before a Senate subcommittee holding hearings on the former.[65] Section members were also active, offering specific recommendations to the State Department in order to minimize the opposition's criticism of the draft covenant. The link between human rights treaties and a possible constitutional amendment was reflected in 1950 by the formation within the section of a Committee on Constitutional Aspects of International Agreements, a committee formed particularly to study the constitutional effect of the human rights treaties.[66] One reason given for the establishment of a special committee on this subject was the great interest being shown in human rights treaties by the Committee on Peace and Law and the need for an authoritative report by a group of international and constitutional law experts. It is likely that this committee was formed as a defensive action, in order to retain jurisdiction over human rights treaties and provide specific responses to the constitutional law critique that had been devised by the Committee on Peace and Law.

The report of this new section committee listed the various alternatives for dealing with some of the problems that had been raised about human rights treaties. One of the options rejected was that of a constitutional amendment. Instead the members supported a recommendation that the treaties be ratified with two "saving clauses": one making the treaty "operative within the United States only when and as implemented by appropriate congressional action" and a second declaring that the treaty "shall not alter the respective constitutional powers of the states and federal government."[67] They also recommended a resolution offering two options for a combined non-self-executing and federal-state article to be included in all multilateral treaties in social or economic areas to which the United States intended to become a party.[68]

During 1950, the concerns of the Committee on Peace and Law in regard to the human rights treaties continued to grow. The committee provided an even more detailed analysis of the threats posed by the latest form of the draft covenant. The members called for renewed activity to warn Americans of the dangers posed to their fundamental rights and proposed a resolution linking severe criticism of human rights treaties with the need for immediate and serious study of a constitutional amendment.[69] On the committee's recommendation, the House of Delegates passed three resolutions: one authorizing the members of the committee to present the association's views on the Genocide Convention and the draft covenant to the State Department, Congress, and other governmental officials; another disapproving the draft covenant; and a third calling for a study to propose a constitutional amendment protecting the Bill of Rights and states' rights from any treaty infringement.[70] Once again, the resolutions and debate revealed the increasing power of the committee and the close connection between human rights treaties and the call for a constitutional amendment.

The section once again proposed an alternative strategy—rejecting the need for a constitutional amendment and instead offering the refinement of a general reservation that could be attached to all human rights treaties at the time of ratification. The purpose of the reservation was to declare the treaty non-self-executing and to attach a federal-state clause.[71] This proposal, resulting from a study done by the section's Committee on Constitutional Aspects of International Agreements, was passed by the House of Delegates. The section enunciated a shared concern with the Committee on Peace and Law over protecting states' rights and the federal system but argued that a reservation would be more suitable than a constitutional amendment.[72] The section's willingness to concede the need for such a measure is a sign of the early influence of the committee's work within and beyond the ABA and also of the changing terms of the general debate over human rights treaties.

In October 1950 something of a scandal erupted when the Carnegie Endowment for International Peace accused the ABA of misusing a grant received from the endowment. The endowment claimed that the organization, particularly through the Committee on Peace and Law, had misused funds that had been granted "for impartial work for peace and law through the United Nations" to instead "fight one of the Administration's principal world-wide programs."[73] The funds had been under the control of the committee, and William Ransom, its chair, was requested "to refrain in future from employing any of the endowment's grant for purposes of influencing public or Congressional attitudes with respect to matters pending before the Congress or either House thereof, except with written approval from the endowment." According to Joseph E. Johnson, president of the Carnegie Endowment, the committee had repeatedly failed to respond to requests from his organization for an accounting of the funds. He had concluded from the committee's publications against the Genocide Convention that "the spirit, if not the letter, of the grant from the endowment has been violated."[74] Cody Fowler, to whom the letter was addressed as president of the ABA, denied that the organization had even been accused of misusing funds.[75] This denial was strange given the fact that two members of the committee, Frank Holman and Arthur Schweppe, both discussed the charges at length.

Holman explained that the money was used for the U.S.-Canadian seminars held in 1949 to discuss the draft covenant and the Genocide Convention. The grant had been obtained through the efforts of George Finch, a member of the committee as well as secretary and trustee of the Carnegie Endowment. Holman was quick to point out that the accusing Johnson was the successor to Alger Hiss, former president of the endowment. Holman contended that the charge was a "smear tactic" aimed at undermining the committee's work.[76]

Schweppe also claimed that the charges were false and resulted from pressure by the State Department to discredit the committee and its work. Specifically, he accused U.S. Solicitor General Philip Perlman of instigating the Johnson charge. Schweppe, too, pointed out that Johnson had succeeded Alger Hiss. He held that the seminars and the committee's analysis of the Genocide Convention had been "strictly impartial" and that the committee had never "campaigned against the

Convention."[77] At the February 1950 Senate hearings on the Genocide Convention, Schweppe had also defended the seminars as "serious study groups, . . . not for propaganda." According to him, they were led by committee members Orie Phillips, Carl Rix, Finch, and Holman and one non-committee member, Manley O. Hudson, a well-respected international legal scholar.[78] All of the committee members noted by Schweppe were strongly opposed to human rights treaties.

By 14 September 1951, Senator John Bricker was moved to introduce a constitutional amendment aimed at protecting the "sacred rights which [U.S. citizens] enjoy under the Bill of Rights and the Constitution."[79] The amendment would have increased the role of Congress and decreased the role of the executive in concluding treaties. It became S.J. Res. 102 and was referred to the Senate Judiciary Committee.[80]

The formal introduction of a constitutional amendment increased the desire of committee members to put ABA support on record. Dissension between committee and section again arose. An earlier meeting in 1951 had produced reports and resolutions for further study, with the section continuing to favor reservations and the committee urging a constitutional amendment. No compromise had been reached between the warring factions by the time of the annual meeting.[81] Harold Stassen, chair of the section's Committee on Constitutional Aspects of International Agreements, was able to persuade the Committee on Peace and Law to delay any pressure for a constitutional amendment by arguing that in time the section might alter its position. Holman believed that the committee had been "outmaneuvered" by Stassen.[82] The section and committee jointly proposed a resolution to continue their mutual and separate studies, and the House of Delegates approved, leaving it to the two groups to forge a compromise. During the House of Delegates meeting, Holman expressed his disappointment at the postponement of the adoption of a recommended constitutional amendment. He argued that the proposals being discussed outside the ABA, including within Congress, were seriously flawed; the expertise of the organization was badly needed. He urged that the amendment be limited to addressing the protection of states' rights and the prohibition of trials of Americans abroad and urged action on such an amendment immediately. However, the joint section-committee resolution was adopted instead.

At the same meeting, the Committee on Peace and Law once again succeeded in obtaining the approval of the House of Delegates for a resolution disapproving the draft covenant. Charles Tillett, chair of the section, attempted to mitigate the resolution by proposing an amendment that would have asked that the draft be referred back to the United Nations Human Rights Commission. Holman pressed for the defeat of the amendment, which he claimed amounted to "quasi approval of the Draft Covenant."[83] The amendment was defeated.

The failure of the ABA to arrive at a consensus on a constitutional amendment did not affect Senator Bricker's advocacy, and on 7 February 1952 he introduced a longer version of his constitutional amendment.[84] Senator Bricker paid special tribute to the ABA for "alerting the American people" to the dangers this amendment was designed to meet. During the debate he also specifically mentioned his hopes that the ABA would soon complete a proposal for a constitutional amendment covering the same issues as his new amendment, S.J. 130.[85]

By 26 February 1952, the two disputing ABA factions had reached a partial agreement on the general controversy over human rights treaties. They jointly recommended, and the House of Delegates adopted, a resolution advising that the United States pursue human rights implementation through the creation of a framework like that of the International Labor Organization (ILO). In suitably ambiguous language, the resolution implied that general multilateral treaties were not necessary or perhaps should be avoided.[86]

The committee, however, did not view this program as sufficiently reliable and sought greater protection for American rights through a constitutional amendment. Its report expressed continued fears about the human rights treaties.

> Since the State Department has undertaken to negotiate so extensively with foreign nations in this new area, covered in part by the federal Bill of Rights, and the bills of rights and statutes of the several states, regarding the relationship of a government to its own citizens, and on the precautionary assumption that this course might be judicially approved, your Committee has prepared its draft amendment to the Constitution in respect of the treaty-making power with that assumption in view.[87]

The proposed amendment read:

> A provision of a treaty which conflicts with any provision of this Constitution shall not be of any force or effect. A treaty shall become effective as internal law in the United States only through

legislation by Congress which it could enact under its delegated powers in the absence of such a treaty.[88]

The section remained unconvinced of the need for a constitutional amendment. Section members expressed concern over the Bricker Amendment, which they felt was more far reaching than that proposed by the committee. They urged that further study be done before the association take any action. A resolution to this effect was defeated and one embodying the report of the committee adopted.[89]

The section and committee also strongly disagreed about the desirability of the international criminal court that was envisioned by the drafters of the Genocide Convention. The section's resolution called on the ABA to support efforts aimed at establishing such a body. Speakers for the resolution cited the United States' role at the Nuremberg and Tokyo trials and on the World Court as laying a foundation for U.S. leadership in this area.[90] The committee rejected the notion as contrary to Anglo-Saxon legal principles and as unconstitutional,[91] and its resolution, calling for no action, was approved.

Because of the power of the committee, the ABA continued to reflect the anti-Communist hysteria of the time. For example, at a 1952 national meeting of the organization, members voted strong encouragement of the Communist witch-hunt being perpetrated by the Congress. In a resolution from the Committee on Communist Tactics, Strategy, and Objectives, the organization expressed

> its approval of the manner in which the investigation and hearings by the present Committee on Un-American Activities of the House of Representatives and the Subcommittee of the Senate Judiciary Committee on the Internal Security Act are now being conducted and we recommend said committees for their continuing inquiry into the activities of the Communist Party, its members and followers.[92]

This resolution and others similar to it sponsored by the Committee on Communist Tactics supported what have since been established as serious violations of individual legal rights; when one considers that they were adopted by the leading legal organization in the nation, the intensity and extent of the fear of communism during this period is apparent.

All the members of the Committee on Peace and Law testified at the Senate Judiciary Committee hearings on the Bricker Amendment in May and June 1952, arguing that the ABA amendment was preferable to S.J. 130, submitted by Bricker. The Senate committee voted Bricker's bill out in an amended version, by a vote of 9 to 5. Although it went to the Senate floor on 15 June, the bill was not debated before the Senate adjourned for the session.

Critical of the Bricker Amendment provisions on executive agreements, the committee made an extensive study of the issue. In their 1952 report to the organization, committee members argued that there was serious danger of continued executive abuse.[93] They recommended a second constitutional amendment, this one on executive agreements.[94] The section opposed the committee recommendation on the basis of a study by the section's Committee on Constitutional Aspects of International Agreements. They argued that although presidential power to make executive agreements was not well defined, legislation could resolve the problem; a constitutional amendment was unnecessary.[95] The section recommended further study and discussion. After extended debate, a substantial majority reaffirmed the preeminence of the committee's views by adopting their resolution.[96]

When the ABA met in early 1953, Senator Bricker had again introduced a version of his constitutional amendment (this time, S.J. Res. 1).[97] At this time, in a report to the association, the Committee on Peace and Law made it clear once more that the human rights treaties were at the heart of their support of a constitutional amendment. The report opened with a quote from the famous address by Secretary of State John Foster Dulles (before he came to that post)[98] that emphasized his comments about the dangers to "the Constitutional Bill of Rights" posed by these treaties. The committee explained that the significance of the Bricker Amendment was that it would preserve "our form of government against the abuse of the treaty power, originating in the type of agreements which the executive arm of the government has been negotiating in the last few years in the name of human rights."[99] They reported that "after considering all alternatives the only sure safeguard against present and future risk is a constitutional amendment, which while preserving the treaty making power in all effectiveness in matters which are genuine subjects of international agreements, will close the gap for such distortions as those just mentioned."[100]

Committee members' emotions were so deeply engaged over the treaties and the amendment that they challenged the mere filing of a section report on the subject. The report, which opposed the proposed constitutional amendment, contained no recommendations for action. Those opposing acceptance of the report, however, argued that its acceptance would confuse the public about the actual position of the association on the amendment. After heated debate, the decision was made to accept the report and file it with the understanding that nothing in it would be considered an action of the ABA.[101]

On 16 February 1953 Senator Arthur V. Watkins (R.-Utah) introduced into the United States Senate the ABA's proposed amendment, which became S.J. Res. 43. It combined the two recommendations approved by the House of Delegates.[102] The 1953 hearings in the Senate Judiciary Committee were on both S.J. Res. 1 and S.J. Res. 43 and are discussed at length in Chapter 4. These were the major Bricker Amendment hearings. Not only did the members of the ABA Committee on Peace and Law testify at length, but numerous other individuals and organizations delivered testimony for and against.

Within the ABA the debate continued over what action the association should take regarding the Bricker Amendment. The Eisenhower administration continued to oppose the Bricker Amendment but had approved a much weaker proposal, the Knowland version, which had been offered as a substitute for S.J. 1.[103] In an address to the ABA in August, Secretary of State Dulles gave the association credit for publicizing the possible problems with the human rights treaties.

> I believe that this concern, when it arose, was a legitimate one, and those who voiced it performed a genuine service in bringing the situation to the attention of the American public. I point out that the arousing of that concern was a correction of the evil—a correction in the most dependable way, that is, by the vigilance of our citizenry. The danger, never great, has passed.[104]

But he also reiterated his belief that, although there might be problems with the human rights treaties, a constitutional amendment like the one supported by the ABA was unnecessary and would seriously interfere with the executive's ability to conduct foreign affairs.

The committee, however, continued to support the amendment proudly. The close cooperation between the ABA and the amendment supporters within the Senate is clear from the ABA committee chair's remarks:

> The text brought out by the majority of the Senate Judiciary Committee follows rather closely the recommendation of the House of

Delegates. It embodies each of the principles for which we stood, and it accepts a very considerable amount of the language.[105]

Clearly, Dulles's comments failed to persuade the committee that the dangers from human rights treaties had passed. In its 1953 report to the organization, the committee devoted a special section to "The Draft International Covenant." It quoted Dulles's commitment that the administration would not try to recommend that the United States become a party to the covenant. The committee suggested that although the constitutional amendment forces had brought about a change in foreign policy, the Dulles promise would be limited to the present administration. Therefore, they argued that this inadequate solution to the problems of the Human Rights Covenant must be addressed by the constitutional amendment proceedings.[106]

The section, on the other hand, introduced a resolution aimed at putting the ABA on record against the Bricker Amendment. They reiterated Dulles's remarks: that the executive as well as several legislative groups were opposed to the amendment, that it was unnecessary given the executive's reassurances about the human rights treaties, and that it would impair the treaty-making powers of the president.[107] In opposing the resolution, Frank Holman, former chair of the committee, cited the long, arduous work by the ABA to bring about S.J. 1 and defeat of the Genocide Convention and the draft covenant. He suggested that a repudiation at this point would undermine the influence and reputation of the organization. Again the committee triumphed as the section's resolution was overwhelmingly defeated by a vote of 117 to 33.[108]

The ABA, then, was firmly on record in support of the amendment when the Senate, on 20 January 1954, began floor debate on S.J. 1. Numerous recommendations, amendments, and substitutes were offered.[109] When the votes were finally taken, the Bricker version failed (by a 52-40 vote) to receive the requisite two-thirds for a constitutional amendment.[110] A weaker version proposed by Senator Walter F. George (D.-Ga.) came closer, falling one vote short of the requirement (61-30).[111]

On 5 August 1954 Senator Bricker reintroduced a constitutional amendment combining parts of those that had failed in February.[112] He argued that the need for an amendment was greater than ever, in part because the Human Rights Commission had failed to include a provision on private property in the final commission draft of the covenants.[113] The Committee on Peace and Law of the ABA in its 1954 annual report continued to support efforts toward a constitutional amendment.[114] The organization did not begin to change its position on human rights treaties publicly until more than twenty years later.

Conclusion

There is no doubt that the ABA, and especially its Special Committee on Peace and Law Through United Nations, was a leading force in establishing the opposition to human rights treaties that has persisted to the present. The ABA played a crucial role in the story of the opposition to human rights treaties. Aroused by the campaign of Frank Holman, a small group within the ABA decided that the treaties represented a serious danger to the country, and that group was able to mobilize the organization to oppose the treaties officially. It was during the debates within the ABA and also in addresses to the public that the major arguments against the human rights treaties were first outlined.

Not only did the association address the public and its own members, but eventually it won the attention of the United States Senate as well. The ABA consistently held a special status in Senate consideration of the human rights treaties. This unique position was reflected in numerous statements by senators, especially Senator Bricker, that expressed gratitude to the association for its help, including its suggestions on the rewording of legislation.[115] Reports of the ABA committee were widely quoted as authoritative during hearings on human rights treaties, and Senate committees waited to allow ABA positions to be officially approved before making decisions about recommendations on ratification.

The actions within the ABA also reflected the political environment of the period—the fear of communism at home and abroad, the fear of a Communist-controlled world government, and the fear of domestic change, especially in race relations. The general fear expressed was the fear of change—change in the political system, change in the economic system, change in the traditional American way of life. Forces at home and abroad seemed to augur change at a time in history when, perhaps, many Americans were tired and reluctant to face the prospect of more disruption of their routines. These fears for the republic, centered as they were on an external foe with internal allies, were the context into which the human rights treaties were introduced. It is possible to imagine that the traditional U.S. ideals of freedom and equality, so frequently and eloquently voiced by conservatives, might have led to the embracing of these international treaties, but instead the human rights treaties appear to have become a symbol of all those forces that might bring about destructive change. How the treaties came to be seen in this light and the impact that this development has had on subsequent debates are the concerns explored in the remainder of this book.

TWO

The Genocide Convention

This convention provides
chiefly an international FEPC,
together with an international
antilynching bill. It is designed
apparently to take a short cut
which will make unnecessary, or
at least less important, the
passing of FEPC laws by the
Congress or by the legislatures of
the several States. . . . This
measure is an attempt to give
other nations, through an
irresponsible international
body, the right to intervene
in our internal affairs.
—Harry Barger, *Genocide
Convention Hearings*, 1950

The Genocide Convention was the first
postwar treaty on human rights and the
strategic starting point for the opposition. The major arguments enunciated
against *all* human rights treaties were
first articulated against the Genocide
Convention. Conservative anxiety over
racial desegregation was initially fed
by the contention that the treaty references to racial genocide would be interpreted in a manner that could be used to
dismantle racial segregation within the
United States.

Conservatives soon connected the
Genocide Convention to other human
rights treaties, all of which they claimed
would have a dangerous impact on the
United States. As we saw in Chapter 1,
the Cold War and the emerging civil
rights movement created fears that provided the context for a negative reaction
to human rights treaties. The American Bar Association Special Committee
on Peace and Law Through United Nations repeatedly pointed to the Genocide Convention when warning the legal profession and the American public
of a threat to the American way of life.

During the Senate hearings on the
Genocide Convention, members of the
ABA committee testified as almost the
lone opposition to ratification. Their un-
remittingly negative claims ultimately
overcame the forces favoring ratification, which were numerically far larger.
Support for the convention was strong;
representatives of groups claiming a
total combined membership of approxi-
mately 100 million people and covering
a wide political spectrum urged ratifica-

tion. Among those groups testifying in favor of ratification were the American Legion, the Salvation Army, the National Association for the Advancement of Colored People, the Congress of Industrial Organizations, the American Federation of Labor, the Women's Christian Temperance Union, the Federal Council of Churches of Christ, the United Council of Church Women, the American Civil Liberties Union, the American Association of Social Workers, the General Conference of Seventh Day Adventists, the American Veterans Committee, B'nai Brith, and the Supreme Lodge of the Order of Sons of Italy. The only major opposition came from the American Bar Association. The question of how and why the Committee on Peace and Law succeeded is the subject of this chapter.

Focusing on the Genocide Convention, the chapter begins with a brief description of the treaty and its drafting. There follows an explanation of how the Genocide Convention was linked in a critical fashion to subsequent human rights treaties. Those opposed to the convention developed and articulated a series of arguments that were ultimately applied against all human rights treaties. These arguments, elaborated and refined during the 1950s, echoed, with little alteration, through the 1960s and 1970s and on up to the present.

A further purpose of this chapter is to draw attention to the legalism that pervaded the discussion. Political arguments were minimized or ignored as legalistic reasoning took center stage. Supporters of the Genocide Convention, feeling a need to respond to effectively presented opposition arguments that linked the treaty with fears widely held in the Senate and among the public, yielded to the opposition claim that the convention was fundamentally flawed. One significant effect of this concession and the legalistic cast of the debate was that the attention of convention supporters was drawn to the game of designing reservations to address the acknowledged flaws in the treaty. At the conclusion of the early hearings on the Genocide Convention, a treaty that had originally been noncontroversial and publicly popular had come to be viewed as defective and dangerous—a verdict that soon spilled over to human rights treaties in general. Thus, the opponents not only succeeded in defeating the Genocide Convention; they also succeeded in changing the question of the debate from Why not ratify human rights treaties? to Why ratify them?

History and Content of the Genocide Convention

The Genocide Convention was drafted in response to the atrocities of the Third Reich, with the objective of making genocide an international crime. The treaty declared that genocide was a crime under international law and obligated states to attempt to prevent and punish it. The heart of the treaty was in Article II, which defined genocide.

> In the present Convention, genocide means any of the following acts committed with intent to destroy, in whole or in part, a national, ethnical, racial or religious group, as such:
> (a) Killing members of the group;
> (b) Causing serious bodily or mental harm to members of the group;
> (c) Deliberately inflicting on the group conditions of life calculated to bring about its physical destruction in whole or in part;
> (d) Imposing measures intended to prevent births within the group;
> (e) Forcibly transferring children of the group to another group.

Other articles addressed the issues of punishment, implementation, trial of those accused, extradition, the role of the United Nations, and dispute settlement. The treaty was adopted by the General Assembly on 9 December 1948. President Truman transmitted the treaty to the Senate on 16 June 1949 with a recommendation of ratification. It was then referred to a subcommittee of the Committee on Foreign Relations, which held hearings on it in early 1950.

The opposition to the treaty, as explained in Chapter 1, was focused in a small appointed committee of the ABA composed of nine men. This group, the Committee on Peace and Law Through United Nations, began its campaign against the convention with a series of invited seminars, held throughout the country to discuss the provisions of the Genocide Convention and those of the draft of the Covenant on Human Rights. Their alleged purpose was to objectively discuss the treaties and anticipate problems. In the end, they concluded that the problems with the Genocide Convention were so severe that it was unsalvageable even with reservations or understandings and therefore should be rejected. In presenting the committee's report, Carl Rix stated, "The Committee did not feel capable of drafting reservations which would adequately protect the constitutional interests of the United States."[1]

At the 1949 annual meeting of the ABA, a long and heated debate between the committee and the Section on International and Comparative Law resulted in a compromise resolution that both groups would continue to study the treaty and issue reports that would be forwarded to the Senate. Representatives of both groups appeared and testified at the Senate hearings. Philip Perlman, solicitor general of the United States, was an important government spokesperson for the treaty and was also a member of the ABA Section on International Law. He testified that the section represented over a thousand members, while the committee, which was appointed, represented only its own nine members. However, the strong and consistent campaign waged by the committee against the Genocide Convention overcame the dedicated and enthusiastic support of individuals and groups representing a broad spectrum of political opinion.

Linking the Genocide Convention to Other Human Rights Treaties

There can be no doubt that the primary opposition to the genocide treaty was closely linked to other international human rights activities. Throughout the first set of Senate hearings on the Genocide Convention, frequent reference was made to the Human Rights Covenant.[2] As one of the leading opponents explained, "I shall not attempt to segregate the problems as between the Genocide Convention and the Covenant on Human Rights because, in my view, both would have in many respects the same effect."[3] The series of ABA seminars held around the country covered both treaties, as did also a Department of State pamphlet published to answer frequent questions from the public.[4]

Thus, many opponents believed that the immediate need was to block the international human rights movement in general, and their starting point was the defeat of the Genocide Convention. Carl Rix, a major adversary of the treaty and member of the Committee on Peace and Law, expressed this view.

> In order to . . . deal with domestic questions, it has been found necessary to change those questions to international law by the use of treaties. That method of creating international law has

been specifically approved by the International Court. . . . A considerable number of treaties of that kind have been proposed and are now under preparation in the United Nations. . . .

If there is to be a succession of treaties from the United Nations dealing with domestic questions, are we ready to surrender the power of the States over such matters to the Federal Government?[5]

And another opponent expressed similar concern: "The American people are getting very tired of the avalanche of proposed treaties and commitments, with all of their implications."[6]

Some senators expressed open antagonism toward this set of U.N. treaties, including the as-yet-uncompleted Human Rights Covenant. Senator Walter F. George, a member of the Foreign Relations Committee, combined hostility toward the Genocide Convention with ignorance of its provisions and those of other human rights agreements.

We are just not careful enough, gentlemen, in these treaties, and this is one of those loose treaties that should never have been made, and the only thing you can say about it is that it is just not quite as bad as the other one that they drew up on human rights or the universal bill of rights, or whatever you call the thing.[7]

Frank Holman, president of the ABA at this time, also criticized the treaty language, claiming that it was "hastily" and "casually put in final form."[8] A letter to the editor published in the July 1949 *ABA Journal* refuted the idea that there was anything other than careful attention paid during the drafting process. The letter was signed by A. H. Fellers, general counsel in the Legal Department of the United Nations. Fellers detailed the various stages of the drafting process, explaining the great effort that was made to gather opinions of governments and nongovernmental organizations and the many sessions spent by the committees, Secretariat, and Economic and Social Council of the United Nations to ensure a document that was as well drafted as possible.[9] This ABA criticism that the treaties were badly drafted, poorly designed, and written by politicians rather than lawyers was often repeated.[10]

The 1 September 1949 report of the Special Committee on Peace and Law Through United Nations created a new phrase to discredit these conventions, "government by treaty." One section of the report, entitled "The New Concept," began,

At a time in the history of the world when economic conditions, resulting largely from two devastating wars, are forcing nations to demand sacrifices of their individual freedoms to conform to Socialist states or alien ideologies, the same peoples are being asked to adjust themselves to revolutionary changes in their relations with their own people and the people of other nations. It does not seem to be enough that they should be led by example and teaching to new ways of conduct. Under international codes of conduct called treaties they are to accept the changes by law. Government by treaties is the new concept.[11]

The strategy adopted by treaty opponents was to clearly discredit and decisively defeat the Genocide Convention. By linking provisions of the Genocide Convention to encroachments on American sovereignty, states' rights, and racial issues and identifying these "dangers" with human rights treaties generally, they believed an unequivocal statement would be made at home and abroad that the United States would have no part of human rights treaties.[12]

Arguments against the Genocide Convention

Ultimately the tactics of the treaty opponents proved successful, for their campaign effectively stopped serious Senate consideration of human rights treaties for over thirty years. Although knowledge of the link between the Genocide Convention and other human rights treaties does not go far in explaining why and how these treaties were opposed, it does enrich our understanding of the general problem: that these treaties as a group were perceived by opponents as a threat to the American system and that the genocide treaty was the first to be debated. The arguments developed against the Genocide Convention came to transcend that single treaty and reflect criticism of all human rights treaties; the specific arguments are, therefore, worth examining here in some detail.

Diminish Basic Rights

The members of the ABA's Committee on Peace and Law frequently argued that the Genocide Convention and other human rights treaties reflected, either intentionally or as a result of inevitable compromises, a lower standard of rights than that enjoyed by Americans, so that citizens of the United States stood to lose rather than gain from ratification. A section in the ABA report presented at the Senate hearings explicates the substructure of the argument. The report contains the following paragraph:

> Peoples who do not know the meaning of freedoms are to be metamorphosed into judges of the freedoms of others. A common pattern is to be set for billions of people of different languages, religions, standards of living, culture, education and mental and physical capacity. A few people, with beliefs utterly foreign to each other, meet, debate, and by majority vote seek to determine how the people of the world shall live on a common pattern. To bring some people to a higher standard, those far above those standards, under the guise of precarious sacrifice to the common good, are to accept the mediocrity of the average. Are the people of the United States ready for such sweeping changes?[13]

Other opponents of the treaty echoed the ABA committee's report in ascribing the major problem of the treaty to its compromise with inferior systems. As one wrote,

> And in the turmoil of compromise, how many of our freedoms and rights will be given up so we can meet upon the common ground of legal, moral, and political mediocrity of so many of the other nations is something no one can foretell.[14]

Some of the opposition statements at the Senate hearings reflected the interpretation of the convention that Frank Holman had developed in his public crusade.[15] Specifically, these statements cited the "mental harm" language of the treaty, holding that it would result in restrictions on First Amendment rights.[16] Harry Barger, of the National Economic Council, read a statement reflecting this point.

> The convention goes much further than to punish or prevent mass murder. It aims to regulate almost the thought, and certainly the acts, including the words and writings, of individuals. . . . Thus, it is clear that the doing of an act by an individual such as the refusal of employment, or blackballing a person for membership in a union or social club, or the publishing of any comment, no matter how mild, with respect to any member of a

minority, could be deemed by the "international penal tribunal" set up by this convention to constitute "mental harm" and hence, under the clear provisions of the Genocide Convention, to be worthy of punishment. . . . Under some . . . of these provisions, the slightest reference to a member of a minority race or religion—such as a newspaper identifying a man under arrest as a Negro, might be deemed a punishable act. Certain American newspapers have already been "induced" not to identify in their columns an individual by race or color.[17]

The ABA report presented a more sophisticated legal argument making the same point. It contended that the treaty phrase "incitement to commit genocide" constituted an infringement of freedom of speech and press.

Who shall judge if political speeches are incitement to genocide, the civil authorities? . . . Who shall judge as to freedom of the press? As prevention of genocide, shall the censors be provided by the state? . . . No treaty, no matter what its purpose, which seeks to deny those rights should be considered by the Senate of the United States.[18]

Promote World Government

A major line of opposition reasoning emphasized the loss of national sovereignty to an international body. This argument played on nationalism and chauvinism by suggesting that ratification would result in a loss of power and authority. Sometimes this loss is described in general terms: a weakening of the United States government by the very act of involving itself in international agreements and international activity. As one opponent put it: "Like most of the other international agreements we are asked to approve, it calls for the transfer of a substantial measure of our sovereignty as a nation to an international group in which we would have a distinctly minority vote."[19] Opponents then argued that the loss of sovereignty occasioned by the treaty would lead to world government. Once on this track, it was implied, it would be an easy step from loss of sovereignty to "world government." "Government by treaty," opponents claimed, will result in world government.

It is a long step in the path to world government. Do Americans want, or are they ready for, world government? . . . That is what government by treaty will do, sooner or later. . . . Government by treaty is a dangerous approach, and if we wish to retain our freedom, and maintain our American concept of government, we have got to abandon that approach.[20]

The fear expressed for U.S. sovereignty is also reflected in fears of international judgment of U.S. actions. Senator H. Alexander Smith (R.-N.J.) voiced his concern:

We may be charged with [genocide], that is the danger, and the Court of International Justice may say that here is a prima facie case made against the United States of genocide, and there you are, left, condemned in the eyes of the world.[21]

When nationals of any country travel abroad, they are subject to the laws of the state they enter. It is always the case that they may be legitimately or illegitimately charged with a crime in that state. The genocide treaty did not change that situation. It certainly did not make unfounded accusations more likely.

Much of this criticism appears to have grown out of an ethnocentric world view, a perspective suspicious or disdainful of things foreign. A strong belief in the superiority of the United States forms the foundation of this argument. An example of this type of ethnocentric thinking is Senator George's comments in executive session, where he declared,

I don't think the peoples of the earth are in any position where they can tell this great people on morals, politics and religion, how they should live. I still feel that we are ahead of them in that respect, and I would hate to bind ourselves. . . . I am in favor of preventing, if you can by any kind of international arrangement, mass murder; but I am not in favor of leaving it to the interpretation of nations who have been indulging for centuries in just such a thing, and they have been occurring at every drop of the hat, so to speak, so that I want to be careful.[22]

This line of argument also misrepresents the United Nations as a world legislature dominated by interests alien to those of the United States[23] and confuses the treaty process by implying that the United States and other countries have been bound by treaties they have not considered or ratified. This false impression is clear in the ABA special report presented to the Senate from the Committee on Peace and Law, which was discussed above.

Enhance Soviet/Communist Influence

At times the treaty was associated with advancing the interests of the Soviet Union in particular and communism in general.

> The Communist world has already won its cold war against the Western powers with respect to the punishment of genocide. The convention as submitted could not be more perfectly drafted to enable the totalitarian governments to proceed against their minority groups the same as Hitler did.[24]

One member of the ABA Committee linked Communist subversion to the civil rights movement.

> I leave to your imagination as to what would happen in the field of administration or municipal law if subversive elements should teach minorities that the field of civil rights and laws had been removed to the field of international law.[25]

A non-ABA opponent clearly presented another form of the anti-Soviet argument.

> If this genocide treaty is ratified by the United States Senate, it guarantees to Russia the winning of the third world war, for this treaty not only would effectually prevent our being able to defend our own shores and our people but it gives the power to our enemies to lie about and harass our citizens, our police, our FBI, our officials, and our armies with charges of "genocide" or inciting to "genocide." . . . This treaty would be a most effective means to prevent the apprehension of spies and traitors.[26]

One fear seemed to be that the Soviet Union, by use of the treaty, might actually gain custody over and try American citizens according to the practice of the Soviet system of justice. Senator Smith presented this argument:

> I do not want any American citizen to be tried by a tribunal, for example, such as the Russians may have . . . or an international tribunal that might conceivably be governed by the kind of jurisprudence that Russia has![27]

This argument combines concern about the Soviet Union with another important point in the criticism of treaty opponents, the fear that U.S. citizens might be tried abroad.

Subject Citizens to Trial Abroad

A major objection of treaty opponents was to the Genocide Convention's provision calling for the creation of an international criminal court. The court would have had the competence to try for crimes of genocide individuals *from those states that had accepted the jurisdiction of the court.* Moreover, establishment of such a court required a separate treaty that would also have to be submitted to the Senate for consideration and ratification. (In fact, this international criminal court has still not been established, and a treaty for it has never been approved.) The opposition implied that American citizens would be tried in foreign domestic courts and by an international tribunal, both of which, they argued, would lack the extensive judicial safeguards of the U.S. system. The ABA report put it quite clearly:

> The committee is opposed to subjecting our citizens and other persons within our territorial jurisdiction to trial, conviction and sentence, for acts of genocide committed in the United States, by an international penal tribunal where they would not be surrounded by the constitutional safeguards and legal rights accorded persons charged with a domestic crime.[28]

The persistence of this argument in the face of repeated contradictory interpretive evidence is revealed in an exchange between Harry Barger, representing the National Economic Council in opposing the convention, and Senator Henry Cabot Lodge, Jr. (R.-Mass.), of the subcommittee of the Foreign Relations Committee.

> Mr. Barger: We oppose this convention because . . . persons charged with genocide may be tried . . . "by such international penal tribunal as may have *jurisdiction* with respect to those contracting parties which shall have accepted its jurisdiction."
>
> If the Senate should ratify this convention, we would be going back toward one of the odious conditions which prevailed when the Declaration of Independence complained, inter alia, that King George III—"had given his assent to acts of pretended legislation . . . for transporting us beyond seas to be tried for pretended offenses."
>
> Senator Lodge: I just can't follow that argument at all. It seems to me if anybody is to be tried in an international tribunal outside of the United States there would have to be an additional treaty in

which we would express our approval of the setting up of that tribunal.

Mr. Barger: . . . this presently proposed treaty is adequate to accomplish that purpose.

Senator Lodge: It seems to me words have absolutely no meaning if [one] can follow that out. The only way [a person] could be tried in any other tribunal would be in a tribunal "in a country which shall have accepted its jurisdiction." In other words, we would have to have a separate treaty and a separate action. . . . It seems to me that that is just fantastic, and if there are arguments against this I want to know what they are, but this, it seems to me, is no argument at all.

Mr. Barger: . . . the language is very broad.

Senator Lodge: I think it is terribly definite. . . . You could not make it any more definite. If there is to be an international court, we would have to accept the jurisdiction of that court, and that would mean another treaty and another two-thirds vote and another set of hearings.

Mr. Barger: I think, however, you will agree with me that it does not specify the necessity of an additional treaty.

Senator Lodge: . . . How do you accept the jurisdiction? You accept the jurisdiction by treaty.

Mr. Barger: Won't the acceptance of this particular genocide treaty accomplish that?

Senator Lodge: By its expressed terms it does not.[29]

This exchange and others like it did not persuade the opposition. Additionally, Mr. William Fitzpatrick, editor of the *New Orleans State*, presented an argument that extended the problem by charging that the treaty called for the mandatory extradition of Americans:

It not only invades domestic law, it provides for the extradition of Americans for overseas trials should they be accused of having committed genocide in any other country. And proponents of the convention plan an international tribunal to try all Americans overseas, wherever the international court of justice might be sitting, for offenses which might have been committed in his own home. Will the safeguards surrounding accused Americans in this country be found in those trials? Or should we stop and take a long look at these proposals before we accept them as the law of the land?[30]

The anathema of trials abroad became a recurring cry. Senator George accurately predicted continuing problems over this charge when he said,

The genocide thing is dead as it stands, because there is no Senate—I do not think there is going to be a Senate hereafter that will ratify that, because under it, why, we would be obligated or might be obligated—they could certainly claim that we were obligated—to try our individual citizens, even officers of states before foreign courts.[31]

Given the absence of any U.S. extradition treaty specifying genocide as an extraditable offense, and given the general U.S. refusal to extradite its own nationals, there is no reason to believe that Americans would have been extradited or that they would have been tried in the courts of foreign states. Yet a paranoia about overseas trials was fostered. Senator Smith expressed his dismay:

Foreign courts; that is my trouble. I would not consent to that. . . . In the light of what has happened in Hungary and other places, you see, trumped up charges were made that somebody was guilty, and you would not have a chance to protect your citizens.[32]

Threaten the U.S. Form of Government

As discussed in Chapter 1, one of the recurring themes of the opposition was that the series of human rights treaties being produced at the United Nations constituted a threat to the fundamental structure of the American system of government. The officially adopted recommendation of the ABA rejecting the Genocide Convention claimed that the treaty "involves important constitutional questions; . . . the proposed convention raises important fundamental questions but does not resolve them in a manner consistent with our form of government."[33] The effect of the treaty on the U.S. system of government, according to opponents of the treaty, would be "revolutionary."[34] The fear expressed was that the treaty would fundamentally alter the constitutional system. Often the form the alteration would take was unclear; at times it appeared that the federal government would be expanded at grave costs to the states, an argument discussed below. At other times the Constitution was cited vaguely with references to the founding fathers, to the separation of powers, or to the history of the document itself. Testimony from Louisiana district attorney Leander Perez offers one example of these arguments positing vague but very serious threats to the Constitution:

> Are we to throw away those precious heritages, won for the present and future generations, at the cost of the blood of those patriots—those men, because they were men—and if we are men, we will tell those today who are misled and who urge upon you gentlemen of the Senate to ratify this monstrosity, that you will preserve our constitutional form of government, that you will not resort to the dishonest subterfuge of amending and destroying the most precious, blood-bought provisions of our Constitution.[35]

As a result of the alleged constitutional threat posed by the Genocide Convention and other human rights treaties, the Committee on Peace and Law suggested the need for a constitutional amendment. Rix called attention to the problem:

> There is a blind spot in the Constitution. At the time it was drawn, and for years thereafter, operations were under a narrower concept of international law. . . . It has been brought to the fore by the proposed Covenant on Human Rights, the Genocide Convention, and the proposed Treaty on Traffic in Persons.[36]

The conviction that a constitutional corrective was needed in order to protect Americans' traditional rights from international interference came to fruition in the Bricker Amendment movement, already noted in Chapter 1 and fully discussed in Chapter 4.

Infringe on Domestic Jurisdiction

More generally, opponents argued that the treaty, in dealing with a "domestic" topic, by its very nature violated Article 2, paragraph 7, of the United Nations Charter, which provided that the internal jurisdiction of member states would not be violated by U.N. actions.

> How can the United States Senate be asked, or urged, to ratify this so-called Genocide Convention which is a direct encroach-

ment on the domestic affairs of this country under the Constitution of the United States, in face of the fact that adoption by the United Nations of this so-called Genocide Convention is a flagrant violation of the solemn provisions of its own Charter, or a violation of that part of the international agreement by which the United Nations came into being?[37]

Testimony during the hearings on the Genocide Convention was crucial for establishing the impression that human rights treaties were, in fact, designed to infringe on U.S. domestic jurisdiction.

It is plain that the whole purpose of the proposed Genocide Convention is to make the international crime of Genocide apply to individuals and thereby to intervene in matters which are essentially within the domestic jurisdiction of the state.[38]

The belief grew that the treaties were full of challenges to U.S. law and practice, as opposed to being a means of internationalizing traditional U.S. values.

Increase International Entanglements

Opponents of the Genocide Convention also expressed concern that the prevention and punishment of the crimes defined in the treaty would lead the United States into unstated international commitments. They suggested that implementation of the convention would draw the United States into the domestic affairs of other states in contravention of our national interests. The ABA committee report on the Genocide Convention argued that "the policy of the United Nations constitutes a renewal of the intervention theory in international practice which has been discarded and for which has been substituted the good neighbor theory."[39]

The new commitments, some argued, would in fact increase the likelihood of the use of force. George Finch, a member of the Committee on Peace and Law, made this point in the following statement:

The ratification of the present Genocide Convention will raise to the level of an international question many questions now reserved to the domestic jurisdiction. It is submitted that such a result will not be in the interest of preserving peace but of creating additional frictions which might lead to war.[40]

Create Self-Executing Obligations

A technical argument related to the constitutional provision that treaties are the supreme law of the land is that treaty provisions may be
"self-executing." The term means that such provisions are immediately applicable by U.S. courts without implementing legislation. The
Genocide Convention in Article V clearly refers to "the necessary
legislation to give effect to the provisions of the present Convention,"
language that makes the convention non-self-executing. The opposition claimed, however, that it was self-executing. They criticized the
drafters for not considering the United States Constitution by including specific language making the treaty non-self-executing.

> The definitions of crimes of genocide are clearly self-executing
> and become the law of the land. . . . The failure of the drafters of
> the Genocide Convention to recognize the need to meet the con-
> stitutional situation of the United States in any way, in our opin-
> ion, is a fundamental error and a barrier to ratification of the
> Convention by the Senate of the United States *on this ground alone*
> [emphasis added].[41]

Violate States' Rights

In spite of these arguments over international jurisdiction and threats
to sovereignty, the main opposition to the treaty was rooted in states'
rights, and the arguments against the Genocide Convention paralleled contemporaneous objections to federal civil rights action. The
historic context, then, is important to understanding the impact of the
states' rights issue on Senate considerations.

As discussed earlier, the Truman Committee report, desegregation
cases, and other attacks on racial discrimination heightened southern
fears that human rights treaties in general and the Genocide Convention in particular would be used to dismantle southern segregation.
Many southerners felt strongly that their way of life was being singled
out for scrutiny and that federal action was being used as a means of
intervening in their local affairs. Vigorous support of states' rights and
criticism of unconstitutional federal encroachment were dominant
themes. The strong emotional appeal of these issues and the ability to
link them to the Genocide Convention had immediate and lasting
effects.

Some southerners, in their sensitivity to criticism of legally structured racial segregation, even went so far as to argue that the abroga-

tion of states' rights was the major objective of the genocide treaty. One opponent of the treaty put it this way:

> This fake, so-called Genocide Convention . . . was simply no more, no less than a part of the pattern of the conspiracy to destroy our American institutions, to nationalize our domestic relations and to deprive the States and the people of the States of their right of self-government.[42]

The executive branch was accused by states' rights people of seeking approval of the treaty in order to take over residual powers of the states. As Finch said, "I regard the Genocide Convention as a further attempt on the part of the Federal Government to increase its power at the expense of the States."[43]

Even those who did not suggest that the treaty was primarily aimed at usurping essential powers of the states still stressed the potential use of the treaty to introduce or modify existing state law. For example, the 1950 report of the Committee on Peace and Law to the ABA stated:

> To impose a great new body of treaty law which will become the domestic law of the United States is a tremendous change in the structure of the relation of States and the Federal Government under our Constitution [and] is of doubtful constitutionality. . . . To deprive the States of a great field of criminal jurisprudence and place it in the Federal field alone, or under the jurisdiction of an international court, is truly revolutionary.[44]

The writers are here referring to the absence in the treaty of a federal-state clause to provide that in federal systems the treaty provisions would only apply to those areas of authority held by the federal government.

In its most sophisticated form, the states' rights argument presented the Genocide Convention as an attack on the formal separation of powers between state and federal governments. Opponents referred to the treaty as a threat to the "dual system" of government. In the initial ABA report, the treaty was seen as creating "endless confusion in the dual system of the United States."[45]

> Thus there may be created, as law, a third body of treaty law in this country with no constitutional basis whatsoever, of equal dignity with our Constitution, as supreme law of the land, super-

seding all State constitutions, decisions, and laws of the States covering the same subjects, and probably superior to all prior enacted laws of Congress on the subject. . . . The effect in this country of a ratified treaty in a field which has been almost exclusive in the States, is so far-reaching in its consequence that the word "revolutionary" is not fully descriptive.[46]

A similar accusation was made by Senator George in an executive session of the Senate Foreign Relations Committee. According to him, the treaty was "filled with subtle and obscure and doublemeaning things that really aim to attack the constitutional setup that we have under our dual system."[47]

Some of the opponents painted the results of the treaty ratification in dramatic terms. Perez, for instance, portrayed them in the following way:

Thus, at one fell swoop a large part of the municipal sovereignty reserved to all the States of the Union over the domestic affairs of their citizens and their police powers and law enforcement authority would be supplanted. If this ever comes to pass, then State and county criminal judges, prosecutors and law enforcement officers would become largely unnecessary, and they might as well be supplanted by the Federal police, prosecutors, and courts.[48]

The racial component of the opposition argument was seen more clearly in the claim that the treaty would be used by the federal government to invalidate state law in order to dismantle the system of legalized segregation. The ABA report put it simply: "Consent to and ratification of the treaty would transfer all jurisdiction in civil rights to the Federal field to the exclusion of the States."[49]

ABA spokesperson George Finch expressed his fear during the Senate hearings that the convention's terms provided grounds for denouncing segregation laws.

Minority groups in this country are now vigorously seeking to have such discrimination abolished by Federal legislation. Can there be any reasonable doubt that if Congress fails to enact the civil-rights laws now being urged upon it and if this convention is ratified as submitted, members of the affected groups will be in a position to seek legal relief on the ground that this so-called

Genocide Convention has superseded all obnoxious State legislation?[50]

One specific provision of the treaty that was severely criticized as raising civil rights issues was that dealing with "mental harm." The wording was considered by the opposition to be too vague.

> The people who wrote the Genocide Convention were not content with dealing with the evil that everyone deplores, namely, the group massacres engaged in by Hitler and other historical assassins, but saw fit to write into the Genocide Convention "civil rights" ideas, such as inflicting "mental harm" on a group "in whole or in part." . . . It cannot be assumed that the unambiguous words chosen, viz "bodily or mental harm," will be construed by any court except in their usual sense, even if some other hidden and unusual meaning may have in fact been intended.[51]

Finch followed through with this criticism by asking, "Can it be successfully denied that segregation laws are susceptible of being denounced as causing mental harm to all members of the group against which such laws discriminate?"[52]

The best example of criticism of the convention on civil rights issues is the attack linking the treaty to the Fair Employment Practices Commission legislation then under discussion in the House Labor Committee. The argument was that the treaty would establish illegitimate civil rights authority within the federal government that would justify new bureaucracies like the FEPC. Rix, of the ABA, outlined the basis of this linkage, which echoed in this specific issue the southern animosity toward federal civil rights legislation.

> The report of the Civil Rights Committee appointed by the President, after considering the division of power over civil rights between the Federal Government and the States, in two places refers to the added power which may be given to Congress in the field of civil rights. . . . Last year, a bill emanated from the Labor Committee of the House dealing with the entire field of civil rights. It is known as the FEPC bill.[53]

This idea was reiterated and extended by Barger during the hearings on the treaty.

> This convention provides chiefly an international FEPC. . . . It is designed apparently to take a short cut which will make unneces-

sary, or at least less important, the passing of FEPC laws by the Congress or by the legislatures of the several States.[54]

The idea was readapted by Senator Alexander Wiley (R.-Wis.) during an executive session of the Senate Foreign Relations Committee when he suggested that this treaty, along with other United Nations activities, "raises the question whether you need any FEPC legislation at all, because you have it all in the United Nations."[55]

Most specifically, and perhaps most effectively, opponents claimed that the Genocide Convention would apply to racial incidents, notably lynchings and race riots. They argued that the language was too vague and ill defined and that, although the treaty ostensibly dealt with mass murder, it could and would be interpreted to cover acts against an individual. Throughout the hearings, opponents expressed their belief that race riots and lynchings would fall within the treaty's terms. The original ABA report made the claim that race riots and lynchings were possible examples of genocide under the terms of the treaty.[56] Arthur Schweppe, presenting the ABA position, stated, "It would be entirely reasonable to include race riots under the present definition, and also lynching, if engaged in with intent to destroy part of a group."[57] The very mention of lynching and race riots aroused racial associations and this linking of the treaty with efforts to address acts that had not been successfully addressed in Congress became a key weapon in the opposition arsenal.

The issue of lynching was raised again and again, growing to such proportions that members of the Foreign Relations Committee consistently raised questions about it at public hearings and in private sessions, and it became a part of the broader public debate. As one supporter of the treaty pointed out during an executive session of the Senate Foreign Relations Committee:

> Let me say one thing before I finish, in getting down to realities here: The objection, that is, the practical objection, the thing that is behind a lot of people's minds on this convention is—is it aimed at lynching in the South? You have to face that. That is a thing that a lot of people are worried about.[58]

The specific discussion of lynching became so widespread that even black groups testifying before the Foreign Relations Committee felt it necessary to deny the treaty's application to lynching. Eunice Carter of the National Council of Negro Women avowed,

[We are] under no misapprehension as to the meaning of genocide or as to the implications of the [treaty]. . . . The situation of
the Negro people in the country is in no way involved. The
lynching of an individual or of several individuals has no relation
to the extinction of masses of peoples because of race, religion, or
political belief.[59]

Supporters, forced to refute the farfetched and unfounded treaty interpretations, found themselves in a strange and dehumanizing
position.

A typical example of exchanges at the hearings on the treaty's application to lynching and other racial incidents took place between Senator Brien McMahon (D.-Conn.), chair of the Senate Foreign Relations
Committee, and Arthur Schweppe of the ABA Special Committee on
Peace and Law Through United Nations.

Senator McMahon: I want to direct your attention to Article 2,
because you have devoted [a considerable part] of your case to the
proposition that "in part" could mean one single individual.

Mr. Schweppe: In some given case.

Senator McMahon: Yes.

Mr. Schweppe: If you want to drive five Chinamen out of town or,
I think, driving one Chinaman out of town could be "in part" with
the group.

Senator McMahon: Now, quoting [reading]: "Article 2 defines
genocide as any of the five acts enumerated therein, committed
with the intent"—of course, you are not overlooking the word
"intent"—"to destroy in whole or in part a national, ethnical,
racial, or religious group as such." Of course, the words "as much
[*sic*]" cannot be disregarded either.

Mr. Schweppe: No.

Senator McMahon: They are certainly words of limitation, aren't
they?

Mr. Schweppe: Definitely, and were deliberately put in for that
purpose, as the record shows. . . .

Senator McMahon: Now, let's take a lynching case, for example.
Let's assume that there is a lynching and a colored man is mur-

dered in that fashion. Is it your contention that that could be construed as being within the confines of this definition; namely, with intent to destroy him as part of a group?

Mr. Schweppe: Well, Mr. Chairman, I don't want to answer that categorically. Let me give you this illustration, though, and I will give you an opinion on it, just one man's opinion, and not that of the International Court, which will ultimately tell us. Let's assume a little town where I live, where the colored groups are small, a very infinitesimal part of the population. Suppose we have the little town of Rendon, which is 10 miles from Seattle, and they have five colored people living in the town and, we'll say, that sometimes [sic] some crime of violence occurs, and as a result of it, some ill-meaning citizens in that community—I wouldn't call them well-meaning—decide that they want to get rid of all of those people.

Well are they proceeding against them because they want to get rid of them as a group, as a racial group? Are they proceeding against them because they thing [sic] some one of them may have been guilty of this heinous offense? I don't know. I say there is a question. Actually, a race riot of some substantial character would be more clearly within my concept of genocide within the meaning of this language. Now again, as I say, I don't want to put out these views as positive convictions. I can no more put them out as my opinions, but this whole concept of part of a group, which may be part of a group in a town, doesn't mean the whole group. Certainly it doesn't mean if I want to drive 5 Chinamen out of town, to use that invidious illustration, that I must have the intent to destroy all the 400,000,000 Chinese in the world or the 250,000 within the United States. It is part of a racial group, and if it is a group of 5, a group of 10, a group of 15, and I proceed after them with guns in some community to get rid of them solely because they belong to some racial group that the dictators don't like, I think you have got a serious question. That is what bothers me. . . .

Senator McMahon: More complicated is the question of intent with regard to the subjective appraisal of the guilty; namely, whether the culprit intended to destroy the group or the destruction was achieved without such intent. . . . A majority of the Commission was, however, of the opinion that there was no genocide without intent and that if intent was absent, the act would become simple homicide. Therefore, according to the wording of article 2, acts of destruction would not be classified as genocide unless the intent to destroy the group existed or could be proven, regardless of the results achieved.

Mr. Schweppe: I am in agreement with that.[60]

Thus, some opponents of the Genocide Convention manifested a complete refusal to reject the idea that it was designed or would be interpreted to cover individual cases normally defined as homicide.

Public concern about lynching and other racial incidents was reflected in a pamphlet issued by the Department of State entitled "Questions and Answers on the U.N. Charter, Genocide Convention, and Proposed Covenant on Human Rights." The pamphlet was written "in response to the numerous queries being received by the Department of State regarding [these treaties] from individuals and organizations."[61] Nestled among the legal issues of constitutionality and conflicts of jurisdiction is the question "Does it [the Genocide Convention] apply to lynching?" The answer given is a clear, fully explained "no."[62]

Legalization of the Debate

A measure of the success of the opposition was the extent to which a legal framework and legal arguments came to dominate the debate over human rights treaties. The process of legalization was launched during the discussions of the Genocide Convention and reached an advanced plateau during the Senate hearings. One sign of the legalization was the lengthy and solemn analysis of possible attachments to the treaties.

Very early in the discussion of U.S. ratification of the Genocide Convention, supporters within the ABA began to acknowledge the legitimacy of the opposition's criticism by proposing attachments to the treaty to address the problems the opposition had identified. The effect of this strategy was to strengthen the position of the opposition, who cited these attachments as evidence of the treaty's serious flaws. The strategic nature of the proposals was made clear by Solicitor General Philip Perlman, a strong advocate of the Genocide Convention. In his testimony during the Senate hearings, he explained the strategy.

> I think that it is fair to say, and I think you will be told, if any of the members of the [ABA] section are permitted to make a statement here, that even the reservations that they have suggested were adopted by the section in the hope of mollifying those who were seeking to defeat the whole proposition before the American Bar Association, and do not actually represent what might be thought to be a need, a pressing need, for reservations. It was an attempt to arrive at something that would answer the objections that had been made.[63]

The result, then, of the ABA debates and the 1950 hearings was the development of a set of reservations and understandings to be attached to the U.S. instrument of ratification. The reservations, it was hoped, would answer the worst of the critics' allegations and keep alive hopes for ratification.[64] To address the concern about treaty references to "part of a group" and "mental harm," which had been so severely criticized, especially as applicable to racial matters, the Foreign Relations Committee recommended the inclusion of the following understanding:

> That the United States Government understands and construes the crime of genocide, which it undertakes to punish in accordance with this convention, to mean the commission of any of the acts enumerated in article II of the convention, with the intent to destroy an entire national, ethnical, racial, or religious group within the territory of the United States, in such manner as to affect a substantial portion of the group concerned; That the United States government understands and construes the words "mental harm" appearing in article II of the convention to mean permanent physical injury to mental faculties.[65]

To answer the objection that the treaty would infringe on freedom of speech and freedom of the press, the committee recommended another understanding related to Article II.

> That the United States Government understands and construes the words "complicity in genocide" appearing in article II of this convention to mean participation before and after the fact and aiding and abetting in the commission of the crime of genocide.[66]

Because the states' rights issue dominated the hearings, the Foreign Relations Committee also devised a declaration to respond to this set of criticisms. The committee report, however, emphasized that the declaration was unnecessary, that the federal government already had the authority to punish genocide, and that in doing so it did not infringe the powers of the states. The report stated:

Much was made by the opponents of the convention of the alleged interference with the jurisdiction of the states by the United States, and of the fact that the convention deprived the states of jurisdiction which they were supposed to have exercised over genocide up to now. Obviously the latter assertion cannot be correct in that genocide was first declared to be a crime under international law in 1946, and today neither the United States nor any state has a law on its books either defining or punishing genocide.[67]

The author of the report, committee chair McMahon, also expressed his frustration over the claim that the treaty would cover a whole host of criminal acts presently defined by the states. The report contained the explanation,

It cannot be overemphasized that while the Federal Government now undertakes the punishment of the crime of genocide, there is nothing in the convention that changes the powers of the States to define and punish the killing of human beings under state laws. Murder still remains murder triable and punishable under State law. Similarly manslaughter remains manslaughter; assault remains assault; lynching remains lynching; and rioting remains rioting. All this still remains true even though the crime of genocide is now added to the roster of crimes which fall within the province of the Federal Government.[68]

The opposition success, however, is apparent since in spite of these caveats, the committee went on to suggest that a declaration might be desirable "in order to allay any fears that may still exist as to the Federal Government infringing upon the so-called rights of the several States." The declaration read:

In giving its advice and consent to the ratification of the Convention on the Prevention and Punishment of the Crime of Genocide, the Senate of the United States of America does so considering this to be an exercise of the authority of the Federal Government to define and punish offenses against the law of nations, expressly conferred by article I, section 8, clause 10, of the United States Constitution, and consequently, the traditional jurisdiction of the several States of the Union with regard to crime is in no way abridged.[69]

These reservations and understandings designed by supporters of the treaty reveal the success of the opposition in challenging the treaty and in moving the debate onto legal terrain. The effect was to raise the salience of the discussion of legalities, increase the authoritativeness of the lawyers who composed the core opposition, cloud the issues for the public at large, and mask the political nature of the opposition.

Conclusion

The Genocide Convention was the first United Nations human rights treaty transmitted to the United States Senate for approval. Although at first it appeared that the overwhelming support of a wide range of organizations representing millions of people would ensure passage, the treaty soon became one of the most controversial items on the Senate agenda. The transformation of the convention from a simple document outlawing a heinous offense to a subversive document undermining cherished constitutional rights was the work of a small special committee of the American Bar Association acting in an environment particularly favorable to its objectives. The nine committee members who presented themselves as offering special expertise on the dangerous but unrecognized implications of the Genocide Convention carried out a careful and well-designed campaign to prevent ratification. Relying on contemporary fears of communism and world government, and claiming that the treaty would lead to abrogation of states' rights and to federal interference in segregation and race-related crimes in the South, they succeeded in labeling the Genocide Convention and all human rights treaties as un-American. Once they persuaded the nation's leading organization of lawyers that only their special professional help and advice would avert the destruction of the American federal system, support for the genocide treaty in the Senate began to fade.

One measure of the ABA's successful strategy is the attitude reflected in a December 1950 *Congressional Digest* article allegedly providing a balanced, objective presentation of the Genocide Convention controversy. The report stated:

> The Genocide Treaty deals in matters which in America are traditionally and legally within the province of the States. Hence the question: Is this Treaty, and other similar ones now being drafted, a step toward "government by treaty"? Regardless of the answer, the asking of the question seems entirely in order.[70]

The acceptance of the opposition assumption that the treaty dealt with matters of states' rights, the use of the opposition bugaboo of government by treaty, and the shifting of the burden of proof to the proponents rather than the opponents of the convention are all indicative of the complete victory of the opposition. The *Congressional Digest* accurately represented the mood in the Senate by stating, "The tone of the controversy is presently pitched to why the U.S. should reject the Treaty rather than why it should be ratified."[71] This reversal of the question, with a follow-up section containing statements pro (that is, rejecting the treaty) and con (supporting the treaty), exemplified the legitimation of the opposition frame of reference and basic tenets. Given the pragmatism of the Senate, as well as the senators' preoccupation with short-term effects and their strong desire to avoid controversy, the opponents' success in halting the momentum for ratification and changing the terms of the debate was a milestone in the history of this treaty and the human rights treaties that followed.

THREE

The Human Rights Covenants

The Genocide Convention was the focal point of opposition to human rights treaties, but it was not seen as the greatest threat. According to the critics of human rights treaties, the most dangerous document produced by the United Nations was the Covenant on Human Rights, the treaty that formally codified the principles in the Universal Declaration of Human Rights. The covenant and declaration were vilified by Frank Holman throughout his crusade against the human rights treaties. Senator Bricker named the covenant as the immediate reason for his introduction of an amendment to the United States Constitution. The covenant was cited by those engaged in elucidating the dangers of human rights treaties during American Bar Association debates and at congressional hearings. Long before a draft of the covenant was completed, it had become in the minds of opponents the embodiment par excellence of their worst fears.

Senator Bricker eloquently articulated his criticism of the covenant when, prior to the introduction of his constitutional amendment, he proposed that the Senate adopt a resolution requiring the executive branch to withdraw from any participation in the completion of the treaty. In the course of his remarks he characterized the covenant as "a Covenant on Human Slavery," a legalization of "the most vicious restrictions of dictators," a "legal basis for the most repressive measures of atheistic tyranny," "an attempt to repeal the Bill of Rights," a threat to freedom of religion, and "a blueprint for tyranny."[1]

What was this document that the opposition believed to be so dangerous that only an amendment to the Constitution would effectively safeguard the United States of America from it? How did it come to be drafted, and what role had the executive branch played in its creation? Had U.S. representatives at the United Nations purposely or inadvertently failed to attend to Western concepts of human rights? These questions can only be answered through a thorough examination of the United States' role in the drafting process.

This chapter begins by providing a brief history and background of the covenant. Then it explores the particulars of opposition charges against the covenant and its drafters. Bricker, Holman, and the members of the ABA Committee on Peace and Law Through United Nations claimed that the covenant would diminish basic rights, abrogate states' rights, enhance Soviet and Communist influence, and imperil U.S. sovereignty. These, of course, are the same basic charges that they leveled against the Genocide Convention, as seen in Chapter 2. They also argued that the Human Rights Covenant was the product of Soviet domination of the United Nations and that the U.S. representatives had conspired with or been duped by advocates of world government and communism.

The primary purpose of the chapter is to achieve a better understanding of the actual document that proved so pivotal for opponents of human rights treaties and their efforts to amend the United States Constitution. A major part of the chapter, therefore, examines the history of the drafting of the covenant up to 1954 (when a draft was completed by the Commission on Human Rights), paying special attention to the specific criticisms made by the opposition within the United States at this time. Four critical issues debated during the development of the covenant are selected to illustrate that the fears and allegations of the treaty's opponents were groundless. These issues are the treatment of economic and social rights, the inclusion of a provision on private property, the wording of the article on freedom of expression, and the statement of a right to self-determination.

Were the U.S. representatives at the United Nations active and effective participants in the drafting process? Did they affect the outcome in any important ways? If so, were their proposals new and radical, or were they in line with traditional U.S. positions on human rights? The detailed analysis of the drafting process presented here is designed to answer these crucial questions.

History of the Universal Declaration and the Covenant

Although the United Nations Charter did not define a set of basic human rights, it made seven references to human rights, including instructions that the Economic and Social Council set up a commission "for the promotion of human rights."[2] As one of its earliest acts, the council established the Commission on Human Rights and directed it to provide proposals, recommendations, and reports on an "international bill of human rights."[3] The initial debate within the commission centered on whether to produce a declaration stating general principles or a convention signed and ratified by states as a binding treaty.[4] The latter would be clear international law, while the former would be "moral" and suggestive, interpretive of the human rights provisions of the U.N. Charter, and perhaps nascent customary law. The commission at its 1947 meeting decided to divide the task into three parts: (1) a declaration of rights, (2) a treaty codifying these rights, and (3) measures of implementation. In final form the "International Bill of Rights" included the Universal Declaration, the Covenant on Economic, Social, and Cultural Rights, and the Covenant on Civil and Political Rights (with an optional protocol).

The Human Rights Commission was chaired by Eleanor Roosevelt, the U.S. representative, who actively supported its work. She, Charles Malik (Lebanon), and P. C. Chang (China)[5] made up the subcommittee that was to draft the declaration, aided by the director of the Human Rights Division at the United Nations, John Humphrey. Owing to irreconcilable philosophical differences among the subcommittee members, the task was ultimately referred to Humphrey, a Canadian.[6] He decided to add economic and social rights to a set of rights that was otherwise drawn entirely from the Western rights tradition. He believed that these "new" rights should be included and that they would be easier to delete than to add at a later date. His assessment of the debate over the declaration was that if he had not included them in the draft, they would not have been in the declaration.[7] The Soviet Union, however, was not satisfied with the draft; it abstained when the commission voted on the draft in June 1948, as did the Byelorussian, Ukrainian, and Yugoslav representatives.[8] Contrary to the rhetoric of the treaty opposition, the Soviet Union and its allies were not, in fact, very influential at this period in the history of the United Nations and were unable to make significant changes in this or later drafts of the Universal Declaration.[9] Eleanor Roosevelt strongly endorsed the declaration, expressing the United States' view that it was an encouragement to and guide for understanding and interpreting the human rights provisions of the United Nations Charter and an inspiration to all to work individually and collectively for the advancement of human rights.[10]

The United Nations Social, Humanitarian, and Cultural Committee (the Third Committee) reviewed the draft declaration in great detail, devoting 81 sessions to it and considering 168 resolutions, with amendments. The representative of the Soviet Union attempted to have the committee adopt a resolution calling for further study of the declaration (exactly what the ABA Special Committee was calling for at this time). He argued that the commission draft had been unacceptable and had been left unchanged by the committee. This resolution was defeated 26 to 6, with 1 abstention,[11] an indication of the relatively weak influence the Soviet Union was able to exercise at the United Nations at this time. On 6 December 1948, in the closing days of the session, the committee approved a text very similar to that which it had received from the Human Rights Commission.[12] Six Communist states (the Soviet Union, Poland, Yugoslavia, Byelorussia, the Ukraine, and Czechoslovakia) and Canada abstained. Saudi Arabia and South Africa did not vote.[13]

When the Universal Declaration was discussed before the General Assembly, the United States supported its adoption, arguing that the instrument did not impose legal obligations but was a statement of inalienable rights and a set of common international standards. The Soviet Union again attempted to delay and alter the declaration, proposing several amendments.[14] A resolution for further study was also offered[15] and was defeated 6 to 45, with 3 abstentions. The declaration was approved with 48 votes in favor, none opposed, and 8 abstentions (the Soviet Union, Yugoslavia, Poland, the Ukraine, Byelorussia, Czechoslovakia, Saudi Arabia, and South Africa).[16] Ironically, this declaration that was considered by some within the United States to be a Communist plot was not supported by the Soviet Union or its allies. The Soviets tried, during committee discussions and in the General Assembly, to delay consideration of the declaration, hoping to be able to bring their influence to bear. Many Human Rights Commission members felt that a victory had been won when the Soviet Union abstained rather than cast a vote against the declaration. In explaining his vote, the Soviet representative stated that he felt the declaration did not provide clear and concrete means of implementing and guaranteeing rights, that it undermined the independence and sovereignty of the state, and that it did not incorporate several important Soviet suggestions, including a statement of the duties of individuals to their nations.

The representative from South Africa accurately predicted that, in spite of its nonlegal form, the declaration would "be interpreted as an authoritative definition of fundamental rights and freedoms which had been left undefined in the Charter."[17] As this representative had argued at commission meetings, the document would establish grounds for interference in the internal affairs of states. Both these fears of South Africa were later realized in the series of International Court of Justice decisions and General Assembly and Security Council resolutions on apartheid in Namibia and South Africa itself. Many legal scholars today argue that the Universal Declaration is in fact a statement of customary international law. These scholars point to the numerous invocations of the declaration in resolutions of the United Nations and regional organizations and by national and international courts. They also cite international statements such as the Montreal Statement of the Assembly for Human Rights and the Proclamation of Teheran, as well as numerous national constitutions and the founding charters of regional human rights organizations.[18]

Even before the completion of the Universal Declaration, the Human Rights Commission focused attention on a draft convention, and early on there was sentiment for introducing the declaration and treaty simultaneously to the General Assembly.[19] The objective of the commission was to define and codify the rights contained in the declaration in a formal multilateral treaty capable of establishing international obligations for the maintenance, promotion, and implementation of human rights. The commission began with one treaty draft, which they submitted to governments for their responses. At the time of the initial controversy within the United States, there was a single draft covenant. However, as explained below, the decision was reached to separate civil and political rights from economic and social rights, so, in the end, the commission drafted two treaties, which were termed "covenants" in order to indicate the importance of their special subject.

Opposition to the Covenant

Criticism of the Content of the Covenant

The Covenant on Human Rights was a key source of concern for the group that came to lead the opposition to human rights treaties and to support the Bricker Amendment. The scope of the treaty was broad, and its declared intent was to provide a universal code of internationally defined human rights. At times, the opposition appeared determined to reject any such code that did not look exactly like the United States Bill of Rights, and, for some, even this form would have been unacceptable.[20] The covenant in draft form was central to the program outlined in 1948 by Frank Holman, president of the ABA, to alert America to the dangers of human rights treaties. He warned the California State Bar Association on 17 September 1948 that the Universal Declaration and the Covenant on Human Rights amounted to a program that "will promote state socialism, if not communism, throughout the world."[21] Some of the objectives of the drafts, he asserted, were to waive the right to private property, allow "increased trespass in the guise of 'liberty of movement,' " encourage civil disorders as "freedom of religion," and "nullify immigration laws by accepting a blanket 'right of asylum.' "[22]

Holman also argued that the covenant would destroy the U.S. Constitution and legal system.[23] In a speech before the House of Delegates of the ABA Holman claimed that the covenant was part of a new system under which

> not only a city, or a county or a state but any individual in this country may be complained against, not only by some pressure group in this country, but by some pressure group in Russia, and may be brought before an international tribunal and tried and punished by imprisonment or death.[24]

Previous ABA president William L. Ransom asserted that upon Senate ratification the covenant would "immediately become part of the supreme law of the land, coordinate with the Constitution itself, and superseding state, Federal, and local laws and state constitutions."[25] Ransom expressed his belief that the United States was being singled out by the drafters of the covenant because it was the only country where treaties had a direct effect on domestic legislation. He claimed that "the Constitution and laws of the United States were 'in violation' of the declaration at many points."[26]

The *ABA Journal* in 1951 carried a lengthy two-part series on the Human Rights Covenant, outlining the serious threats that it posed to the American way of life. The dominant themes were the loss of basic rights, the defense of states' rights, the protection of U.S. sovereignty, and anticommunism.

The primary accusation made by the author, William Fleming, was that acceptance of the covenant would mean the destruction of basic U.S. rights. "The American system is clearly put in jeopardy" since the treaty will lead to the "whittling away of those liberties which are so dear to the great majority of Americans."[27] He firmly rejected the idea that the rights in the covenant were well established in American law, claiming that "nothing could be farther from the truth" because the covenant promotes "extreme egalitarianism."[28] The concept of rights as known to Americans, according to the author, was essentially missing from the treaty:

> The efforts of the United States to bestow the blessings of liberty on the world as a whole have boomeranged. The crusading missionary returning home from abroad finds himself converted to the creed of the nonbelievers to whom he was supposed to teach the gospel! What a spectacle, ludicrous and tragic at once.[29]

Not only the United States' system of rights but also its system of government was threatened by the treaty. In one crucial area, the division of power between states and the federal government would be undermined according to Fleming.

> Ratification of the Draft Covenant by the United States would result in the destruction of the American federal system of government as we know it today. . . . Were the Covenant, then, to become the supreme law of the land, the traditional distribution of power between governments on the national and state levels would give way to a unitary state with almost all power therein exercised by the Government in Washington.[30]

Fleming also had great fear for the sovereignty of the United States, which he believed would be completely destroyed by the covenant.

> The very moment the Covenant is put in force, the Declaration of Independence will be legislated out of existence. . . . The war of 1776 will have been fought in vain, the principles of the Revolution undone, self-government abolished, with the international

bureaucracy as the new sovereign in the field of human rights taking the place of George III.[31]

Criticism of the Drafters of the Covenant

A crucial part of the opposition strategy was the undermining of the credibility and standing of the Commission on Human Rights, which drafted the declaration and covenant. Often the U.S. representatives were criticized for their lack of legal expertise or their political naiveté, which had resulted in the dangerous document they had participated in creating. Eleanor Roosevelt, as the leading U.S. participant,[32] as well as chair of the commission, came in for the heaviest attacks. Holman, in November 1948, claimed that the members of the commission were inexperienced.

> Mrs. Eleanor Roosevelt is its Chairman and the sole United States representative. She is not a person in any sense trained in legal draftsmanship; she is primarily a social reformer.[33]

The Daughters of the American Revolution (DAR) also viewed Roosevelt as, at best, a dupe of the Communists, chiding her,

> Well, Mrs. Roosevelt, . . . you have been associated with many of these members of the [U.N.] Secretariat for years and either did not recognize their Communist sympathies or purposely ignored them.[34]

Senator Bricker, discussing the "dangerously inept draftsmanship" of the covenant, commented, "We need not pause to consider whether this is due to Mrs. Roosevelt's lack of legal training or to a conscious effort to appease Socialist and Communist nations."[35]

In some sense they may have been right in blaming Roosevelt for whatever they disliked about the Universal Declaration. Many observers believe that she was central to the drafting process and to the decision to begin with a declaration rather than a draft treaty.[36] She worked tirelessly and for long hours and asked the other commission members to do likewise.[37] Although she had some influence in determining U.S. policies, she was guided by the U.S. position papers[38] and was concerned about constitutional issues.[39]

She consistently "stood up to" Soviet criticism of U.S. domestic policies and practices. As commission chair she frequently ruled against the Soviet Union and Soviet bloc countries,[40] who were in a clear minority.[41] Members of the Soviet bloc, as noted above, felt that they had lost out in the drafting of the declaration and abstained when the declaration was adopted in the General Assembly.

In his 17 September 1948 address to the California Bar Association, Holman, then president of the ABA, attacked the "Anglo-Saxon" members of the commission on the grounds that all three lacked legal experience and implied that the language of the draft, which he decried as "indefinite and elastic," was due to this shortcoming.[42] Although Roosevelt had no legal training, she was aided by lawyers from the State Department and relied on them for advice. "All my advisers are lawyers," she explained, "or I would be lost."[43] She did, however, in the case of the Universal Declaration, feel that the language should be easily accessible to common people and argued for simple language whenever possible.[44] Since the declaration was not a treaty, but a resolution stating principles, the use of legal language was not essential. The State Department concurred in this assessment and was less responsive to legal criticism since the document would not require Senate approval.[45] Also, future secretary of state John Foster Dulles wrote to the American Bar Association to defend Roosevelt and the declaration, explaining that she had had a strong legal staff and that the declaration was nonbinding.[46]

There is evidence that Roosevelt was mindful of the problem of a reluctant Senate and, with the covenant, worked to enhance the likelihood of Senate ratification.[47] She held no illusions that the Economic, Social, and Cultural Rights Covenant had "the slightest chance" of Senate approval.[48]

One explanation offered by opponents to explain how the covenant had come into existence with U.S. representatives present was that these Americans had been duped by the Communists or by the world federalists. According to William Fleming, in the previously mentioned *ABA Journal* article, the Soviets undoubtedly "scored" with the covenant:

> It is impossible not to recognize the heavy imprint of Eastern philosophy. As a matter of fact, Part III is nothing else but the perfect embodiment of the unadulterated welfare state and unmitigated socialism.[49]

The advocates of communism, he argued, not only succeeded in incorporating economic rights into the covenant, but they also accomplished the objective of destroying a major obstacle to their success in the undermining of the educational system in the West.

> The adoption of the Covenant, of course, would mean the end of education as we have it in America today. The private liberal arts colleges, important bulwarks of the free world in the struggle against communism and totalitarianism, would be driven from the American scene.[50]

Holman, too, was disturbed by the composition of the Commission on Human Rights in that "all the other [except Eleanor Roosevelt] members . . . were foreigners, including three Russians."[51] Apparently, in Fleming's mind, the U.S. representatives involved in the formulation of the human rights treaties had been outwitted by the Soviets:

> The United States delegation has, unfortunately, not realized that the struggle against communism is a global one, indeed. It is waged not only on the battlefields of Korea, but everywhere, including the Council chambers of the United Nations and the Human Rights Commission. American boys in Korea bearing the brunt of the communist onslaught are fighting for the same ideas and ideals that ought to be upheld at the conference table. . . . Our sacrifice of fundamental principles [by ratifying the covenant] would be a victory for the Kremlin, far greater than it has won up to the present time.[52]

The U.S. representatives, according to Fleming, were also hoodwinked by world government proponents, who would be unable to have their objective accepted openly. Instead they developed "a substitute device—the conclusion of a world-wide international treaty, the Covenant on Human Rights. Ratification of the Covenant would amount to introducing world government through a back door."[53]

There is, however, every reason to believe that the positions of the United States were well developed and effectively implemented by the U.S. delegation; on most points the U.S. representatives carried their positions through, successfully blocking Soviet bloc or other conflicting proposals and amendments. Contrary to the accusations of opponents, it can be argued that the United States won on most of the disputed issues and that the codification reflected the Western human rights tradition. One example not atypical of the general success of the

U.S. delegation was the treatment of economic, social, and cultural rights, the major item on the agenda of the Soviet Union.

Economic and Social Rights

One of the general problems facing the Commission on Human Rights was whether to include economic, social, and cultural rights in the same treaty with civil and political rights.[54] Only six articles of the Universal Declaration dealt with economic and social matters, and although the commission members agreed that an expanded treatment of these rights would be desirable, they differed about how to accomplish this objective. The initial work included these rights with civil and political rights in a single treaty; the single declaration of international rights, it was felt, should be transformed into a single international convention. Early on, however, the United States, India, and the United Kingdom began to argue for a division of rights. Considering civil and political rights most ripe for codification, the commission drafted a covenant dealing with these rights and submitted it to governments for comments. At the 1950 commission session, proposals were received from Australia, Yugoslavia, and the Soviet Union calling for the inclusion of economic, social, and cultural rights. The United States argued that any effort to include these rights would prevent the completion of the commission's work. Eleanor Roosevelt suggested that reference to them be included instead in the preamble to the proposed covenant.[55]

The Soviet Union, in protest over Chinese representation, did not participate in the next session. The commission, again chaired by the U.S. representative, decided to complete the draft covenant without including economic, social, and cultural rights but expressed an intention to draft related instruments in the future. The members presented the draft as the first of a series that would be needed in order to translate the entire Universal Declaration into treaty law.

At the 1950 session of the Economic and Social Council, to which the Human Rights Commission reported, the council decided to approve the commission's decision to separate the two groups of rights, but it requested that the General Assembly also make a decision on this issue.[56] The General Assembly declared that the two sets of rights were "interconnected and interdependent."[57] The representatives proposed that the draft include "a clear expression of economic, social and cultural rights in a manner which relates them to the civil and political freedoms proclaimed by the draft covenant."[58] At its seventh session (1951) the commission concentrated on economic, social, and cultural rights, having before it comments of governments, a memorandum on the subject from the secretary general, and communications from several specialized agencies, including the ILO and the United Nations Economic, Social, and Cultural Organization. The commission completed fourteen articles on economic, social, and cultural rights, but the issue of division was again raised. The U.S. representative, maintaining her opposition to the single-treaty approach, shifted her argument from a utilitarian "not enough time" to a contention that there was need for a qualitative differentiation of the two groups of rights. She held that "economic and social rights were of a different nature from the other rights enunciated in the Covenant, since they were not justiciable, and therefore could not be enforced in the same way."[59] The Soviet Union denied this notion:

> The segregation of the rights contained in the Covenant into two separate categories according to whether they were justiciable or not was completely arbitrary. . . . [The] proposal was based on the assumption that the individual could defend his civil and political rights by legal action, whereas he could not defend his economic, social and cultural rights by the same process. That assumption, however, would not bear scrutiny, as in many countries certain civil and political rights, such as for instance, the right to vote, could not easily be defended by legal action initiated by the individual.[60]

The strategy of the United States was, first of all, to attempt to reverse the General Assembly instructions. Thus, Roosevelt argued that even though the Economic and Social Council and the General Assembly had decided that the two groups of rights should be in one treaty, the commission could ask that the decision be reversed.[61] She supported an Indian proposal[62] that asked the council to recommend to the General Assembly that it reconsider the decision on this point.[63] This proposal was not adopted.[64] The Soviet representative predictably rejected the United States' contentions, opposed the reconsideration proposal, and argued for the unified treatment of the two groups of rights.[65]

The representative of Lebanon, voting against the Indian proposal, suggested that support for economic, social, and cultural rights was rooted in anticolonialism rather than socialism:

During the past 150 years, certain peoples, who had not been in as privileged a position as others, had made their claims with regard to their economic, social and cultural position felt with growing insistence. It was essential to recognize that such rights were of equal importance with others.[66]

Since the commission had already adopted eighteen articles on civil and political rights, the Soviet Union urged the priority of dealing with a large number of economic, social, and cultural rights.[67] The commission proceeded to draft additional articles on economic, social, and cultural rights and on implementation, enlarging the covenant to seventy-three articles. Having failed to win acceptance of the two-treaty plan, the U.S. representative moved to incorporate into the treaty the idea that the two sets of rights were qualitatively different and, together with the French representative, sponsored an amendment to this effect to be included in the introductory general clause to the economic, social, and cultural rights section of the covenant.[68]

At its next session, the Economic and Social Council, in its review of the annual report of the Human Rights Commission's work, discussed the draft and forwarded it to the General Assembly with a recommendation that the Assembly reconsider its decision requesting a unified instrument.[69] After a long debate, the U.S. representative was able to bring American influence to bear, and the Assembly adopted a resolution requesting the Economic and Social Council to ask the commission

> to draft two covenants on human rights, . . . one to contain civil and political rights and the other to contain economic, social and cultural rights, in order that the General Assembly may approve the two covenants simultaneously and open them at the same time for signature, the two covenants to contain . . . as many similar provisions as possible.[70]

The 1952 session of the commission saw a reiteration of the basic arguments about the two groups of rights. The major dispute crystallized around the introductory article for the Economic, Social, and Cultural Rights Covenant. The U.S. State Department was interested in clearly establishing these rights as goals, stressing that they could not be given immediate legal effect. Thus, Roosevelt pressed for a strong limiting clause in the proposed first article that emphasized the idea of "progressive achievement."[71] The Soviet Union accused the United States of attempting to weaken the covenant:

The Commission was now being asked to adopt a mere empty declaration. If the general clause was adopted in the form proposed by the United States delegation, the succeeding articles would be stillborn.[72]

The Soviet Union and the United States continued to disagree on which rights should be given priority. The U.S. representative, for example, stated that

it was felt by some that economic and social rights were more important than civil and political rights, but many countries with a long democratic tradition knew well that civil and political rights were indispensable for the attainment of economic and social rights and freedoms.[73]

The Soviet Union reversed this dictum:

Without the implementation of economic, social, and cultural rights, the implementation of civil and political rights would be illusory.[74]

At the next two sessions of the commission the drafts were completed. The Soviet Union made a further effort to recombine the treaties into a unified convention, but failed.[75]

The convention on economic, social, and cultural rights met the expectations of neither the Soviet Union nor the United States. The Soviet Union wanted a treaty with clearer immediate state obligations, preferably combined in a treaty with civil and political rights. The United States would have preferred postponement of the entire issue or the inclusion of a vague general statement that represented little advancement over the language of the Universal Declaration.

In summary, the U.S. representative forcefully resisted a single treaty that would have codified a concept of human rights different from traditional Western ideas of human rights. Generally, three main arguments were made by Eleanor Roosevelt, on behalf of the United States, in supporting separate treaties. One was that the drafting would be difficult and would unnecessarily delay the commission's work, which was proceeding well in the area of civil and political rights. A second line of reasoning was that the rights were different in kind: civil and political rights were justiciable, while economic, social, and cultural rights were not. More significantly, economic, social, and cultural rights were not immediately realizable. These rights could only be "progressively achieved," and that major distinguishing quality made it inappropriate to include them in the same legal document with civil and political rights. Third, opponents of the single instrument held that the measures of implementation that would be necessary to make a treaty on civil and political rights meaningful would be inapplicable to economic, social, and cultural rights. Civil and political rights could best be implemented through the establishment of a special committee responding to complaints through good offices and inquiry; on the other hand, a system of periodic reporting would constitute the main mechanism for the implementation of economic, social, and cultural rights.

The desire for a single treaty sprang mainly from a belief in the equal significance of all the rights. Proponents of a single treaty rejected the notion that civil and political rights were more important than economic, social, and cultural ones. Including all the rights in *one* document would emphasize the lack of hierarchy. The socialist states in particular felt that separation reflected a downgrading of economic rights. Additionally, arguments were made that separation of rights into "protected" (normally civil and political) and "program" rights (normally economic and social) was not a simple matter. If all rights were included in one treaty, states could indicate, through reservations and understandings, which would be immediately implemented and which would be the object of progressive development.

The U.S. representative stood well in the forefront of the move to separate the two groups of rights. Given the ideological preference of the United States for civil and political rights and its substantial suspicion about economic, social, and cultural rights, the division was seen as simplifying domestic acceptance and solidifying an international definition of human rights more clearly in the Western tradition. Roosevelt's success in obtaining the separation of the two sets of rights as well as the inclusion in the Economic, Social, and Cultural Rights Covenant of the language of goals to be "progressively" achieved, should have significantly reduced one obvious source of domestic objection to the treaties.

The Right to Private Property

The efforts of the U.S. representative to the Human Rights Commission did not, however, appease the committed opposition, who considered any treaty on economic and social rights to be dangerous. In fact, the only thing worse than a treaty on economic rights, in the opposition's view, was a treaty on economic rights without a provision on private property. In other words, the inclusion of economic rights was evidence enough of socialistic influence according to opponents, but the failure to include the right to private property was proof positive of Communist control. This argument was consistently raised against the covenant. Frank Holman in 1948, as head of the ABA, cited the lack as an indication of the "socialistic" nature of the covenant. Even before the covenant was initially drafted, he claimed it would "waive the concept of private property."[76] In 1949 he pointed to the omission as evidence that the covenant would mean a loss of "the basic rights which it took our forebears centuries to achieve."[77]

Initially, the United States placed much emphasis on the inclusion in the covenant of an article on private property. It is difficult for most U.S. citizens to imagine a statement of human rights that fails to mention this right so basic to the Western tradition. There had been little disagreement within the commission over the formulation of the private property provision in Article 17 of the Universal Declaration. It reads:

1. Everyone has the right to own property alone as well as in association with others.
2. No one shall be arbitrarily deprived of his property.

The original set of articles drawn up by the commission's drafting committee did not include an article on private property. The U.S. representative submitted a proposal for discussion at the seventh session, which read,

The States Parties to the Covenant recognize the right of everyone to own property alone as well as in association with others and to be protected from arbitrary deprivation of property.[78]

All the commission members agreed on the individual's right to own property, but there was considerable diversity of opinion about how to formulate the right, given the variety of national constitutional provisions on it, and the limits or restrictions that could be made on individual ownership and state action.

The Soviet Union's representative supported the inclusion of a private property provision, stating that the Soviet constitution

guaranteed the legal protection of the personal right of citizens in their incomes and savings from work, in their dwelling houses and subsidiary home enterprises, in articles of domestic economy and uses and articles of personal use and convenience, as well as the right of citizens to inherit personal property.[79]

The problem, he said, was with the new form of the U.S. proposal and its amendments. He then suggested that the U.S. proposal be amended by adding at the end of the first sentence "in accordance with the laws of the country in which that property is found."[80] Roosevelt rejected this amendment. She presented the view that this formulation might legitimize illegal expropriations.[81] No decision was reached on the provision, although the issue was discussed at this session and the next.[82] At that time the United States submitted a revised provision, the text of which was as follows:

> The States Parties to the Covenant recognize the rights of everyone to own property alone as well as in association with others and to be protected from arbitrary deprivation of property. Private property shall not be taken for public use without just compensation.[83]

However, no provision was then adopted.[84] At its eighth session, the commission again discussed the right, this time focusing on a proposal from France,[85] but again adjourned debate without any adoption.[86]

In 1954 the issue of a provision on private property was raised once more. This time the commission had before it a subcommittee draft[87] requiring states to respect the right of everyone to own property in accordance with the law of the country in which the property was located and including a provision for compensation. Even so, the United States opposed this formulation and introduced a draft article following the language found in Article 17 of the Universal Declaration. The U.S. representative would not accept the language of the subcommittee proposal, but she continued to work for an article on this topic in the covenant. She argued that the subcommittee proposal, if adopted, would weaken the Universal Declaration provision on private property, a provision that had been adopted unanimously. She reiterated the classical international legal requirement that property could only be taken for public purposes and in return for just compensation. She also suggested that failure to include some provision on private property would be a retrogressive step, reversing Article 17 of the Universal Declaration.[88]

It is likely that had the United States agreed to the subcommittee draft for this article, it would have been included in the covenant. The

Soviet representative, for example, argued that the subcommittee proposal obligated states to "respect the right of everyone to own property alone as well as in association with others, in accordance with the law in countries where the property is situated."[89] The language that was so objectionable to the United States conforms with general international law and does not approve illegal expropriations.[90]

The Human Rights Commission remained divided between those who wanted the article to include restrictions on state action against private property, especially traditional international law obligations for expropriations, and those who wanted a provision indicating the dominant position of the law of the place. The result was another commission decision to adjourn consideration of the article, and the commission's final draft contained no private property provision at all. In the 1950s, treaty opponents were able to cite the absence of such a provision as evidence of the Communist nature of the draft treaty. Their attack, however, was on political rather than legal grounds. The inclusion of an article clearly stating that nothing in the treaty could be interpreted in a manner that would reduce the level of human rights protection within a country removed any legal grounds for concern that the treaty in any way endangered the private property rights of U.S. nationals.

In summary, then, the U.S. representatives worked to include an article on private property in the Economic, Social, and Cultural Rights Covenant. First the U.S. representative offered a general private property article; when this effort failed, she suggested a provision that would reiterate traditional international legal requirements for legitimate expropriation. When a commission subcommittee agreed to an article recognizing the law of the place as a dominant element in the treatment of property, the U.S. executive decided that a treaty with no provision on private property was preferable to one that might be interpreted as condoning expropriation. One suspects that the opponents of human rights treaties could never have been satisfied on this issue. The U.S. representatives did the best they could at a time when strong feelings about colonial exploitation were coming to the fore in many U.N. member states. Certainly the draft provision that the United States refused to support, which would have included a private property article, would also have been unacceptable to the 1950s opposition.

Freedom of Expression

One of the persistent arguments against human rights treaties was that they would diminish the rights of citizens of the United States. Among the most frequently cited rights likely to be lost was that of freedom of expression. Members of the United Nations were also concerned about fashioning protections for freedom of expression, with special emphasis on the press. In fact, while the Human Rights Commission was drafting the covenants, the United Nations was developing three other documents dealing with the same subject as that of the declaration's Article 19, freedom of expression: a Convention on Freedom of Information, a Convention on the Gathering and International Transmission of News, and a Convention Concerning the Institution of an International Right of Correction.[91] This effort at elaborating the right of freedom to information affected the commission's work primarily by offering an alternative to those opposed to a detailed provision on the right in the covenant. Like representatives with special concerns in other areas, such as labor and health, these representatives were reminded of the opportunity to have their views reflected in other international agreements already focusing on the particular problem.

One of the first difficulties to arise for the commission was the issue of what constituted freedom of "expression" as presented in Article 19 of the Universal Declaration:

Everyone has the right to freedom of opinion and expression; this right includes freedom to hold opinions without interference and to seek, receive and impart information and ideas through any media and regardless of frontiers.

The commission debate clarified and distinguished between freedom of opinion and freedom of expression. The latter was manifestly in the realm of the public; the former, held individually and being of the mind, was a private matter. Since freedom of opinion could not be regulated or dictated by law, it raised different issues from those related to freedom of expression, and the commission decided to treat them separately. Thus, the first paragraph of the commission's draft declares, "Everyone shall have the right to hold opinions without interference."[92] The remainder of the discussion was devoted entirely to the problems surrounding freedom of expression.

Here again there was complete agreement that this right was essential and ought to be included in the covenant. Disagreement arose over the constraints that might legitimately be placed upon the right. The text proposed by the United States revealed its basic approach to this issue: a broad statement of the freedom, an emphasis on the fear of governmental interference, and a general limitation linked to national security and public order—in short, the previously adopted formula for other articles.[93] Interestingly enough, the major opposition to the U.S. text came from other Western democracies rather than the Soviet bloc, although here, too, there were some important difficulties.

The major difference of opinion was with Britain and France over the issue of abuse of rights. Commission members in general were concerned about preventing abuse of this particular right and felt protection was especially urgent given the tremendous influence of the contemporary media. The proposal from the United Kingdom emphasized that the right "carries with it duties and responsibilities and may therefore be subject to certain penalties, liabilities, and restrictions but those shall be such only as are provided by law, and necessary."[94] The French representative also felt strongly about this issue, expressing his feelings as follows: "Every freedom has two aspects: that of the protection of the individual against the State and that of the protection of the freedom itself by the enforcement of the individual's respect for it."[95]

The Soviet Union, too, stressed the need for some statement of responsibilities, but with a different area of emphasis.

> In the interests of democracy, everyone shall be guaranteed by law the right of free expression of opinion, and in particular freedom of speech, of the Press and of artistic expression, provided that freedom of speech and of the Press is not used for war propaganda for inciting enmity among nations, racial discrimination and the dissemination of slanderous rumors.[96]

The U.S. representative, however, objected strongly to the formula of including duties in this one article, arguing that they are not mentioned elsewhere.[97]

A dispute arose over whether to draft the limitation clause in a brief general form or a specific list. The latter approach gave rise to a large number of amendments suggesting over thirty limitations. The United Kingdom was in the forefront of the move to draft specific limits. The British representative pointed out that such a list was necessary because there was no guarantee that the Convention on Freedom of Information would be drafted. Indicative of some of the British concerns was a provision covering governmental control of imported foreign news print based on balance of payments problems.[98] The British also proposed several restrictions on coverage of trials by the press, arguing that restrictions were necessary in order to maintain "the authority and impartiality of the judiciary."[99] The U.S. representative argued that the former proposal was unnecessary since the government always retained its option "to decide whatever restrictions or prohibitions on the import of news material they deemed necessary."[100] The United States also opposed the latter suggestion because it felt that the general limitation clause covered this problem.[101]

The United States disagreed with both the United Kingdom and France over the wording of the general limitation. This difference revealed the complexity of the issue, the major role of the United States, and the fact that the pressure for the article came from other Western democracies rather than from the Soviet Union. The U.S. representative rejected part of the French suggestion, as well as a similar phrase in the British text.

> The United States could not support the phrase "respect for law" which appeared in the French text because in its view that expression was equivalent to the United Kingdom wording "for the prevention of disorder or crime" which might serve as an arbitrary basis for limiting freedom of information. Governments would merely have to enact legislation designating any act as a crime in order to be able to prohibit or punish any expression relating to that act. In the absence of any possible test or standard to evaluate the reasonableness of such a measure, the United States delegation deemed that provision an improper and unreasonable limitation for an article on freedom of information.[102]

Furthermore, the United States was concerned about the inclusion of a provision on interference. Article 19 of the Universal Declaration simply provides for "the right to hold opinions without interference." The commission discussed whether the "interference" referred to would be solely state interference or rather interference from any source. Roosevelt stressed from early on a need to include the phrase "free from governmental interference"; she saw this as the necessary method of avoiding government censorship.[103] The French felt that governmental interference was too narrow a concept. Roosevelt explicated this dispute:

> The French delegation felt that the article on freedom of information should not be limited to governmental interference alone while the United States believed that any attempt to broaden the scope of the article beyond governmental interference would involve serious complications and difficulties.[104]

Therefore, the U.S. representative also rejected the French amendment, which read, "Steps shall be taken to eliminate political, economic, technical, and other obstacles likely to impair freedom of information," because "she felt that the phrase . . . was obscure and secondly, because the amendment was not couched in the legal form appropriate to a covenant."[105]

The commission adopted a three-part text which followed closely the recommended U.S. text:

> 1. Everyone shall have the right to hold opinions without interference.
> 2. Everyone shall have the right to freedom of expression; this right shall include freedom to seek, receive and impart information and ideas of all kinds, regardless of frontiers, either orally, in writing or in print, in the form of art, or through any other media of his choice.
> 3. The exercise of the rights provided for in the foregoing paragraph carries with it special duties and responsibilities. It may therefore be subject to certain restrictions, but these shall be such only as are provided by law and are necessary, (1) for respect of the rights or reputations of others, (2) for the protection of national security or of public order ("ordre public"), or of public health or morals.[106]

A further issue was that of the relationship between Article 19 and proposed Article 26 prohibiting racial hostility and incitement to violence. Since the purpose of Article 19 was to protect the right of the individual to freedom of expression and information, many felt that it should contain as few restrictions as possible. Many of the amendments, however, contained important restrictions, some similar to those in draft Article 26. A Brazilian amendment would have added "for preventing any manifestations of racial, religious or class prejudices" to the list of reasons why it might be necessary to impose restrictions on freedom of expression and would have deleted proposed Article 26. The Soviet Union proposed adding the following after "and are necessary":

> (1) for the prevention of war propaganda, incitement to enmity among nations, racial discrimination, and the dissemination of slanderous rumors.[107]

Eleanor Roosevelt initially had taken a position in full support of the draft article of the commission, which she described as

> a clear and balanced text which adequately stated the principle of freedom of information. Propaganda and prejudice could be overcome only by the best possible flow of information making the facts available to the people.[108]

Later, however, the United States introduced an amendment to paragraph 3 partly to counter the amendments on this issue of incitement.

> The above-mentioned rights shall not be subject to any restrictions except those which are provided by law, are necessary to protect national security, public order ("ordre public"), public health or morals or the rights and freedoms of others, to prevent incitement to violence by fostering national, racial or religious hatred, and are consistent with the other rights recognized in this Covenant. However, these limitations shall not be deemed to justify the imposition by any State of prior censorship on news, comments and political opinions and may not be used as grounds for restricting the right to criticize the Government.[109]

In explanation of her proposal, Roosevelt said that the clause on incitement to violence

> had been inserted in an attempt to meet a point raised by delegations, the verb "prevent" being used to preclude an interpretation that would open the door to prior censorship. The clause was intended to combat hate-mongerers and hate-propaganda groups. Its inclusion indicated that the methodical defamation by which the Nazis had come to power had not been forgotten in her country, any more than it had in other parts of the world. She believed that the clause overlapped sufficiently with the Soviet proposal concerning prevention of war propaganda to obviate the necessity for including such a separate concept in the third paragraph.[110]

This effort of the United States was obviously aimed at avoiding the incorporation of the language of draft Article 26 into Article 19. Later this amendment was withdrawn, and none of the amendments to the article was accepted.[111] As we have seen, then, the basic provision in the Civil and Political Rights Covenant on freedom of expression represented a complete success for the U.S. position. The final text of Article 19 of the Covenant on Civil and Political Rights was basically drafted by the Human Rights Commission, working primarily from a text designed by the United States.[112] The complexity of the issue and the dominant role of the United States were evident; this pattern was characteristic of most of the debate over the provisions of the covenant.

Self-Determination

Probably the most important addition made to the covenants when codifying the principles of the Universal Declaration was the article on self-determination. The Universal Declaration was accepted without any reference to self-determination; however, given the growing anticolonial sentiment at the United Nations, it is not surprising that the General Assembly requested an addition dealing with the issue when the covenants were being drafted and decided that the same article should be included in both treaties. By the early 1950s, there was an emergent international consensus on the illegality of colonialism reflected in treaties, declarations, and numerous U.N. resolutions. The dominant issue for the Third World had become the elimination of Western "remnants of imperialism."

The General Assembly resolution specified certain provisions for the self-determination article.

> This article shall be drafted in the following terms: "All peoples shall have the right of self-determination," and shall stipulate that all States, including those having responsibility for the administration of Non-Self-Governing Territories, should promote the realization of that right, in conformity with the purposes and principles of the United Nations, and States having responsibility for the administration of Non-Self-Governing Territories should promote the realization of that right in relation to the peoples of such territories.[113]

As might be expected with a controversial topic such as this one, there were numerous disagreements in the commission about how the article should be written. The members eventually agreed on three paragraphs to cover the major points raised during the discussions, and the United States played a major role in achieving that agreement.

The first difficulty encountered was that of defining the term "self-determination" and reaching a satisfactory understanding of what the concept included. Some members contended that self-determination was, in fact, a principle rather than a right and not appropriate for the body of a legal instrument. Different representatives pointed out some of the many different meanings that have been attached to the term: local autonomy, self-government, sovereignty, secession, statehood, and independence.

Because of these complex problems, it was suggested that a special declaration or covenant should be prepared on this topic or that it should be included in the preamble rather than in the operative body of the treaties. These suggestions were rejected by a majority of the commission members, who felt that self-determination was a right and had to be included in the body of the covenants. There is little doubt that the intensity of feeling about the self-determination provision was a reflection of the increasing frustration of many governments with the persistence of Western colonialism; this priority was well reflected in the preeminent positioning of the self-determination article as Article 1 of Part I in both treaties.

Eleanor Roosevelt voiced her support for a provision on self-determination during the early debates.[114] She submitted amendments to the Soviet draft that was the basis for the commission's early discussions.[115]

The second paragraph of the article indicated the broad extent of the application of the right of self-determination and referred to the U.N. Charter provisions as the basis for its validity. Those supporting the second paragraph stressed these charter provisions.[116] Even though some argued that it was not legitimate to link the *principle* of self-determination discussed in Articles 1 and 55 of the charter with the term "self-government," the majority of the commission believed that the two were interdependent. This belief explains the addition of the words "all nations" to the General Assembly wording "all people." The desire was to include people of all states, countries, and territories—trust, autonomous, or non-self-governing. The right and its concomitant realization were accordingly seen as necessarily joined; the right of self-determination was proclaimed to be universal, and all people and nations, whether or not they were presently independent, were entitled to exercise it.

The United States supported the second paragraph. Roosevelt pointed out that the reference to the U.N. Charter was essential. "The object of that was to make it clear that the principle was already recognized in the Charter and was not a new principle to be applied only to countries which ratified the covenants on human rights."[117] She also favored making it clear that self-determination was an explicit responsibility that all states must accept. She criticized the alternate draft submitted by the Soviet Union.

> The USSR draft resolution referred only to States which had responsibility for the administration of Non-Self-Governing Territories, whereas the General Assembly resolution referred to all States unreservedly. In the view of the United States delegation, the principle of self-determination applied not only to people which had not yet attained independence, but also to politically independent States which needed protection from external pressure, threats, the use of force and subversive activities.[118]

The Soviet Union responded to the U.S. critique with one of its own.

> [The Soviet representative] was, however, opposed to the first United States amendment for, contrary to Mrs. Roosevelt's assertions . . . , that text was not in line with General Assembly resolution 545 (VI). It placed on the same footing States entrusted with the administration of Non-Self-Governing Territories and all other States, and left out the last sentence of the first paragraph of the operative part of the General Assembly resolution.[119]

But the Soviet Union was unable to persuade the commission. The Soviets also proposed adding to the article a provision for the protection of minorities.[120] This proposal, opposed by the United States,[121] was also rejected. The commission adopted, with the concurring vote of the United States, the following text:

> All States, including those having responsibility for the administration of Non-Self-Governing and Trust Territories and those controlling in whatsoever manner the exercise of that right by another person, shall promote the realization of that right in all their territories, and shall respect the maintenance of that right in

other States, in conformity with the provision of the United Nations Charter.[122]

By far the most controversial paragraph in the self-determination article, for reasons similar to those pertaining to the article on private property, was the third. A Chilean draft was the basis for the commission debate. It read,

> The right of the peoples to self-determination shall also include permanent sovereignty over their natural wealth and resources. In no case may a people be deprived of its own means of subsistence on the grounds of any rights that may be claimed by other States.[123]

The connection of "permanent sovereignty over natural resources" with self-determination reflects an effort by the developing states to correct perceived injustices and prevent further exploitation. Valenzuela of Chile clearly explicated this goal in advocating his government's proposal.

> It has been argued that its adoption would deter private foreign investment at a time when the under-developed countries were crying out for it. It was in fact designed to end that existing paradoxical situation in which the under-developed countries had to appeal desperately to the more advanced countries for hard currency while private investors from the latter were draining the under-developed countries' natural resources. . . . It was not an attempt to suggest that international obligations should not be respected nor to deprive any investor of his investment nor to justify expropriation.[124]

The U.S. representative, however, opposed this paragraph from its initiation, and opposed it more consistently than any other part of the draft. Alternatively, in Roosevelt's view,

> The correct way to remedy the problem [referred to in the Chilean remarks] would be to include in all contracts and concessions a provision for their renegotiation within a certain period or if certain conditions were or were not fulfilled. The Chilean proposal ignored existing contracts and international law, which provided a remedy in expropriation, provided that adequate, effective and prompt compensation was paid.[125]

The Soviet Union presented its own view and that of many of the other delegates in defending the Chilean proposal.

All that the draft resolution implied was that people could not be deprived of their natural resources, the very basis of their existence, which in turn was the basis of their possibility of exercising the right to self-determination. Nothing in the Chilean draft resolution infringed existing international law, of which the concept of sovereignty was an abiding principle. The Chilean draft resolution was merely a development of the principle just adopted by the Commission that all people and all nations should have the right freely to determine their economic, as well as their political, social and cultural status. It did not in any way conflict with international law nor with contracts or trade agreements, provided that they were not unfair nor obsolete, imposed often by force of arms in the course of colonization.[126]

The U.S. response was predictable.

No one would contend that all existing contracts were fair, but the correct remedy existed in international law, namely expropriation with due compensation. No one would say that fairer contracts should not be negotiated, with every possible safeguard; but to give the right to ignore the fact that a contract existed would be a questionable procedure from the ethical point of view and even of that of self-interest.[127]

The French position, like that of the United States, reflected the view of the developed states, but it also made reference to the use of an international organizational approach and the need, at times, to surrender some sovereignty.[128] After much debate, the Chilean proposal was adopted,[129] and the entire article, in accord with an earlier vote, was included in both treaties.[130]

The United States was sensitive to the widespread desire within the United Nations for an article on self-determination. The first and second paragraphs of the article met U.S. concerns. The third paragraph raised the issues that surrounded the expropriation question discussed in connection with the debate over a private property provision. The article on self-determination again created a complex task for U.S. representatives, which they handled effectively. The covenant was, of course, only in draft form during the entire 1950s debates within the United States. Drafts, in fact, do change, and, in the case of the self-determination article, subsequent qualifying language removed any legal basis for criticism of the controversial paragraph.[131]

Conclusion

The opposition to human rights treaties in the 1950s focused major attention on the Covenant on Human Rights. This treaty, opponents argued, exemplified all the dangers of the movement for international human rights laws: loss of basic American rights, abrogation of states' rights, promotion of world government, increased Communist and Soviet influence, and reduction of U.S. sovereignty. Their attack on the treaty extended from its contents to its drafters, including Eleanor Roosevelt and other representatives of the U.S. executive branch appointed to work on the text.

As we have seen in this chapter, four core issues took center stage during the drafting process and became relevant to the opposition's criticism. And in regard to all of these issues U.S. representatives exhibited a thorough understanding of the political and legal problems involved in codification, combining traditional U.S. foreign policy positions with an awareness of potential domestic objections to proposed treaty provisions.

First, on the question of one or two treaties, the United States took an early lead in moving for separation. Of the issues discussed here, the one on separation or integration of the two groups of rights was most revelatory of the United States' general influence in the Human Rights Commission. The representatives presented strong substantive arguments and used the full range of procedural and parliamentary tactics in obtaining their goal. Second, on the issue of freedom of expression, U.S. arguments and tactics likewise prevailed.[132]

Study of the two remaining issues revealed the United States to be an active and well-prepared participant in their resolution also. On these issues, however, the outcome was a compromise rather than a "win" for the United States. On the issue of private property, the United States wanted a provision protecting private property rights as well as a reaffirmation of classical international legal requirements for expropriations. Once the U.S. delegation determined that their proposals would not be approved, they decided it was preferable to have no private property provision rather than to have one altering "existing" (in the U.S. view) standards for treatment of the property of non-nationals. The self-determination article also reflected a compromise, with two paragraphs in accord with U.S. aims, and one that was not. Subsequent actions at the United Nations addressed the legal issues raised in connection with these two provisions.

U.S. representatives evinced a strong commitment to the Human Rights Covenants and participated actively in their preparation by submitting articles, developing amendments and compromise alternatives, and articulately advocating well-defined positions. Criticism of the treaties cannot be attributed to unable or unwilling U.S. representation at the drafting; nor can it reasonably be claimed that U.S. representatives were duped by more active or more able participants from the Soviet Union. U.S. proposals reflected a conservative constitutional position protective of a traditional American view of individual rights. These proposals were for the most part accepted, and on the rare occasions when they were not, compromises protective of the U.S. system were reached. The one exception, a provision on propaganda for racial hatred and war, was added after the 1954 draft was completed (see Chapter 6). That the U.S. representatives were unable to prevent a particular outcome on two provisions reflected the fact that their perceptions and values were not always shared by a majority of the commission; this majority included not only the Soviet representative but frequently commission members from leading Western democracies as well. In the array of opposition arguments against human rights treaties in the 1950s, there was precious little legal basis for the U.S. opposition's attacks on the drafters of the covenant or the draft document they formulated. Nevertheless, the opposition's political interpretation of the treaty produced an ingenious legal solution to thwart the perceived dangers of the Human Rights Covenant: the demand for an amendment to the United States Constitution.

FOUR

The Bricker Amendment

America has been caught in a noose which can only be removed by a Constitutional amendment along the lines of that introduced by Senator Bricker . . . to prevent the present "blank check" form of treaty-making being proposed at the United Nations from changing the rights and liberties of the American people as guaranteed by the Constitution.
—Frank Holman, speech to Tacoma Council of World Affairs, 1951

Human rights treaties received their most extensive review by the Senate during the period of debate over the so-called Bricker Amendment. Opponents of the treaties, led by Senator John Bricker, focused their efforts on the adoption of a constitutional amendment which was primarily motivated by the alleged dangers arising from the treaties. Although international legal scholars have often acknowledged this connection between the human rights treaties and the effort in the early 1950s to amend the treaty-making provisions of the Constitution, most international relations scholars have not. Most major works on U.S. foreign policy that mention the Bricker Amendment imply that its major purpose was the curtailment of the president's power to conclude executive agreements.[1] While criticism of the increased use of executive agreements was reflected in one section of the amendment and did later become an important issue during the debates, the original impetus for the Bricker Amendment was a concern about the U.N. human rights treaties, especially the covenant discussed in the previous chapter. During the Bricker Amendment debates, human rights treaties were effectively branded as dangerous to the American way of life and cast into a senatorial limbo from which they have never been released.

As explained in Chapter 2, prior to consideration of the Bricker Amendment the only extensive postwar Senate deliberations on human rights treaties concerned the Genocide Convention. In the 1950 hearings (see Chapters 1 and 2), opponents did not consider the Genocide Convention to be an isolated problem but rather part of a much larger movement—the international recognition and legal codification of individual human rights—that they feared would alter the nature and process of the American political system and way of life. The arguments that germinated during the Genocide Convention hearings subsequently blossomed into full-fledged opposition to all human rights treaties during the hearings on the Bricker Amendment.

This chapter is divided into three sections. The first section is an analysis of the Bricker Amendment itself, highlighting the explicit and implicit arguments against human rights treaties, and the second is a summary of Senate consideration of the Bricker Amendment. In the third section, the various arguments against the treaty are organized according to a typology in order to clarify their basis, examine their frequency, and, at a later point, compare their consistency and importance over time.

The Bricker Amendment

The movement surrounding the proposal, modification, and support of the Bricker Amendment reflected a widespread concern within the American electorate. Steve Garrett identifies two important dimensions of the movement: (1) a "substantive" concern about increasing U.S. involvement internationally and (2) an "institutional" dismay at the increased power and independence of the executive in foreign affairs.[2] However, if we look closely at the immediate cause of concern, we can see that human rights treaties played the most important role in initiating and maintaining the spirited attack on the treaty-making powers of the executive branch.

Although there are many different reasons why various members of the Senate in the 1950s supported the collection of proposals now subsumed under the general term "Bricker Amendment," concern over the effects of human rights treaties was in the forefront. Senator Bricker himself linked his proposal to his opposition to the human rights treaties and their international implementation:

There is a singleness of purpose of course on the part of all of us . . . who have joined in the presentation of this Resolution. . . . The American people want to make certain that no treaty or executive agreement will be effective to deny or abridge their fundamental rights. Also, they do not want their basic human rights to be supervised or controlled by international agencies over which they have no control.[3]

As explained in Chapter 1, Frank Holman and the ABA Special Committee on Peace and Law Through United Nations developed their plan to amend the Constitution in order to protect the country from what they saw as the dangers posed by human rights treaties. The Eisenhower administration also perceived the Bricker Amendment forces as primarily motivated by opposition to human rights treaties.[4] This belief led to the administration's decision not to ratify any human rights treaties; the secretary of state made this announcement during his testimony at the Bricker Amendment hearings with the expectation that it would mollify senators supporting the amendment.[5]

The treaties were also perceived as pro-Communist and pro-Soviet, which added emotion and urgency to the opposition attacks on the treaties and support for the amendment.

> Iron Curtain countries would no doubt welcome a new Roosevelt-Litvinov agreement to make their confiscatory decrees effective in the United States. . . . Reactionary one-worlders [are] trying to vest legislative powers in non-elected officials of the UN and its satellite bodies with a socialist-communist majority.[6]

If we examine each section of the 1953 form of the amendment, we can see reflected there a variety of political and legal concerns raised by the human rights treaties.

Section 1

The first section of the Bricker Amendment simply states,

> A provision of a treaty which denies or abridges *any right* enumerated in this Constitution shall not be of any force or effect [emphasis added].

In defending Section 1, Bricker said it would ensure that "no [humanitarian] treaty can be effective to undermine the constitutional rights of American citizens."[7] The issue here is the nature and extent of the limits on the content of treaties. Some constitutional law scholars had argued that treaties, being the supreme law of the land, were not subject to normal constitutional restrictions. Such would be a broad reading of Article VI, paragraph 2, of the Constitution:

This Constitution and the Laws of the United States which shall be made in Pursuance thereof; and all Treaties made, or which shall be made, under the Authority of the United States, shall be supreme Law of the land; and the Judges in every State shall be bound thereby, any thing in the Constitution or Laws of any State to the Contrary notwithstanding.

Senator Bricker described Section 1 in the following manner:

Section 1 subjects the President and the Senate to constitutional restraints in the exercise of the treaty-making power comparable to those which limit their action as participants in the enactment of ordinary legislation. This was, of course, the original intent of the framers of the Constitution and was reflected in early judicial dicta.[8]

He was referring, in this last comment, to the decision in *Geofroy v. Riggs*, in which Justice Stephen J. Field explained,

That the treaty power of the United States extends to all proper subjects of negotiation between our government and the government of other nations is clear. . . . The treaty power, as expressed in the Constitution, is in terms, unlimited except by those restraints which are found in that instrument.[9]

And Justice Field went on to explain that the treaty power does not extend "so far as to authorize what the Constitution forbids."[10] The difficulty, as Bricker viewed it, was the subsequent decision of the Supreme Court in *Missouri v. Holland*, which left ambiguous the meaning of Article VI, paragraph 2, of the Constitution. Justice Oliver Wendell Holmes, in delivering the judgment, did not, in Bricker's eyes, hold to the proper interpretation of this provision when he stated,

Acts of Congress are the supreme law of the land only when made in pursuance of the Constitution, while treaties are declared to be so when made under the authority of the United States. It is open to question whether the authority of the United States means more than the formal acts prescribed to make the convention.[11]

Bricker saw this 1919 decision as effectively reversing that of *Geofroy v. Riggs*, and he argued that the lack of clarity on this crucial issue made amendment of the Constitution a necessity. He argued that most of the rights contained in the Bill of Rights would be "repealed" by ratification of the Human Rights Covenant.[12] His amendment would prevent this travesty and therefore be in the interest of all citizens:

The American people resent the argument that rights which they regard as God-given and inalienable can be alienated by the President and two-thirds of the Senate present and voting.[13]

Opponents of Section 1 argued that it was unnecessary. Secretary of State John Foster Dulles, in testifying against the amendment, stated:

No limitations upon the treaty-making powers are explicitly defined in the Constitution or decisions of the Supreme Court. But the treaty-making power is not an unlimited power. All of the Supreme Court cases which deal with the subject are uniform to that effect.

Furthermore, while the Constitution provides that treaties made under the authority of the United States shall be the supreme law of the land, they only rank on an equality with congressional enactments.

The effect of any treaty as internal law can be overcome by a simple act of Congress.

That is a constitutional fact which must be, and is, accepted by all other nations which make treaties with us.[14]

Section 2

Section 2 reveals most clearly the institutional line of attack laid by the Bricker proponents. They wished to secure greater protection for states' rights, arguing the constitutional grounds of the Tenth Amendment. Section 2 of the Bricker Amendment proposed,

No treaty shall authorize or permit any foreign power or any international organization to supervise, control, or adjudicate rights of citizens of the United States within the United States enumerated in this constitution or any other matter essentially within the domestic jurisdiction of the United States.

The purpose of this section was to restrain the federal government from further encroaching upon states' rights via the treaty-making power. As has already been mentioned, a great concern was that these treaties could be used to establish a federal basis for desegregation. This section would have enabled Congress to review all treaties before they had any domestic application, thereby preventing the federal government from using treaties as a basis for expanding its authority into areas where power is otherwise reserved to the states under the Tenth Amendment to the Constitution:

> The powers not delegated to the United States by the Constitution, nor prohibited by it to the States, are reserved to the States respectively, or to the people.

This issue arose from one possible interpretation of the *Missouri v. Holland* decision. The case concerned a treaty between the United States and Great Britain regulating, for conservation purposes, the taking of migratory birds. Congress had enacted legislation prohibiting the hunting of migratory birds, and this legislation had been declared invalid by two lower federal courts. Before the Supreme Court heard the case, the United States had entered into a treaty with Canada establishing a cooperative system of conservation of migratory birds and Congress passed an implementing statute. The state of Missouri challenged the validity of the treaty and the implementing legislation on the grounds that it interfered with states' rights and violated the Tenth Amendment of the Constitution. In upholding the treaty and federal statute, Justice Holmes stated:

> We do not mean to imply that there are no qualifications to the treaty-making power; but they must be ascertained in a different way. It is obvious that there may be matters of the sharpest exigency for the national well being that the act of Congress could not deal with but that a treaty followed by such an act could. . . .
>
> The treaty in question does not contravene any prohibitory words to be found in the Constitution. The only question is whether it is forbidden by some invisible radiation from the general terms of the Tenth Amendment.[15]

To this question he answered no. And it is this issue that led to the drafting of Section 2 of the Bricker Amendment. Senator Bricker stated:

> Section 2 prevents the President and the Senate from using treaties as an instrument of domestic legislation without the participation of the House of Representatives. In addition, section 2

protects the reserved powers of the states by preventing Congress
from acquiring by treaty legislative power which it does not pos-
sess in the absence of treaty. . . . [It] reverses the doctrine of
Missouri v. Holland which holds that a treaty may empower Congress to legislate in areas prohibited by the Tenth Amendment in
the absence of treaty.[16]

It could be argued, however, that *Missouri v. Holland* did not significantly alter what the executive or Congress could do. And certainly,
by the 1950s, a great deal of authority had moved to Congress as well
as the executive in areas previously viewed as the domain of states.
Rather than view the treaty-making power as moving a subject out of
the state realm, Louis Henkin has reversed the line of reasoning
beginning with the international rather than state level.

The subject of a treaty must be of international concern. And
because the matter is of international concern one may say that it
is ever in the federal domain and might become the subject of a
treaty. If, before a treaty, it is left to the States, it is only
"defeasibly" so, subject at any time to the assertion of the federal
interest by treaty, just as in some other areas of federal power the
States may act in the absence of federal regulation. Any matter,
then, which is or becomes of international concern is "lifted"
when Congress taxes it and regulates it to protect the reve-
nue. . . . Congress makes the lives, and actions, and the most
"local" interests of any citizen of any State subject to federal
regulation because they are of "war concern." This is what Justice
Holmes was saying, more succinctly, in *Missouri v. Holland*.
Holmes assumed in that case that migratory birds were not subject to congressional regulation apart from the treaty; he did not
assume that they were without the federal domain. Indeed, the
point of the case is that migratory birds, being of international
concern, were in the federal domain and subject to the exercise of
federal jurisdiction.

It is no matter that—on Holmes' assumption—the federal jurisdiction to which they were subject was an exercise not of congressional power but of the treaty power. It was because they were
subject to such federal jurisdiction that, said Holmes, they were
not "reserved" to the States by the tenth amendment.[17]

In addition to states' rights concerns, Section 2 was designed to protect U.S. domestic jurisdiction. Bricker cited Article 2, paragraph 7, of the United Nations Charter and argued that the human rights treaties were violating this provision.

> Are human rights essentially within the domestic jurisdiction? Dr. Philip Jessup and many others who have represented us at the U.N. say, "No." If that is true, then nothing is essentially within the domestic jurisdiction. Those who oppose section 2 must believe that the relationship between the American people and their own government is not purely a domestic matter.[18]

He then explained that this reason was the motivating force behind all his efforts to amend the Constitution.

> What this amendment would in essence do is to keep the rights of the American people in the spiritual realm and not place them in the temporal power of an international government which is controlled by countries which are totalitarian in their philosophy and seem to have no concept of the God-given inalienable rights that the people of America enjoy.[19]

Section 3

A further concern of those supporting the Bricker Amendment was that courts might apply provisions of the human rights treaties directly, without implementing legislation from Congress. Since the treaties generally have no explicit provision that they are not self-executing, this interpretation might be possible. Bricker described Section 3 as an effort to prevent the invasion of U.S. domestic jurisdiction through the instrumentality of human rights treaties. Section 3 read:

> A treaty shall become effective as internal law in the United States only through the enactment of appropriate legislation by the Congress.

Bricker cited the Fujii case as a "reminder that treaties may have far-reaching and unintended consequences."[20] In this case the intermediate California court cited Articles 55 and 56, human rights provisions of the United Nations Charter, and the Universal Declaration of Human Rights when holding that the state's alien land act was invalid. Bricker concluded,

> If the Supreme Court of the United States should adopt the reasoning of the lower California Court, thousands of Federal and State laws will be nullified. . . . All treaties affecting domestic law must be made non-self-executing to avoid unintentional alteration of the rights of the American people under Federal and State laws.[21]

This section was, in effect, a second line of defense in the event that a human rights treaty was actually approved by the Senate without a non-self-executing provision or reservation.[22] Courts, then, would have been prevented from citing treaty provisions that had not first been implemented by domestic legislation.

Section 4

The increase in the use of executive agreements and their effect on the rights of Americans also troubled Senator Bricker and his supporters. Section 4 responded to the fear of abrogation of rights by agreements not submitted to Congress:

> All executive and other agreements between the President and any international organization, foreign power, or official thereof shall be made only in the manner and to the extent to be prescribed by law. Such agreements shall be subject to the limitations imposed on treaties, or the making of treaties, by this article.

This section was a reaction to the Supreme Court's decisions in the Belmont and Pink cases. At issue in these cases was the Litvinov agreement, signed as part of the settlement surrounding the recognition of the Soviet government. It was not submitted to Congress, and it did result in property transfers that were contrary to the state law of New York. Bricker bitterly presented the case in the following manner,

> Foreign creditors were entitled to the protection of the fifth amendment. Both Russia and the United States were powerless to deprive them of that property. However, the Supreme Court held that an agreement between Franklin Roosevelt and Maxim Litvinov cancelled out property rights otherwise protected by the fifth amendment and the public policy of the State of New York.[23]

The more general issue was the determination by the Court that "a treaty is a 'law of the land' under the supremacy clause . . . of the

Constitution. Such international compacts and agreements as the Litvinov assignment have a similar dignity."[24] In other words, executive agreements have the same constitutional status as treaties. Thus, the Bricker forces argued that if human rights treaties and agreements were acceded to by the United States as executive agreements without the consent of the Senate, they could then be used to deprive Americans of their basic rights, including the right to private property.

In the final analysis, the crucial topic of debate became whether or not human rights are an appropriate subject for treaty-making. Opposition to the conclusion of human rights treaties came to signify protection of domestic jurisdiction, maintenance of states' rights, and defense against communism and the encroachment of international organizations. As Bricker put it, "The peace of the world is endangered by the U.N.'s ambition to supervise and control the purely domestic affairs of its members."[25] He specifically attacked the Human Rights Covenant, of which he snidely observed,

> The State Department of the previous administration contended that the U.N. draft Covenants on Human Rights were great humanitarian treaties, and that the American people should cheerfully submit their political, civil, and economic rights to United Nations definition, supervision, and control.[26]

Formal Congressional Deliberations

On 17 July 1951 Bricker made a direct attack on the human rights treaties by proposing that the Senate adopt a resolution requiring the president to announce that the covenant was unacceptable and withdraw the United States from participation in drafting it and other human rights treaties (see Chapter 3). By 14 September 1951, Bricker moved to introduce a constitutional amendment aimed at protecting the "sacred rights which [U.S. citizens] enjoy under the Bill of Rights and the Constitution."[27] This resolution became S.J. Res. 102 and was referred to the Senate Judiciary Committee. There were no hearings and it died with that session of Congress. On 7 February 1952 Senator Bricker introduced, with fifty-nine co-sponsors, a second constitutional amendment.[28] In introducing the amendment, Bricker made specific mention of the Human Rights Covenant.

There is not the remotest chance that even one-third of the present Senate would undermine the rights of the American people by voting for the U.N. Covenant on Human Rights or any other treaty of similar import. However, the rights and freedoms enumerated in the Constitution must be protected in perpetuity, and not merely by the suffrance of the President and two-thirds of the Senators present and voting.[29]

The Senate Judiciary Committee held hearings on the Bricker Amendment in May and June of 1952. By a vote of 9 to 5, the committee approved an amended version, but the Senate adjourned without debating the issue.

On 7 January 1953 Bricker once again introduced a constitutional amendment, this time co-sponsored by sixty-two senators.[30] Support had grown for some form of the amendment and passage appeared likely. At the hearings held in 1953 by the Senate Judiciary Committee, the Eisenhower administration expressed its opposition to the amendment through testimony by Secretary of State John Foster Dulles. Dulles had the difficult task of reversing himself publicly on human rights treaties. Supporters of the Bricker Amendment had frequently cited a speech by Dulles in which he stated that treaties

can take powers from the States and give them to the Federal Government or to some international body, and they can cut across the rights given the people by their constitutional Bill of Rights.[31]

In an effort to assuage the fears of the Bricker followers and undercut support for the amendment, Dulles made the following conciliatory statement:

This administration is committed to the exercise of the treaty making power only within traditional limits. . . . While we [i.e., the administration] shall not withhold our counsel from those who seek to draft a treaty or covenant on human rights, we do not ourselves look upon a treaty as the means which we would now select as the proper and most effective way to spread throughout the world the goals of human liberty. . . . We, therefore, do not intend to become a party to any such covenant or present it as a treaty for consideration by the Senate.[32]

He also said that the administration had no intention of recommending ratification of the Genocide Convention or the Convention on the Political Rights of Women, not because they objected to the rights contained therein, but

> because we do not believe that this goal can be achieved by treaty coercion or that it constitutes a proper field for exercise of the treaty making power. . . . These same principles will guide our action in other fields which have been suggested by some as fields for multilateral treaties.[33]

Despite this appeal, the Senate Committee on Foreign Relations voted to approve the amendment.

Floor debate began on 20 January 1954. The Eisenhower administration continued to oppose the Bricker Amendment but had approved a much weaker proposal, the Knowland version, which had been offered as a substitute.[34] When the vote was finally taken, the Bricker version failed to receive the requisite two-thirds vote for a constitutional amendment—52 senators voted in favor, while 40 were opposed.[35] A weaker version proposed by Senator George came closer, falling one vote short of the requirement.[36]

What is important to remember in assessing these deliberations is that, while supporters of the amendment were reacting against human rights treaties, opponents of the amendment were not arguing in favor of the treaties. Arguments against the Bricker Amendment had little relevance to the debate over human rights treaties, and the defeat of the Bricker Amendment revealed nothing about support for the treaties. Opponents argued, for example, that the amendment would interfere with the day-to-day conduct of foreign affairs, significantly alter a constitutional balance of power that had worked well for 160 years, endanger national survival, limit the president's ability to conduct and end a war, impede arrangements for the control of atomic energy and nuclear weapons, and embarrass the president in front of both allies and enemies.[37]

The examination of the American Bar Association presented in Chapter 1 revealed that the human rights treaties provided the initial impetus for the formulation of the amendment and a substantial reason for the strong ABA support of it. In fact, the determination within the ABA that human rights treaties posed a threat to Americans' basic rights and to their system of government was crucial to the popularity of the Bricker proposal. In introducing the amendment in 1953, Bricker said:

> I should like to pay tribute to the magnificent work of the American Bar Association and its Committee on Peace and Law through United Nations in alerting the American people to the dangers inherent in the treaty-making power.[38]

The uniqueness of the ABA position was reflected in numerous statements by Senator Bricker in which he expressed his gratitude to the ABA for their help, including their suggestions on the rewording of the amendment.[39] ABA members testifying in favor of the amendment were given special consideration; for example, they were invited by the chair of the subcommittee conducting the hearings to sit at his table.[40] Special care was taken to consider their convenience for attending, and they were informed when important witnesses were testifying against the amendment. During the hearings they frequently questioned other witnesses, a privilege normally reserved to members of the subcommittee. Arrangements were made so that one member could testify after all the opponents had finished their testimony in order to respond to any arguments that had been made.[41] And, as with the Genocide Convention (see Chapter 2), throughout the deliberations, ABA positions on the amendment and on various treaties were cited by others as authoritative.

A Typology of Arguments against Ratification

Previous sections have examined the arguments against human rights treaties found within the Bricker Amendment itself and within formal congressional deliberations. Chapter 2 presented an early form of the opposition arguments. This section presents a refined typology of arguments offered in opposition to ratification of human rights treaties in the 1950s. While numerous hearings were held on the Bricker Amendment during this period, the single best source of antiratification arguments is the set of hearings held by the Senate Judiciary Committee in February and April of 1953. These were the most extensive, and they occurred when Senate support was at its strongest. During these hearings, the Eisenhower administration made its commitment not to ratify the human rights treaties. This action made

Table 1. Analysis of Testimony in Support of the Bricker
Amendment, Senate Judiciary Committee Hearings, 1953

	Percentage of		
Topic	ABA Testimony ($n = 208$)	Non-ABA Testimony[a] ($n = 92$)	All Testimony ($n = 300$)
Human rights treaties	49.5[b]	51.1	50.0
General abuse of treaty power	31.2	46.7	36.0
Executive agreements	11.1	0.0	7.7
Other[c]	8.2	2.2	6.3

[a] Included in this category were representatives from the Veterans of Foreign Wars of the United States, the *New Orleans State*, the American Flag Committee, and the National Society of the Daughters of the American Revolution.

[b] Figures were computed by dividing the number of pages of testimony devoted to each topic by the total number of pages of testimony. The hearing included 300 pages of testimony in support of the Bricker Amendment.

[c] This category includes other topics discussed by witnesses, discussions related to the procedure of the hearings themselves, and supplementary materials provided by the witnesses—such as texts of treaties and lists of organizations and countries.

subsequent hearings less fruitful for this study, because it reduced the number of references to the treaties made by witnesses.

Content analysis of the 1953 hearings, the procedures for which are described and analyzed in greater detail in Chapter 7, reaffirmed the appropriateness of using these hearings to explore arguments against human rights treaties. Each page of testimony in support of the Bricker Amendment was coded according to the dominant topic of discussion. The results indicated a clear focus on human rights treaties. As can be seen in Table 1, the topic of human rights treaties accounted for 50 percent of the testimony. The other major issues of the hearings, executive agreements and the general abuse of the treaty-making power, together accounted for 43.7 percent. Also evident from the data presented in the table is the significance of the role of the ABA. The testimony of members of the ABA's Special Committee on Peace and Law Through United Nations accounted for 69 percent of all testimony in support of the Bricker Amendment.

Diminish Basic Rights

Although the rudimentary form of this argument was expressed at the Genocide Convention hearings, it was fully developed during the Bricker hearings. In fact, the indictment that the treaties would diminish basic American rights became the most frequently mentioned argument made against them. The argument rests on the contention that once a human rights treaty is ratified, constitutional protections would be superseded. Arthur J. Schweppe, chair of the ABA Committee on Peace and Law, stressed this idea in his testimony:

> The limitations in the first amendment with respect to freedom of speech, press, and religion are only limitations on Congress. They are not a limitation on the treatymaking power.[42]

And Frank Holman, former ABA president, presented this argument dramatically:

> The "internationalists" and the State Department move step by step—first aspirations, then ratification of these aspirations in treaty form, then international courts to enforce the aspirations. Thus our internal rights under our own Constitution, and Bill of Rights, are to be undermined step by step and will continue to be undermined unless the American people shut off this insidious process by an appropriate constitutional amendment.[43]

Various specific rights that were thought to be endangered, including most of those in the Bill of Rights, were discussed throughout the hearings. The testimony of ABA member Eberhard Deutsch on the freedom of the press conveys the flavor of these attacks: "[The treaties] contain the festering germs of destruction of a free press beyond the antiseptic properties of the first amendment."[44]

Violate States' Rights

The claim that the treaties would violate states' rights had been the most important argument raised during the Genocide Convention hearings, and it continued in prominence during the hearings on the Bricker Amendment as well. The treaties, it was argued, would legitimize federal action in areas formerly reserved to the states. Some opponents identified supremacy of the federal government as the ultimate objective of the treaties. Deutsch stated clearly,

It is impossible to overemphasize the significance of present con-stitutionally possible abuses of the treatymaking power in the United States. The unquestionable objective of at least some of the opponents of constitutional limitation of that power is early elimination of State and local political entities except as adminis-trative agencies of the Nation. . . . The gilding of multipartite treaties with such idealistic immediate goals as the prevention of genocide and the promotion of human rights cannot conceal their underlying long-range objective to destroy local government while expanding the sphere of national power.[45]

Federal action on civil rights was very much on the minds of those supporting the Bricker Amendment. Frank Holman described his concern.

[A treaty] can increase the powers of the Federal Government at the expense of the States. For example, in the so-called field of civil rights, a treaty can do what the Congress has theretofore refused to do. The Congress has to date refused to enact the civil rights program.[46]

He went on to explain that the federal government could accomplish this objective through ratification of the human rights treaties. Deutsch articulated the common concern that the treaties would be used specifically to legitimize federal legislation on racial matters, complaining that "the same instrument has recently been cited with great force as a prohibition of race segregation in the District of Co-lumbia, in Kansas, and in other States."[47]

A common metaphor that was often applied to the treaties during the hearings was that of the Trojan Horse. Deutsch explained the metaphor well.

The treaty clause of the Constitution (article VI) [is] as a "Trojan Horse," ready to unload its hidden soldiery into our midst, de-stroying State laws and constitutions and leaving behind the wreckage of the dream of the Founding Fathers which envisioned maintenance of the established constitutional balance between State and Federal power, and preservation of the Bill of Rights intact.[48]

Some of the specific states' rights which were mentioned during the hearings as being in danger of encroachment were the rights to restrict land sales on the basis of race and national origin, set criminal and civil liabilities, determine the political rights of women, establish qualifications for public school teachers, and regulate membership in the medical and legal professions—which seemed especially unsettling to the testifying ABA members.[49]

Promote World Government

Fears about the potentially subversive action of the United Nations continued from the Genocide Convention hearings. The third-most-often-heard argument during the Bricker Amendment hearings was that human rights treaties constituted a move in the direction of establishing a world government. An ABA memorandum on the amendment that was included in the testimony of Vernon Hatch referred to this matter.

> Not only is the treaty power a threat to the States, it is a threat to the very Federal Government itself through the pressures of internationally minded groups who would favor erecting a world government by the treaty route in whose favor we would abdicate much, if not all, of our sovereignty.[50]

Frank Holman evoked the danger of Americans waking up to find that they are living under world government:

> We [could] have had a full-fledged world government overnight, and this is exactly what may happen under so-called treaty law unless a constitutional amendment is passed protecting American rights.[51]

Opponents of the amendment were portrayed as at best misguided and at worst ill intentioned. The testimony of Special Committee member George Finch exemplifies the former portrayal.

> The adoption of the proposed constitutional amendment now before this committee relating to the treatymaking power would stop the prevailing trend to regard the United Nations as but the first step in the ultimate establishment of a world government in which the United States would occupy the position of a province. . . . Now, the so-called liberals, the people who are opposing things that we are trying to do here would take us back into

that era from which we emerged 300 years ago and subordinate our sovereignty, which means our freedom and our independence, to some foreign power in which we would have but one vote among many.[52]

The latter portrayal is presented by Deutsch.

> It is difficult to believe that objections to a constitutional bulwark against direct legislative participation by Poland and the Argentine in the local affairs of Louisiana and North Dakota and Ohio and Utah can be rooted in good faith.[53]

Subject Citizens to Trial Abroad

A continuing argument that aroused strong emotional response was the allegation that human rights treaties would lead to the trial of Americans in foreign courts. The major points of the allegation are described in the testimony of ABA member Frank Ober:

> Among the 200 treaties that are being proposed is a treaty creating an international criminal court . . . a court composed of all but one of foreign judges, including judges from other countries who have no conception of our independent judiciary but think only of the judges as an arm of the political government.[54]

As implied in this statement, aversion to the idea of trials abroad carried with it a suspicion of foreign judicial systems and accusations that procedural safeguards would be lost. In other statements the suspicion was more forthrightly expressed:

> Meanwhile, the Genocide Convention is still on the agenda of the Senate for ratification, which, if ratified, would, among other things, commit us to the principle of the trial of American citizens in foreign courts . . . where our constitutional trial procedures and Bill of Rights would not operate.[55]

Threaten the U.S. Form of Government

A fifth line of opposition to human rights treaties was the allegation that they constitute a serious threat to the American form of government. Testimony before the Senate Judiciary Committee frequently predicted, in addition to the disintegration of the line between federal and state powers, the general destruction of the American political system. The report of the ABA Committee on Peace and Law exemplified this line of reasoning, suggesting that "the real significance" of the amendment was "the preservation of our form of government against the abuse of the treaty power."[56] Holman made a similar argument, speaking of the human rights treaties and the need for the amendment:

> Our own Bill of Rights forbids the Congress to change our basic rights but as the Constitution now stands it does not prevent our basic rights from being changed by a treaty made by the treatymaking agency which consists of the President and two-thirds of the Senators present and voting. This is the loophole in the Constitution that we now face and through which the internationalists propose to move and by treaty law change and level out our American rights (both State and individual) and thereby change our form of government.[57]

Enhance Soviet/Communist Influence

McCarthyism and the Cold War, which dominated the politics of the early 1950s, had a decisive impact on the debates about human rights treaties. Arguments related to the Communist scare appeared in two different forms. One, closely related to the preceding argument, emphasized the direct threat posed by the Soviet Union. The treaties were presented as manifestations of Soviet efforts to undermine the American system. Again the testimony of Finch is instructive.

> The United States should not participate in the negotiation of treaties, the effect of which would be to build around us a wall of socialistic and communist containment in anticipation of the withering away of our principles of human freedom and of the decay of the free institutions we have established to secure them. Are we so certain of our internal strength that we can resist indefinitely the communistic softening to which we are being subjected?[58]

More frequently, the specter of communism appeared in allegations that the treaties contained socialist rights. The dangers outlined were multiple:

> One of the first documents produced under this program of world-wide reform . . . was the so-called Declaration of Human

Rights. . . . This declaration, among other things, is a complete blueprint for socializing the world, including the United States. Article 23 provides that everyone has the right to "just and favorable conditions of work and to protection against unemployment" and that everyone has the right to "just and favorable remuneration." . . . The purpose provided was to liquidate our individual enterprise system.[59]

Senator Bricker also presented his concern that the treaties would alter our "control over our domestic, social, and economic rights, world medicine, socialized medicine. . . . I am trying to plug that loophole so that there will be no possibility of it."[60] He also addressed the issue by stating, "You know that the American Medical Society is greatly disturbed about the possibility of socialized medicine in this country coming in by the back door of treaties."[61]

Infringe on Domestic Jurisdiction

The human rights treaties were consistently criticized on the grounds that they infringed upon U.S. domestic jurisdiction and violated the domestic jurisdiction clause of the United Nations Charter. Some opponents believed that the very objective of the treaties was to legitimize U.N. consideration of matters that were essentially domestic and beyond the legitimate reach of an international organization. Holman made this claim in citing a member of the United Nations Human Rights Division

> who stated that what the Commission [on Human Rights] was proposing constituted an intervention in matters "within the domestic jurisdiction" of the member states. And he exposed this whole program which has since been under way in the United Nations, in my opinion not a program of peace at all, but a program for meddling in the affairs of the member states.[62]

Deutsch expressed the contention that domestic jurisdiction was threatened by human rights treaties:

> With similar suavity, albeit with greater logic, we were assured that section 7 of article II of the Charter of the United Nations gave us added protection against interference by that world organization in our domestic affairs. But today even the opponents of constitutional limitations on treatymaking power can no longer

sustain their confidence in understandings and reservations as adequate safeguards against the destructive potentialities of international conventions.[63]

Create Self-Executing Obligations

As explained in Chapter 2, self-executing treaties need no implementing legislation to be effective and can be cited and applied by domestic courts. As we have seen, one provision of the Bricker Amendment was that no treaty would be implemented without congressional legislation. Finch explained this purpose of the amendment: "The purpose of the American Bar Association amendment [is] to make all treaties non-self-executing as internal law and thus require legislation to make them internally effective."[64] He also elaborated upon the special problems of the human rights treaties as self-executing:

> That is why we had all this discussion about the Treaty on Human Rights. . . . The United Nations itself cannot by any declaration or resolution or draft treaty make law within the United States. When they do try to do it, it is through the treaty method because of our peculiar provision of our Constitution. What we are trying to do now is to plug that gap so they cannot do it that way and would be obliged to resort to legislation by the whole Congress.[65]

Increase International Entanglements

Other arguments were generated by antipathy toward the United Nations and its agencies and by a fear of foreign entanglements. Non-ABA witnesses were particularly outspoken about their suspicions of U.N. activities, especially action related to human rights. For example, the Reverend DeLoss Scott appeared on behalf of the American Council of Christian Churches and spoke against the United Nations and especially against the Covenant on Human Rights and the Genocide Convention. He cited the opening words of the U.N. Charter, which "brings the United Nations down into the realm of human affairs, affairs which affect our daily lives as individuals" and praised Senator Patrick McCarran (D.-Nev.) for his regret "to my dying day that I ever voted for the U.N. Charter."[66]

W. L. McGrath, speaking on behalf of the United States Chamber of Commerce, presented a very critical view of the United Nations and its agencies. In speaking of the treaties produced by the United Nations, he said,

> Don't you see how devious these people plan how they move into the back door if they can't deal with you at the front door? They go around to the back door. And that is dangerous. . . . The issue cannot be dismissed by saying casually that of course even a bare quorum of the Senate could not conceivably ratify anything that would not be in conformity with the Constitution.[67]

Associated with the neo-isolationism of the time was an ethnocentric suspicion of foreign states and a fear of entangling alliances. Holman also expressed the first of these concerns.

> Why should we overlay our inherent and precious rights and freedoms with a pattern of international rights drawn to suit the concepts of more than 60 nations with varying and antagonistic concepts?[68]

And Mrs. Enid Griswold, representing the National Economic Council, referred to the second of these issues.

> The role of world leadership which . . . has been thrust upon us, can best be fulfilled by preserving our American Republic and by limiting our international commitments to what we can do without weakening ourselves.[69]

Conclusion

Without doubt, the 1950s movement to amend the United States Constitution was fundamentally a response to human rights treaties. Senator Bricker himself identified the Covenant on Human Rights and other human rights treaties as the immediate impetus for his efforts. His statements confirm what is apparent from the events and opinions analyzed in the previous three chapters: that support for a constitutional amendment within the ABA was also directly linked to opposition to human rights treaties. The analysis of the four sections of the amendment proposed by Bricker highlights the extent to which the amendment was explicitly designed to respond to perceived threats posed by human rights treaties.

The 1953 Bricker Amendment hearings provided the most intensive formal and public criticism of human rights treaties. The widest range of opposition arguments ever elaborated emerged at that time. A typology of these arguments, drawn from the hearings, reflects the refinement of the arguments initially introduced during the 1949–50 Genocide Convention hearings. Content analysis, using this typology, reveals the persistence and development of the major arguments described in Chapter 2: abrogation of states' rights by the federal government, especially for purposes of desegregation; advancement of communism and of the power of the Soviet Union; deterioration of U.S. sovereignty, moving toward world government; and weakening of the U.S. constitutional system, including constitutional protection of individual rights.

The short-term effect of the Bricker Amendment hearings, and of the public debate surrounding them, was the defeat of efforts to ratify human rights treaties, most explicitly contained in the Dulles policy statement of the Eisenhower administration. This defeat was definite even though the Bricker Amendment did not pass. The Eisenhower administration respected its commitment and did not request Senate consideration of any human rights treaties. The long-term effect was also executive and legislative resistance to action on human rights treaties. The proponents of the Bricker Amendment, with official ABA sanction, successfully branded human rights treaties as dangerous and, perhaps more important, as controversial—labels most likely to deter consideration by members of the United States Senate.

PART TWO

Legacy
of Fear

FIVE

Two Treaties
That Passed

We are told that the year 1968 is to be designated as Human Rights Year and that this is an occasion when America should manifest its good faith by subscribing to these proposed treaties. To my mind this is a snare and a delusion. Every year is Human Rights Year in the United States. . . . Let the countries practicing slavery and denying women their just deserts observe Human Rights Year and let us not be trapped by this type of propaganda into relinquishing our most valuable heritage.—David F. Maxwell, *Human Rights Treaties Hearings*, 1967

The Bricker Amendment debate, and the Eisenhower administration's effort to head it off, put a temporary end to the consideration of human rights treaties in the Senate. In 1963, however, President John F. Kennedy revived three treaties, sending them to the Senate with no reservations and only one understanding. The Senate responded by not holding hearings on these treaties until 1967. When the three treaties were debated, they were considered together by a subcommittee of the Senate Foreign Relations Committee. Of these three, the Supplementary Slavery Convention was approved by the Senate after the hearings and debate in 1967. The Convention on the Political Rights of Women eventually gained acceptance in 1975. And the Convention Concerning the Abolition of Forced Labor remains unratified today.

The Senate's consideration of these three treaties, and particularly the two that passed, says much about U.S. reaction to human rights treaties generally. These treaties were introduced by President Kennedy as a trial balloon, a conscious decision to see if a set of seemingly uncontroversial agreements, the contents of which were in complete harmony with state and federal law, would encounter difficulty in the Senate. Once these accords were approved, the administration planned a renewed effort to gain approval for the Human Rights Covenants, the Genocide Convention, and other human rights instruments that might be considered more innovative.[1] After one set of subcommittee hearings, with overwhelmingly supportive testimony, the treaties were sent to the full committee with a recommendation to accept all three.[2] Why were two ultimately accepted and the other rejected by the United States Senate?

Looking at the two treaties that have been approved, we find that the question is difficult to answer. The Supplementary Slavery Convention extends an already ratified treaty and was supported by the United States at all stages of codification. However, its provisions could raise questions of domestic jurisdiction, federal-state conflict, and international adjudication. The treaty was accepted internationally in 1956, was sent to the Senate in 1963, and was passed by the Senate in 1967. Even more confusing in terms of the time under consideration and the controversy surrounding ratification was the Convention on the Political Rights of Women. Although this treaty received little attention during the Bricker Amendment hearings, Secretary of State Dulles, in announcing the Eisenhower administration's withdrawal of support for U.N. treaty-making on human rights, explicitly included this treaty in his statement. For twenty-one years it awaited Senate floor consideration and approval, until 1975 when the Senate deliberated less than a month and unanimously voted for ratification with no reservations.

Those voting for the treaty included members who consistently and vocally opposed other human rights treaties. How and why did this occur? How can we explain the unceremonious passage of this treaty which shares so much with agreements which remain on the dusty shelf of Senate inaction? These questions are examined in this chapter. First, the background of the treaties is examined, revealing active U.S. support and participation in the drafting process. Second, the politics of the initial Senate consideration is explained. Third, the Senate hearings and the internal debate within the ABA are analyzed to illustrate the continued centrality of this interest group in Senate consideration of human rights treaties. Fourth, the arguments against the treaties presented at the Senate hearings are discussed, using the typology introduced in Chapter 4. The final section of the chapter recounts the fate of the treaties and the lessons to be learned about the perplexing forces that appear to influence the Senate consideration process—in particular, the determination of what is controversial, the impact of interest groups, and the politics of Senate review.

Background and Content of the Three Treaties

In order to understand the domestic opposition to the three treaties, it is helpful to explain the background and contents of the documents themselves. Slavery was perhaps the first human rights violation to be addressed by international law. Throughout the nineteenth century numerous agreements were reached in efforts to suppress traffic in slaves. These arrangements culminated in the 1926 Slavery Convention in which states accepted the obligation to prevent the slave trade and to work to abolish slavery within their own countries. The Supplementary Slavery Convention was drafted in response to studies showing that although traditional slavery was diminishing, other practices with similar results were still widespread. The Economic and Social Council of the United Nations in 1955 established a committee to prepare a draft convention. This draft was adopted on 4 September 1956 by the United Nations Plenipotentiary Conference. The United States was active in the drafting of the treaty and voted for its adoption.

The Supplementary Slavery Convention primarily serves to extend the 1926 Slavery Convention to which the United States is a party. The treaty requires states to take steps to abolish certain practices similar to slavery, including debt bondage, serfdom, involuntary marriage or transfer of women for money, child marriage, and inheritance of widows. It requires the setting of a minimum age for marriage and the registration of marriages, and it contains provisions outlawing the slave trade and providing for the freeing of any slaves taking refuge on board vessels of the states that were parties to the convention. The mutilation of slaves or people in servile status is a criminal offense under its terms, and states are obliged to work cooperatively with one another and with the United Nations to implement the treaty's provisions. There is also an article providing for disputes arising under the treaty and not settled by negotiation to be referred to the International Court of Justice.

The Convention Concerning the Abolition of Forced Labor also supplements an earlier treaty, the Forced Labor Convention. The first treaty was drafted by the International Labor Organization and was adopted on 28 June 1930. Its objective was the abolition of forced or compulsory labor in all its forms. The Economic and Social Council of the United Nations initially reconsidered the issue of forced labor in

response to a 1947 letter from the American Federation of Labor pointing to the continued existence of forced labor and urging consideration of steps to secure its abolition. The council's response was to
invite the ILO to cooperate with it in making an impartial study of the
nature and extent of the problem. After its study, the ILO recommended in 1956 that a treaty would be the most appropriate form for
addressing the issue. By 1957 a draft of the Convention Concerning
the Abolition of Forced Labor was completed, and it was approved by
the General Conference of the ILO on 21 June of that year by a vote of
240 to 0, with 1 abstention. The U.S. representatives played an active
part in the drafting of the treaty, and the U.S. government voted in
favor of it.[3] The treaty came into force on 17 January 1959; at the time
of the Kennedy request for ratification, sixty states were parties to the
treaty. The convention obligates states to suppress any form of forced
or compulsory labor, including labor used as (1) a means of political
coercion or education or a punishment for holding certain political
views, (2) a method of mobilization for economic development, (3) a
means of labor discipline, (4) punishment for participation in strikes,
or (5) a form of racial, social, national, or religious discrimination.

Of the three treaties under discussion here, the Convention on the
Political Rights of Women represents the newest topic for international
legal treatment. It was drafted by the United Nations Commission on
the Status of Women[4] but was twice rejected by the Economic and
Social Council on the grounds that its subject was not appropriate for
international legal formulation and should be handled through education and social programs.[5] In 1952, however, the council accepted the
draft convention and sent it to the General Assembly, where it was
approved on 20 December.[6] The treaty came into force on 7 July 1954,
and as of December 1988 eighty-seven countries had ratified or
acceded to it. There is a voluntary reporting system, established in
1953, which includes nonratifying states and has been merged with
the system set up in 1963 in conjunction with the Declaration on the
Elimination of Discrimination Against Women. Article 1 provides that
women be eligible to vote in all elections on equal terms with men,
without any discrimination. In the United States this provision is
already covered in the Nineteenth Amendment to the Constitution,
which stipulates, "The right of citizens of the United States to vote
shall not be denied or abridged by the United States or by any State on
account of sex." Article 2 of the convention requires that women be
eligible for election to all publicly elected bodies, established by na-

tional law, on equal terms with men, without any discrimination. Article 3 provides that women be entitled to hold public office and to exercise all public functions, established by national law, on equal terms with men, without any discrimination. It may be helpful to note here, as the Senate report does, that "articles II and III apply only to bodies, offices, and functions established by 'national law.' "[7] For the United States this wording means that state and local offices, bodies, and functions are not included in the scope of the convention.

At the time the treaty was sent to the Senate, the State Department recommended an understanding "that in article III the phrase 'public office' does not include military service and that the phrase 'public function' is coterminous with 'public office.' "[8] By the time of the 1967 hearings, the executive no longer felt this understanding was necessary. The view expressed then[9] was that the legislative history of the convention and a statement from Eleanor Roosevelt at the time of its drafting clarified and illuminated this provision.[10]

The convention's remaining articles are procedural and, with the exception of Article 9, relatively noncontroversial. Article 9 provides that disputes arising under the treaty that are not settled by negotiation should be referred to the International Court of Justice. The treaty then would fall under Article 36, paragraph 2, of the Statute of the International Court of Justice. The executive did not feel that any reservation or understanding was appropriate on this issue, even though questions were raised about the applicability of the Connally Amendment, which reserves to the United States the right to determine which issues are essentially domestic and therefore not subject to international adjudication. The Connally Amendment refers only to paragraph 1 of Article 36, however, and therefore would not apply to this treaty. The Convention on the Political Rights of Women has never been the basis of a dispute before the International Court of Justice.

Initial Senate Consideration of the Three Treaties

As we have seen, the hearings on the Genocide Convention were the first official postwar consideration of human rights treaties, as such, in the Senate. Although the focus of the hearings was on the Genocide Convention, the U.N. covenants and other human rights treaties were very much in evidence. The opposition frequently pointed to the other agreements as examples of the growing threat to the U.S. legal system, the Genocide Convention being painted as but the first strategic maneuver in a planned full-scale legal invasion of the United States' domestic jurisdiction.

One of the many occasions on which other human rights treaties were mentioned during the genocide hearings is especially relevant here. George Finch, while testifying to his belief that the Genocide Convention was being supported by the federal government in an effort to increase its power vis-à-vis the states, added wryly:

> I would like to give the ladies in the audience a bit of free advice, should the Senate put its approval upon this form of Federal legislation by treaty. Some of their organizations are now trying to get the Congress to agree to an amendment to the Constitution giving them what they call equal rights. Should that amendment pass the Congress and its backers be unable to obtain its ratification by the State legislatures, as required by the Constitution, then they would have an easier method of making it the law of the land by having the United States Government enter into a treaty on that subject. Such a treaty is already in existence for several Latin-American Republics.[11]

During the Bricker Amendment hearings these human rights treaties were not the major focus of attention, but the Convention on the Political Rights of Women did haunt the debate as one of the group of four treaties that had been described as threatening to the American way of life. The most important testimony related to it was that given by the secretary of state, John Foster Dulles. As discussed in Chapter 4, Dulles explained that the administration had established a new trend, away from using treaties as a method of effecting internal changes and back to confining treaty-making to traditional limits. In accord with this commitment he announced that the administration would not sign the Convention on the Political Rights of Women.

> This is not because we do not believe in the equal political status of men and women, or because we shall not seek to promote that equality. Rather it is because we do not believe that this goal can be achieved by treaty coercion or that it constitutes a proper field for exercise of the treatymaking power. We do not now see any clear or necessary relation between the interest and welfare of the United States and the eligibility of women to political office in other nations.[12]

Following this statement, human rights treaties were generally ignored by the executive and legislature until 22 July 1963, when President Kennedy recommended that the United States ratify all three of
the treaties under examination in this chapter. Senate consideration
began almost four years later. At that time, Senator Thomas Dodd (D.-
Conn.) made a request to chair a subcommittee of the Committee on
Foreign Relations to look into the conventions, in hopes that the
successful passage of these treaties would help bring him some favorable attention at a time when his affairs were being investigated.[13] The
subcommittee held hearings on 23 February and 8 March 1967. The
three treaties were considered together at the hearings, and, although
the testimony often addressed only one, the arguments against them
usually merged. Almost all of the testimony at the hearings favored
ratification. On 5 June 1967 the subcommittee voted to support approval of all three treaties.

American Bar Association Consideration of the Treaties

The ABA first debated these treaties in 1967 after they had been
brought up by Senator Dodd's subcommittee. The Committee on
Peace and Law Through United Nations, the same committee that had
opposed the genocide treaty and had testified so strongly on behalf of
the Bricker Amendment, studied the three treaties and recommended
against ratification of all three on the grounds that the treaties were
"concerned with matters essentially within the domestic jurisdiction
of the United States."[14] The ghost of the Bricker Amendment was
apparent in the committee's report. The committee reminded its read-
ers that during the Bricker discussions "the American Bar Association
was assured that it could trust the Executive Department not to sign
and submit treaties affecting the internal affairs of the United States."
The report then went on to suggest, "If such treaties as are now
proposed for accession or ratification should be approved, it will again
become necessary to seek constitutional limitations on treaty-making
power."[15] The committee was most adamant in its opposition to the
Convention on the Political Rights of Women stating,

> It is difficult to conceive of any area more peculiarly within the
> domestic jurisdiction [than the subject of the Convention on the
> Political Rights of Women]. To prescribe who shall vote and on
> what terms, who shall be eligible for election to publicly elected

bodies, who shall hold public office and on what terms, is clearly at the very heart of every domestic political system.[16]

Most of the time, however, the ABA committee considered the three treaties together. The basic objections were that the treaties would alter existing federal-state relations, that they would set lower standards that those in the United States, that they would contribute to increased international authority, and that they would violate U.S. domestic jurisdiction. These arguments are those that were raised earlier in debates over other human rights instruments.

The opposition arguments were interwoven in the committee's report, with the emphasis falling on alteration of federal-state relations through "internationalization." Even though committee members did not object to the content of the treaties per se and agreed that the operational parts were already law in the United States, they felt that the rules being formalized should not have been considered at the international level. They held that international bodies were wrong in addressing such a domestic issue through codification and rejected the idea that the drafting of the treaty itself and its ratification by many countries could transform a domestic subject into an international one.

The Section on International and Comparative Law of the ABA also made a study of the three treaties. The section council concluded that the ABA should support ratification of the Supplementary Slavery Convention but oppose the Convention on the Political Rights of Women. It recommended that the Convention Concerning Forced Labor be adopted with certain understandings on imprisonment for illegal strikes. Council members' main opposition to the Convention on the Political Rights of Women was that it dealt with an area of domestic jurisdiction. Speaking on behalf of the section, Max Chopnick said that "the rights sought for women contemplated by this treaty must develop in each country from education and the desire of the women themselves."[17]

The House of Delegates of the ABA adopted a compromise recommendation, and by a 115-92 vote the ABA went on record officially supporting the Supplementary Slavery Convention while rejecting the Convention on the Political Rights of Women and urging delay of the Convention Concerning Forced Labor.

As explained in Chapter 1, the ABA played a special role in all Senate considerations of human rights treaties. After the subcommittee of the Senate Foreign Relations Committee had completed its hearings on these three treaties, the full committee delayed consideration of the subcommittee report at the request of the ABA. Although the organization had been invited to attend the subcommittee hearings, it did not send representatives because internal disagreements made it impossible to reach a unified position on the treaties. Several senators objected to the delay, claiming that no new information was likely to be forthcoming. As Senator Dodd put it, "I don't like to be in position of refusing the American Bar Association, but I don't believe we will learn anything we don't already know."[18] Senator John Sherman Cooper (R.-Ky.) pointed out that the ABA had been offered many opportunities to appear and that the subcommittee chair had tried all year to arrange testimony.[19] Favorable communications had been submitted by other bar groups: the Committee on International Law of the New York State Bar Association, the Committee on International Law of the Bar of the City of New York, the New Jersey State Bar Association, the Board of Trustees of the Los Angeles Bar Association, the Alaska Bar Association, and the Philadelphia Bar Association.

The senators' informal discussion, however, clearly revealed the special role of the ABA in providing the definitive response on ratification.[20] Finally, a special session of the Foreign Relations Committee was agreed upon, the ABA representatives having insisted upon appearing before the full committee. The 13 September 1967 session was held exclusively in order for two ABA members to present the arguments of the organization. The references to the ABA during the summer 1967 executive sessions of the Committee on Foreign Relations indicated clearly the very special position of the organization. On numerous occasions senators asked about or cited traditional (1950s) ABA arguments against the treaties. Senator Bourke B. Hickenlooper (R.-Iowa), originally opposed to all three treaties, openly admitted his complete faith in the validity of any position taken by the ABA on treaty ratification. Speaking of the treaties he said:

> We do not need them. . . . I do not see any real reason why we should get into a treaty situation on the things which we already cover in every particular in our own laws within the country, and while I asked [U.S. representative to the United Nations Arthur] Goldberg, his opinion is not worth a hoot. . . . I am generally opposed to the principle. Now, if after studying, if the American Bar Association feels that the safeguards are adequate there, I could change my mind. I am not so hard-nosed about it.[21]

After the favorable ABA recommendation, Hickenlooper voted in favor of the Supplementary Slavery Convention.

Arguments against the Treaties

The opposition arguments presented at the September 1967 hearings
before the full Senate Committee on Foreign Relations repeated the
major arguments made in the 1950s. Although the subject matter was
different, the fears expressed were the same. They were primarily that
the treaties would diminish basic American rights, reduce the power
of the states, promote world government, and violate U.S. domestic
jurisdiction.

Diminish Basic Rights

Since the treaties covered already existing law, concern about the
possible loss of rights was not as frequently expressed in the hearings
on these three treaties as it had been at earlier debates. The argument
was made, however, that because the standards reflected in these
treaties were less rigorous than those of U.S. law, deterioration of our
protections could result. Eberhard Deutsch expressed it in this way:

> In the United States we have long since established much
> higher standards in the bills of rights to our federal and state
> constitutions, than those sought to be drawn out of the domestic
> field into the international domain; and the real question is sim-
> ply as to whether the ephemeral tissue of international ideals
> should be substituted for the enduring fiber of our domestic con-
> stitutional limitations.[22]

Deutsch took advantage of the hearings to air his opposition to
human rights treaties generally. One of his basic fears was that the
treaties would result in a loss of rights, but his argument was weakened by the fact that none of the three treaties being discussed would
have had such an impact; nothing in them contravened U.S. law.
Therefore, he declaimed against human rights treaties per se and
especially the threat they posed to private property rights, a potential
if weak source of criticism for the Economic, Social, and Cultural
Rights Covenant,[23] but completely irrelevant to the three treaties under consideration at the hearings. After lambasting the entire U.N.
effort in codification of human rights law, Deutsch explained that

in this entire mass of treaties on so-called human rights, there is not a single guarantee of the right to own private property. . . . The rights to own property are not included in a single one of these treaties which protects all such other rights, like the right to leisure and holidays with pay and so on.[24]

Violate States' Rights

It is easy to find within much of the protest about domestic jurisdiction a concern about states' rights. The language of the opposition in these hearings was very similar to that of earlier objections to the use of treaties by the federal government to usurp the power of the states. The intervening civil rights legislation, its implementation, and actual changes in society seem only to have exacerbated the antipathy toward these agreements on the part of the ABA's Committee on Peace and Law Through United Nations. That committee's report on the conventions emphasized the states' rights issue, as exemplified in the following excerpt:

The federal Government, being a government of limited powers, is still precluded from regulating large areas of intrastate matters. It is unnecessary and unsound to cut down this area of intrastate jurisdiction over human rights through the medium of international agreements.[25]

Deutsch explained his opposition on this point by citing *Missouri v. Holland*, a case so often mentioned at earlier hearings. He explained the significance of the judgment.

The case ultimately went to the Supreme Court of the United States, which held that the treaty had effectively given the Federal Government that power over that subject matter which it did not have in the absence of that treaty because of the 10th amendment.[26]

According to Deutsch, maintaining the federal-state system intact was the primary reason for rejecting the treaties. He described the opposition

as based on various grounds, principal among them being that the treaties do not deal with matters of genuine international concern, but invade the domestic jurisdiction of the United States and disturb the constitutional relationship of the state and federal governments to each other.[27]

A source of repeated attack was the decision by the State Department in 1966 not to continue to press for the inclusion of a federal-state clause in international agreements.[28] Thus the treaties were repeatedly challenged on the grounds that, lacking such a provision, they would place increased power in the federal government at the expense of the states. The ABA committee report addressed this problem:

> As to the treaties, if ratified without the federal-state clauses, the question must ultimately inevitably be raised as to whether a treaty may override the Constitution of the United States, to the extent, at least, of bringing within the jurisdiction of the federal government, subjects theretofore within the exclusive competence of the states. . . . The position apparently taken by our Department of State on this point is shocking. The United States is still a federation of states. If any attempt to alter our form of government is to be made through the use of the treaty-making power, the people of the United States should be so advised.[29]

It was to so advise the people that the ABA committee acted as it did before and during the genocide treaty hearings and during the Bricker Amendment debates.

Again, the most extensive discussion of this problem came in connection with the Convention on the Political Rights of Women. Canada had attached a form of federal-state clause to its acceptance of the treaty, and opponents took this action as evidence of the difficulties the treaty presented for federal-state systems. The ABA report identified the federal-state problem as one of the major reasons for its recommendation not to ratify.[30] The Committee on Peace and Law clearly felt, however, that a reservation to this effect would still not make the treaty acceptable, because the domestic jurisdiction objection would remain.

Senator Sam Ervin (D.-N.C.) was especially disturbed by this treaty and recommended that if it were accepted by the Senate, a reservation should be included to the effect that the preamble of the treaty

> is not to be interpreted to alter or limit in any way the existing powers of the United States of America and the several states to

prescribe qualifications for voting and qualifications for office holding which are applicable to men and women alike.[31]

The Convention Concerning Forced Labor was also criticized on these grounds. Here the problem was a bit more complex, for it involved the right of punishment for participation in illegal strikes. The opposition interpreted the treaty as prohibiting any disciplining for involvement in illegal strikes and felt this prohibition constituted an important invasion of state jurisdiction. Senator Cooper brought attention to the issue in his questioning of Deutsch. He asked,

> Would you say if this convention is adopted and thereby becomes the law of the land that that would provide to the Federal Government then a power which it might not have now to make legislation in the field of States and prohibit the enactment by States of laws which would prohibit their employees from striking or imposing penalties for striking?

Deutsch's response was in the affirmative.[32]

Senator Ervin was also worried about the preamble to the Supplementary Slavery Convention, which contained a reference to the Universal Declaration of Human Rights, so often criticized by the ABA Committee on Peace and Law. His fear was that

> the Universal Declaration of Human Rights contains a number of provisions which can be reasonably construed to conflict with the provisions of our Constitution separating the powers of the Federal Government and those of the States, to nullify various existing national and State laws.[33]

A further indication of states' rights advocacy was the criticism of civil rights legislation already passed by Congress. The ABA committee report strongly criticized the potential involvement of the World Court in U.S. domestic jurisdiction. Again, their major fear, as with the Genocide Convention, had to do with civil rights violations. The committee implied that there was more civil rights legislation and enforcement than the country needed and that international adjudication would only compound an already complex set of legal arrangements.

Probably no other country in the world has as much civil rights legislation as has been enacted in the United States during the last ten years. . . .

It will take many years for us to determine and evaluate the consequences of the civil-rights legislation now on the statute books of the United States. How can it be said that we now need, in addition, international legislation, international decision-making, and an international level of enforcement?[34]

Promote World Government

A further fear of the opponents was that ratifying international agreements on the topics covered in these treaties would expand the powers of the United Nations and thereby increase the influence of nations critical of the United States. One danger of this expanded power, it was argued, was that it would lead to charges against the United States at the international level. The report of the ABA committee expressed this concern in a clear manner, claiming,

> There are those who would overlook no opportunity to use the enforcement provisions of the human rights convention to embarrass or to attack us.[35]

In connection with the Convention Concerning Forced Labor, for example, opponents argued that if the United States ratified the treaty, the country would be attacked for imprisoning illegal strikers. The debate within the ABA on this treaty centered on this very point and on fears of the United States' being brought before the World Court, especially by socialist states.[36]

The Genocide Convention was not far from the hearts and minds of the members of the ABA committee during their 1967 consideration of the three treaties. Deutsch resurrected the scare stories from the Genocide Convention hearings to attack these treaties as well. One of the major fears expressed then, we may recall, was that of international adjudication. Allegedly, by ratifying the Genocide Convention, the United States would be susceptible to criticism in international political forums and before the International Court of Justice as well. Interestingly, and as had been suggested by supporters of the Genocide Convention, failure to ratify would not insulate the United States from accusations. Deutsch, without addressing this contradiction, referred to such criticism.

Although the Genocide Convention has been pending in the Senate since 1949, it has never been ratified. In that connection, it is interesting to note that the United States has now been charged at least twice by leaders of Communist countries with committing the crime of Genocide in Viet Nam.[37]

In connection with these fears about international charges, treaty opponents expressed concern about the effect of these conventions on the Connally Amendment. The amendment was attached by the United States when accepting the Statute of the International Court of Justice in order to retain the right to determine for itself which issues were domestic and therefore not subject to the court's jurisdiction. The International Labor Organization Statute includes a provision requiring states to submit disputes concerning ILO treaties to the World Court. Thus, even though the Convention Concerning Forced Labor does not contain a provision requiring states to submit disputes about it to the World Court, the United States could not escape the court's jurisdiction by citing the Connally Amendment. Some ABA members felt that the Connally Amendment was in jeopardy from all three treaties. As they complained,

> It is clear that by unconditional adherence to these treaties, the Connally reservation would no longer be effective to prevent the World Court from assuming jurisdiction of a matter solely within our domestic domain, thus establishing a precedent by which the principle of the Connally reservation could be effectively by-passed through the medium of separate international treaties.[38]

As in all Senate hearings on human rights treaties, the particular treaty in question was criticized as part of a series of treaties that, as a group, pose critical problems for the United States. The Human Rights Covenants were also frequently cited at the hearings as extremist measures indicating the dangerous direction the nation would be turned toward by ratifying the three proposed treaties. One particularly noxious development, according to critics, was the Optional Protocol to the Civil and Political Rights Covenant. The protocol provided for the right of individual petition of alleged violations of the covenant. Deutsch was horrified by the implications of such an avenue for individual appeal.

> The Protocol provides that citizens of ratifying countries may file complaints directly with an international Human-Rights Commit-

tee, against their own governments, charging deprivation of their rights under the Covenant. . . . While this Protocol does not yet provide international enforcement machinery to compel redress of such grievances, efforts to bring such a right into being are already underway.[39]

Deutsch expressed the fear that steps such as these could lead to the "erosion of the constitutional structure of the United States."[40] He viewed the petition system as a transfer of authority from the United States to the United Nations. Deutsch argued forcefully that granting the right of an individual to file a claim with an international body was a dangerous step toward moving authority outside the country.[41]

> In other words [individuals] may go outside the borders of the United States to a tribunal. . . . It is now being advocated . . . that citizens should have the right to adjudication of their grievances before an international tribunal.[42]

Enhance Soviet/Communist Influence

These three treaties did not raise the extensive anti-Communist rhetoric of the 1950s. However, anxiety over Soviet and Communist influence was still an important factor in the opposition. In the case of these treaties, most of the Communist influence was seen as stemming from international organizational power—at the ILO and within the central United Nations organization. The myth of Communist domination of these bodies continued to function as a basic assumption for the strongest opponents of the treaties; from their discussions there is no doubt that significant anti–United Nations feeling survived the McCarthy period and the 1950s crusade against the United Nations as a propaganda forum for Communist ideas. For example, George Winthrop Haight, the ABA observer at the ILO, argued that the Soviet Union had used the debates over the Convention Concerning Forced Labor to expound propaganda against the United States. He also claimed that the Soviet Union had insisted on widening the scope of the treaty, making it difficult for non-Communist states to ratify it.[43]

The Communist menace at the United Nations was also cited in attacks on human rights treaties generally. One example of such thinking is apparent in Deutsch's introductory statement.

The only provision of the Universal Declaration which has not reached fruition in any completed or even embryonic international convention, is that guaranteeing the right to hold private property. Every effort by the Western nations, to incorporate that fundamental right in a treaty on human rights, has been defeated by the Communist countries.[44]

The inclusion of economic and social rights in the Universal Declaration and some treaties continued to raise the specter of Communist erosion of the American system. Deutsch indicated his concern when discussing some of the treaties that formed part of the larger human rights package of which these three were, to him, but an initial driving wedge.

Another provides that everybody must be given favorable conditions of work, and now I quote "including rest, leisure, and reasonable limitation of working hours and periodic holidays with pay." That is the subject of an international convention which has been adopted by the General Assembly of the United Nations. That is just one of the many provisions of a similar texture in that document. . . . Another provides that working mothers are to be accorded paid leave before and after childbirth. This is an international convention in this series adopted by the General Assembly of the United Nations.[45]

Subject Citizens to Trial Abroad

In addition to worrying about the United States' being brought before the International Court of Justice against its wishes and being criticized in international forums, opponents expressed concerns similar to those raised so strongly against the Genocide Convention—that the treaty would result in trials of American citizens abroad. During these trials, opponents claimed, U.S. citizens would be denied all normal constitutional protections. David F. Maxwell of the ABA lucidly summarized these concerns.

All of the proposed conventions carry sanctions enforcible in forums and by procedures fundamentally different from our own. Our Constitution guarantees certain safeguards to our citizens charged with crimes, such as the right to trial by jury, the right to a speedy trial, the right to counsel, and the right to stand trial in the place where the crime has been committed. Together these constitute the so-called accusatory system which is the American way of administering criminal justice in contrast to the prosecutory method generally practiced in Europe. Under the Human Rights Conventions we would jeopardize these precious keystones of our freedom and internationalize our criminal procedures.[46]

Threaten the U.S. Form of Government

All three treaties were seen as threatening the American system of government. Maxwell expressed this concern and felt that the treaties would supersede all levels of domestic law.

Consequently there is much merit in the position supported by many authorities that upon the consent of the Senate to adhere to the Human Rights Conventions, the conventions would supersede every city ordinance, every county ordinance, every state law, every state constitution, and every federal statute dealing with the same subject throughout every state in the Union.[47]

The very structure of the U.S. legal and political system was presented as weakened by these treaties, and the ABA was seen as the guardian of freedom, liberty, and the American way.

As during the debates of the 1950s on human rights treaties, the opposition in 1967 characterized the treaties under consideration as "the tip of the iceberg" and simply the beginning of a long line of legal arrangements that the United States was being called upon to accept and that constituted a threat to our government and our way of life. Often provisions of the other treaties were quoted or paraphrased to reveal the absurdity that the opposition believed to be apparent in all these treaties.[48] An example can be seen in the testimony of Deutsch.

Now, the treaties which you have under consideration, these three, are simply the first in a long series of human rights treaties. . . . It is a tremendous mill that is grinding rapidly. . . . There is a treaty actually passed, and I give these merely as examples, a half dozen briefly here, there is a treaty actually passed around 1950 by the General Assembly in which the parties prohibit the keeping or financing of a brothel. That is going pretty far but that is literally a treaty which has been adopted among this series of human rights treaties. . . . There is another which provides that penitentiaries are to be so maintained as to look toward social rehabilitation of prisoners. . . . Another: that everyone is to have the right to take part in cultural life.[49]

The three treaties under discussion, then, at times became simply representatives of a national and international movement that threatened American legal and political institutions.

Infringe on Domestic Jurisdiction

Placing the controversy in historical perspective, the opponents argued that these treaties represented "a radical departure from traditional treaty practice."[50] The argument often drew attention to the unacceptability of attempting to employ international law to alter the relationship between a government and its citizens. Harry Leroy Jones of the ABA explained this view in his testimony:

That the internal affairs of a foreign country are an improper subject of diplomatic negotiation and therefore inappropriate for regulation by treaty is . . . clear. The relationship between Ruritania and its own citizens is essentially within the domestic jurisdiction of Ruritania. The relationship is not governed by international law, and it would therefore be improper for the United States to make diplomatic representations to Ruritania about it.[51]

And other ABA members reiterated this argument in highly ethnocentric terms. Critical of most of the provisions of the Supplementary Slavery Convention for addressing internal practices, they argued:

[These practices] arise not from the slave trade, but from the primitive nature of many societies, notably in Africa, where social development has frequently not progressed beyond feudalism and tribalism. Such practices should eventually be eradicated, and it may be appropriate to assist those in the countries concerned who wish to bring this about. But are these practices matters of international concern to the United States?[52]

And reservations about U.S. involvement in the internal affairs of foreign countries were only part of the basis for rejecting these treaties as inappropriate; they were even more fiercely criticized for addressing the internal affairs of this country. One of the major reasons why these treaties were considered inappropriate was that they were identified as touching on matters that have traditionally been viewed as domestic. As Senator Hickenlooper revealed during the hearings,

Frankly, I have the feeling that none of these treaties is really international in scope. They are primarily domestic and, therefore, may not be the proper subject matter for a treaty under our original concepts of a treaty.[53]

The opponents, very simply, argued that because the treaties dealt with matters that were essentially domestic, the United States should rule out any possibility of ratification. Moreover, they believed that when these documents were drawn up under U.N. auspices, they represented a violation of Article 2, paragraph 7, of the United Nations Charter. As Deutsch put it at the hearings on these treaties:

It will be recalled, of course, that paragraph 7 of article II of the charter states that nothing contained therein shall authorize the United Nations to intervene in matters which are essentially within the domestic jurisdiction of any state, and we think that has meaning or should have meaning; that matters within the domestic jurisdiction should not be governed by international compacts.[54]

A claim was also made that by invading domestic jurisdiction the treaties were unconstitutional. Again, ABA member Jones, whose statement was included in the record of the hearings, argued,

The human rights conventions dealing, as they do, with the political and economic status of citizens, racial discrimination against citizens, the social and cultural rights of citizens, the conditions of labor and education of citizens, and the civil and political rights of citizens, all in great detail, cover a substantial portion of the domestic *corpus juris*. Ratification of the conventions would go far to destroy the domestic jurisdiction into which the International Court of Justice may not now intrude.[55]

A further branch of this argument was that the inclusion of domestic matters in the treaties made it impossible for the United States to accept the treaties under our present legal system. As the ABA report explained, in connection with the Convention Concerning Forced Labor,

The question, however, is whether the United States can, under its Constitution, and whether it should, having regard to fundamental principles, become a party to international legislation of

this character which deals entirely with its domestic jurisdiction.[56]

The Convention on the Political Rights of Women was most severely
criticized as being domestic in nature. The statement of Lyman Tondel
of the ABA was relevant on this point:

> Of the three Conventions now before the Senate, that dealing
> with the political rights of women appears to be the farthest
> removed from matters of genuine international concern. . . . It is
> difficult to see how the internal political structures of other states
> can be made a matter of international concern of the United
> States. Here again, the test would appear to be whether the dim-
> inution in domestic jurisdiction resulting from accession to this
> instrument would be justified by the advantages to this country of
> promoting the cause of universal suffrage throughout the
> world. . . . The content of domestic jurisdiction would be small
> indeed if all human rights matters were to be considered of inter-
> national concern and embodied in international instruments.[57]

And Deutsch, arguing specifically about the Convention on the Political Rights of Women, made the same point:

> The determination as to qualifications of voters within a country
> is a matter for that country to determine for itself. . . . We ap-
> prove the right of women to vote, we demand it, we enforce it as
> strongly as we can but we don't think it is a proper subject for an
> international compact in which one nation binds itself to another
> in that regard.[58]

The opposition cited the unfortunate precedents that they felt these
treaties would set. The ABA report on these treaties explained this
view.

> Clearly, there is nothing in this [Supplementary Slavery] Conven-
> tion which runs counter to United States domestic law. It does,
> however, deal not merely with international traffic in slaves, but
> also with wholly domestic practices which fall within the domes-
> tic jurisdiction of states. To legislate internationally with respect
> to such matters opens the door to an invasion of the domestic
> jurisdiction of nations which may lead to serious prejudice.[59]

And later in the same report, this point is elaborated.

It is argued that no such subversion of the domestic jurisdiction would result from adherence by this country to commitments that do not go beyond legal norms already established by our federal and state constitutions. Granted that the treaties under consideration do not impose novel standards on our own internal governments, participation in them would open a wide area of domestic jurisdiction to international regulation, and would seriously prejudice our concept of domestic jurisdiction in other matters.[60]

Increase International Entanglements

It was an easy step from criticizing the "massive" body of human rights treaties to condemning the organization that had produced them. Hostility toward the United Nations as a Communist forum has already been discussed. Antagonism toward the organization was also fueled by a sense of relative loss of U.S. influence within it. By 1967, the membership of the United Nations had grown dramatically with the admission of former colonies that had recently gained political independence. Developed and developing countries alike were striking out on paths separate from those trod by the United States, many of them rejecting U.S. "guidance" in their foreign policies, including instructions on U.N. voting. Blocs were formed at the United Nations and bloc membership was often a better predictor of voting than any tie to one of the superpowers. Opponents of the treaties cited the loss of U.S. power at the United Nations as one justification of the need to move away from human rights treaty-making at the United Nations. The organization was described as too heterogeneous[61] in cultures, values, and experiences to reach meaningful agreements. The ABA committee report cited at the hearings made this observation:

It is unnecessary and unsound to cut down this area of intrastate jurisdiction over human rights through internal legislation through the medium of international agreements. If that area is to be cut down, the way to do it is through internal legislation, debated and concluded by representatives of the people concerned, and not by a heterogeneous international gathering of officials representing some 125 different countries, each with its own concept of internal social standards.[62]

The organization was also criticized as not competent to draft clear, unambiguous legal instruments.[63]

As in the 1950s, the human rights treaties were additionally depicted as one ploy used by some United Nations members to attack U.S. sovereignty. The ABA committee report concluded,

> Even assuming that it should be considered appropriate to cut down the sphere of domestic jurisdiction to the extent provided in these conventions, the question still remains whether, by so doing (and perhaps later going much further by ratifying other conventions) the door would be opened [for] intervention by the United Nations in the field of human rights generally, and for this field to fall within the domain of international law despite its domestic character. . . .
>
> It is doubtless regarded by many that the sphere of human rights is no longer of purely domestic concern, but that the United Nations, and the international community generally, are concerned not only with the promotion of human rights and fundamental freedoms, but also with their preservation and the enforcement of penal sanctions relating thereto.[64]

The reference here was to the charter provisions, Articles 55 and 56, that committed U.N. members to promote human rights. Opponents argued strongly that obligations under the U.N. Charter did not require the United States to ratify these treaties.

> It has been suggested that failure to ratify the Conventions would be inconsistent with our obligations under the Charter. It is true that Article 56 of the Charter commits us to take action in cooperation with the Organization for the achievement of the ideals set forth in Article 55, of which subparagraph "c" relates to human rights. . . . That the United States has complied with its obligations under Articles 55 and 56 cannot be doubted. Article 56 does not obligate the United States to contract international obligations which do not accord with our Constitution. There is no inconsistency with the Charter in not doing so.[65]

This line of thinking was closely related to that presented by Secretary of State Dulles during the Bricker Amendment hearings. The essential point of his argument was that the United States supported international action on human rights, but that treaties were not the correct way to improve human rights practices. Rather, states and international organizations should stress education, persuasion, resolutions, declarations, and other nonlegal measures. Dulles's statement was quoted numerous times during the 1967 hearings.[66] Critics also rejected the argument that U.N. treaties on human rights were an essential part of the organization's goal of peacekeeping.

> In other statements and declarations, it has been urged that these Conventions are "necessary" for "permanent peace and security"; that they promote human freedom; that this is "an indispensable condition to the achievement of a stable peace"; and that we cannot afford to renounce responsibility for supporting fundamentals that distinguish our concepts from tyranny. . . .
>
> Quite clearly, there is emotional appeal in the reasons given for supporting these conventions. It is not an enviable task to have to examine this subject—not from the standpoint of the moral issues involved, but from the more prosaic standpoint of constitutional limitations, and what the lawyers of this country should regard as the long-term national interest.[67]

Furthermore, opponents also rejected the idea that the United States needed to ratify the treaties in order to protect its leadership role or avoid criticism at the United Nations and elsewhere. To this they countered,

> The United States need not make themselves party to treaties of doubtful validity purely to demonstrate our devotion to human rights. That devotion is firmly established by our Constitution, by adherence to the Charter, . . . by acts of Congress, and by decisions of our Supreme Court.[68]

Create Self-Executing Obligations

The issue of the use of human rights treaties by U.S. courts that had been raised in the 1950s was raised again in the 1967 hearings. The opposition once again argued that the treaties were self-executing and therefore would be applied by courts without implementing legislation. Senator Hickenlooper, who strongly opposed all three treaties initially, gave this argument as one of his primary concerns.

> I think there is language in here that could be, especially in view of the Supreme Court to go into the field and search around for ways and means of altering and changing what has been generally considered to be the intent of the Federal Constitution, and to hold something different, there is language in here that could be so construed. . . . [Once ratified] it is the supreme law of the

land, part of the supreme law of the land. So, there is no question but what they have a right to refer to it once we commit the mayhem on the internal policy.[69]

Hickenlooper also referred to *Missouri v. Holland* when answering an inquiry from Senator Claiborne Pell (D.-R.I.) about the use of treaties to reinterpret domestic laws. "Oh, yes," he replied. "The leading case on that was the Duck case out in Missouri."[70]

Deutsch testified on the self-executing nature of the Convention Concerning Forced Labor, and Chopnick raised the issue in connection with the Convention on the Political Rights of Women. The concern was similar to that raised by Hickenlooper, that ratification of these treaties would result in changes in U.S. law that might go beyond those understood by the Senate at the time of ratification.

The Fate of the Three Treaties

The Senate Foreign Relations Committee decided, in accord with the ABA's opinion, to recommend ratification of the Supplementary Slavery Convention. The Senate, with little floor debate, followed that recommendation. Why, if this treaty could be ratified with no reservations or understandings and no threats of filibuster or cries of imminent destruction of the nation, were the other treaties found to be so objectionable as to delay or prevent their consideration?

First, the fact that the United States was already a party to a treaty on the subject of slavery probably made acceptance much easier. Supporters were able to stress the slave trade and abolition of slavery provisions rather than the domestic practices "similar to slavery." The discussion was thus in terms of the specific treaty, and the unfavorable associations that had been developed during the early 1950s about human rights treaties generally were avoided. The Supplementary Slavery Convention gained acceptability as an extension of a former, quite popular treaty rather than as a new "human rights" treaty. The joint report of the ABA's section and committee observed that the United States had "had a long tradition in the efforts to suppress slavery and the slave trade and a long history of achievement in this field."[71] At the 1967 hearings an exchange between Senator Hickenlooper and Deutsch reflected the core of this argument supporting ratification.

Hickenlooper: I don't like to interrupt your train of thought on this, but is there language in the Bar Association's resolution suggesting that as long as we have a treaty on slavery it doesn't hurt anything to accede to this supplementary convention? . . .

Deutsch: . . . the reasons underlying favoring the Slavery Convention were (a) that it does deal with matters of international concern and . . . (b) that it does deal as a whole or does function as a whole, as a supplement to a prior convention to which the United States is a party.[72]

Second, the treaty was presented as a desirable way for the United States to celebrate the United Nations Human Rights Year. The report of the ABA Section on International Law reveals that consideration of the three treaties by the ABA was evoked, in part, by the designation of 1968 as Human Rights Year. This form of U.S. commemoration of the year was mentioned many times during the hearings as a reason for ratification.[73]

The opposition arguments that the treaty invaded domestic jurisdiction and that it would provide grounds for federal interference in state affairs were as cogent in relation to this treaty as to others. In addition, the provision for compulsory jurisdiction of the World Court in disputes that were not settled through negotiation was at least as strong as dispute settlement mechanisms found in other agreements. There was, then, a major inconsistency in voting to approve this treaty while continuing to give these reasons as the basis for opposing other human rights treaties.

Although it took an additional eight years, the Senate Foreign Relations Committee also eventually recommended ratification of the Convention on the Political Rights of Women. At the second set of hearings, held in 1975, all the testimony favored ratification. The American Bar Association was specially contacted for its position on the treaty. The response was that the stand of the organization had not been changed, but no one was sent to testify against the convention. (No active ABA opposition was expressed.) This passive performance by the ABA unquestionably aided treaty passage. In addition, 1975 had been designated by the United Nations as International Women's Year, and the treaty's passage had been identified as a significant symbol for U.S. observance.

Senator Charles Percy (R.-Ill.) led the move to tie the treaty to the

International Women's Year celebration. Numerous women's groups, which had not been actively seeking ratification of the treaty since 1967, joined in supporting the treaty as a part of their International Women's Year activities. The Foreign Relations Committee report and statements on the floor of the Senate reveal this tie.[74] Thus the treaty was not addressed as a human rights treaty, but as a symbolic gesture of support for improving the general status of women internationally. The rights involved were, of course, already afforded to women in the United States, and supporters pointed out that accession would mandate no changes in U.S. law and would cost nothing. The proponents wisely introduced the proposal for ratification during the closing days of the congressional session, a busy time when more weighty matters of state were likely to hold the attention and energy of the members. The opposition forces from 1967—whether from ignorance, weak memory, higher priorities, or loss of steam—did not mount a campaign against the treaty, and it sailed through the Senate with a unanimous vote of approval.[75]

This treaty, too, contained most of the flaws that the ABA Committee on Peace and Law identified as objectionable in the other human rights treaties. Of the three treaties considered in this chapter, it was the most widely criticized during the 1967 ABA debates; we may recall that not only the committee but also the Section on International Law strongly rejected this treaty. In addition, the treaty most clearly addressed a completely domestic issue, and one that concerned the jurisdiction of the states as well as the federal government. One would find it hard to disagree with Deutsch that the topic of qualifications for voting is as domestic and as clearly state-relevant as that of any of the human rights being codified. It is difficult to understand how the argument of domestic jurisdiction could effectively be applied in regard to other human rights treaties after the acceptance of this treaty. The Convention on the Political Rights of Women also contained a strong provision on compulsory jurisdiction of the World Court for dispute settlement. The dominance of political considerations over legal content is placed in stark relief when one ponders the unanimous vote for this treaty in a Senate that included Jesse Helms (R.-N.C.), present and voting, the same senator who for over ten years led the attack on the Genocide Convention because it addressed domestic issues and would subject the United States to World Court jurisdiction without our consent.

The Convention Concerning the Abolition of Forced Labor was not ratified and has not been the subject of Senate hearings since 1967. The ABA has not discussed the treaty again and, contrary to what has been the case with most other human rights treaties, it has not changed its position to one of support for U.S. ratification.

Conclusion

A review of the process of Senate ratification of the Supplementary Slavery Convention and the Convention on the Political Rights of Women reveals some noteworthy similarities between the two. First, the opportunity for consideration was provided by the United Nations' announcement of a special year for focused attention and activities on human rights. Treaty ratification was presented as a symbolic act, an appropriate action for U.S. commemoration of the year. In the case of the Supplementary Slavery Convention, it was merely an extension of an already ratified treaty; in the case of the Convention on the Political Rights of Women, it was seen as a "gift to the girls."[76]

In addition, the American Bar Association, the central interest group active on human rights treaties, either supported or did not actively oppose ratification. A major result of the relative silence of the ABA was the minimal reintroduction of the 1950s arguments against the ratification of these particular treaties. The Supplementary Slavery Convention was the subject of some criticism from recalcitrant ABA members, but this criticism was responded to by other ABA members voicing the organization's position of support. The 1950s opposition arguments were effectively employed by ABA members in 1967 to prevent ratification of the Convention on the Political Rights of Women. The silence of the ABA in 1975, and the absence of these same arguments, was crucial to acceptance of the treaty at that time. Finally, both treaties were presented as simple documents with no objectionable content and in no way at variance with constitutional or statutory provisions of U.S. law.

Both these treaties clearly deal with domestic law issues; both clearly involve subjects of federal-state controversy; and both clearly provide for World Court jurisdiction over disputes in a manner that would exclude U.S. citation of the Connally Amendment. Thus, we can conclude from these two instances that consideration of human rights treaties is not ineluctably based on the content of the treaties themselves. A treaty may be placed on the agenda and even accepted on the basis of a propitious external event and the passive stance of the major interest group involved. In the absence of the traditional and authoritative litany of furtively concealed dangers lurking in these treaties, the United States Senate can—and in two instances, did—determine that a human rights treaty is fundamentally unobjectionable.

SIX

The Reservations Game

The treaties imperil or restrict existing rights of Americans by using treaty law to restrict or reduce U.S. constitutional rights, to change U.S. domestic Federal or State laws, and to upset the balance of power within our unique system of federalism. . . . The proposed reservations, statements of understanding, and declarations are like shaking hands to make a deal with fingers crossed on the other hand. They constitute an admission that the treaties are unsatisfactory to us and offensive to our Constitution.
—Phyllis Schlafly, *Human Rights Treaties Hearing*, 1979

On 19 February 1986 Senator Jesse Helms, a member of the Senate Foreign Relations Committee, rose to speak about the Genocide Convention on the floor of the Senate. He proposed eight attachments that he claimed were necessary to protect the U.S. political and legal systems as well as our national sovereignty. But the major part of his speech was a resounding condemnation of the treaty. He invoked the spirit of the late Senator Sam Ervin, a consistently vocal opponent of the Genocide Convention, and asked that the entirety of Ervin's testimony before the Senate Foreign Relations Committee in 1970 be included in the record. The Senate went on to ratify the convention with all eight provisos, but Helms was one of eleven senators who still voted against ratification.

Once the American Bar Association Committee on Peace and Law Through United Nations and its supporters succeeded, in the early 1950s, in shifting the debate over treaty ratification from a political to a legal framework, the discussion of reservations became highly significant. Opponents, determined to defeat the treaties, viewed reservations as damage control in the event that ratification actually took place. Proponents designed reservations in direct response to opposition arguments as a way of undercutting those arguments and claiming that the alleged problem could be addressed through a unilateral U.S. attachment. Reservations became a strange sort of meeting ground between opponents and proponents. The former gained legitimacy and validation for their criticism of specific provisions, and the latter offset the criticism with suggestions of how specific attachments could meet all problems raised. Ratification debates became in large measure a legal game with reservations as the tokens of play.

For all of the treaties that have been considered, reservations were recommended by either the executive or members of the legislative branch. The ABA has always approved ratification only on the condition that reservations be attached. The origins of this ritual came with the first postwar treaty, the Genocide Convention.[1] The practice continued throughout the following decades of debate.

The assumedly controversial nature of the treaties, again a product of the 1950s debate, also led treaty supporters to accept or even encourage the formulation of "strategic reservations," attachments designed solely to undercut the opposition by claiming to neutralize the damage that might otherwise occur with adoption of the treaties. On occasion even a supportive executive branch has transmitted treaties laden with recommended attachments designed to forestall opposition arguments and thereby ease ratification. ABA treaty supporters have also voted within ABA organs for reservations that they have defended solely on the grounds that they were necessary to ensure passage within their organization and by the United States Senate.

The purpose of this chapter is to expose the fundamentally political nature of the opposition arguments and the co-optation of treaty proponents through the legitimation of a legalistic framework for debate. To a great extent, the debate over human rights treaties has been removed from the political to the legal realm and delivered into the hands of two warring teams of lawyers. Both teams have accepted a legal playing field and have effectively disqualified nonlegal political players. The persistence of legal rhetoric and the preeminence of legal experts have masked the fundamentally political nature of the opposition arguments and effectively excluded or minimized the impact of a political response. A careful analysis of most of the attachments proposed for human rights treaties reveals that they are legally unnecessary.[2] One of the major arguments against the treaties, that they might contravene the Constitution, has been laid to rest by the Supreme Court's decision in *Reid v. Covert*, which upheld the superiority of the Constitution over executive agreements and treaties. The case dealt with constitutional rights to a jury trial and other procedural safeguards denied dependents of military personnel when, by executive agreements, dependents were subject to the jurisdiction of military courts. Justice Hugo Black made the following statement, which should have provided reassurance on one major problem identified as crucial to the opposition in the 1950s:

> There is nothing in this language [Article VI paragraph 2] which intimates that treaties and laws enacted pursuant to them do not have to comply with the provisions of the Constitution. Nor is there anything in the debates which accompanied the drafting and ratification of the Constitution which even suggests such a result. . . . It would be manifestly contrary to the objective of those who created the Constitution, as well as those who were responsible for the Bill of Rights—let alone alien to our entire constitutional history and tradition—to construe Article VI as permitting the United States to exercise power under an international agreement without observing constitutional prohibitions. In effect, such construction would permit amendment of that document in a manner not sanctioned by Article V. The prohibitions of the Constitution were designed to apply to all branches of the National Government and they cannot be nullified by the Executive or by the Executive and the Senate combined.[3]

The demystification of the reservations game's legal liturgy is carried out in this chapter through a case study, an in-depth analysis of one set of proposed treaty reservations: the attachments recommended by the Carter administration for the U.N.'s Human Rights Covenants. First, a drafting history is provided for each specific treaty provision for which an attachment was recommended. Second, these provisions are examined to determine whether they conflict with the Constitution and whether a need exists for the particular recommended attachment. Finally, conclusions are drawn as to what the reservations game reveals about the underlying assumptions that guide executive and legislative consideration of human rights treaties.

Tailoring the Treaties to the U.S. System

The reservations game was played to the hilt during the Carter administration's consideration of the Human Rights Covenants. The normal bureaucratic process for treaties was followed. The covenants were carefully studied by the White House counsel and the State Department Legal Advisor's Office before the decision was made that the president should sign them. They were sent to the Department of Justice for careful scrutiny and decisions on which provisions needed reservations and understandings. Then, the treaties, with reservations and understandings designed by the Legal Advisor's Office of the State Department, were discussed by the Department of Defense and further attachments considered.[4] None of the bureaucratic divisions would be likely to approve provisions that in any way conflict with or endanger, in their minds, their freedom of action or their perception of the existing legal prerogatives of the state.

The end result was a set of recommended attachments in which the players were engaged in an exercise of one-upsmanship. The game's objective was to foresee any possible objection that might be raised within the Senate; the strategy was to identify each potential objection and obliterate it with the broadest possible attachment. This very strategy revealed the persistence of the 1950s mentality on human rights treaties: the assumption that there were dangerous *legal* complications in the treaties that challenged the American system. The proposed attachments established that the appropriate framework for debate was legal and technical rather than political. By trying to second guess the Senate, the drafters of the attachments raised some issues that probably would not otherwise have been raised and reinforced the sense of controversy that the opposition had settled over the treaties in the 1950s. Most of the proposed attachments addressed specifics that had never been a focus of vocal opposition and hardly seem the creation of a sympathetic executive. The impact of these recommendations was to create an aura of defectiveness rather than desirability (as suggested by Schlafly in the epigraph to this chapter) and to belie the rhetoric of praise that preceded them in the executive letter of transmittal. A review of the recommended attachments to the covenants, in fact, makes plain the effectiveness of the 1950s opposition to these treaties.

The Human Rights Covenants were selected for this case study for two reasons. First, as explained in Chapter 3, the provisions of the covenants were cited by treaty opponents as the best examples of all that they most feared from human rights treaties. Second, the recommendations for attachments to the covenants are the most extensive ones available, and they were designed by a sympathetic administration, the postwar administration that was most sympathetic to human rights treaties. Therefore, the reservations themselves reflect the success of the opposition in persuading strong treaty proponents to acknowledge serious problems in the treaties.

As was seen in Chapter 3, U.S. representatives were successful in influencing the initial draft of the covenants so that they reflected basic U.S. concepts of human rights. One treaty (that on economic, social, and cultural rights) casts the rights as goals, obligating states to work toward their implementation but without any immediate action required. Although today most people associate the Economic, Social, and Cultural Rights Covenant with the socialist countries, the principles behind it, reflected in Articles 22–27 of the Universal Declaration, are those of Franklin D. Roosevelt's Four Freedoms message to Congress on 6 January 1941. President Roosevelt recognized then that the achievement of security and prosperity was dependent upon "freedom from want" and the acceptance of a "second Bill of Rights"; the rights to be addressed in that second bill of rights are the same ones contained in the Economic, Social, and Cultural Rights Covenant. The second covenant, that on civil and political rights, basically internationalizes the U.S. Bill of Rights. As Warren Christopher, assistant secretary of state under Jimmy Carter and author of the letter of submittal sending the covenants to the Senate, has pointed out:

> The rights guaranteed are those civil and political rights with which the United States and the western liberal democratic tradition have always been associated. The rights are primarily limitations upon the power of the State to impose its will upon the people under its jurisdiction.[5]

Adapting the Economic, Social, and Cultural Rights Covenant

As previously explained, the Human Rights Commission originally planned to draft one treaty that would codify and elaborate the principles set forth in the Universal Declaration of Human Rights. The response and strategy of the United States was based, in part, on the notion that the inclusion of economic rights in a binding treaty of the form used for civil and political rights would greatly reduce the possibility of ratification by the U.S. Senate. The United States' success in separating the rights and shaping the treaty's form, as discussed in Chapter 3, ought to have made this ratification a relatively simple proposition.

Restating the Goal Orientation of the Covenant

Some groups will find obvious difficulties associating the United States with the rights set forth in this covenant (the right to work, full employment, rest, leisure, periodic vacation with pay, etc.), because the very idea of the government being concerned with social and economic matters is anathema to them. However, as discussed in Chapter 3, the goal-oriented tenor of the entire document, coupled with interpretation based on the discussion throughout the drafting process that this document reflects goals rather than immediate obligations, lay a strong foundation for support of U.S. ratification. The clearest basis for establishing the nature of this treaty is in Article 2, paragraph 1:

> Each State Party to the present Covenant undertakes to *take steps,* individually and through international assistance and coopera-tion, especially economic and technical, to the maximum of its available resources, *with a view to achieving progressively* the full realization of the rights recognized in the present Covenant by all appropriate means including particularly the adoption of legisla-tive measures [emphasis added].

This language, of taking steps and trying to progressively achieve the realization of rights, is the formula for all the substantive provisions of the treaty, Articles 1 through 15. There is no question that the obliga-tion is one of working toward rather than instituting now. This lan-guage is in clear contrast to that of the Civil and Political Rights Covenant. The United States in ratifying this treaty would go on record as accepting, for its own people and as an international stan-dard, economic and social goals that have been a part of the American scene at least since the New Deal. Compliance with the treaty would not require any specific immediate governmental action.[6]

The administration's recommended understanding was completely unnecessary in that it merely restates the language of the article itself when it declares,

> The United States understands paragraph (1) of Article 2 as estab-lishing that the provisions of Article 1 through 15 of this Cove-nant describe goals to be achieved progressively rather than through immediate implementation.[7]

The administration also engaged in unnecessary limitation when it coupled part of this paragraph with language in Article 11 that asks ratifying states to "take steps individually and through international cooperation to guard against hunger" and states that these provisions "import no legally binding obligation to provide aid to foreign countries."[8]

Asserting Private Property Rights

An issue of economic self-determination arose during debate within the Third Committee of the U.N. General Assembly—the Social, Humanitarian, and Cultural Committee—to which the draft covenants were referred after completion by the Human Rights Commission. The debate was over Article 2 of the Economic, Social, and Cultural Rights Covenant, which includes the provision encouraging international cooperation for economic development and a general nondiscrimination clause. A group of developing states moved to include in Article 2 an additional paragraph that would address the issue of economic rights of non-nationals.[9] The debate, as might be expected, divided along lines of developed versus developing nations. Supporters of the provision were accused of violating the spirit of the covenant by undermining its universality. Revisions to address the concerns of the developed states were generally unsuccessful.[10] However, a majority of the committee accepted the final revised form, which read:

> 3. Developing countries, with due regard to human rights and their national economy, may determine to what extent they would guarantee the economic rights recognized in the present Covenant to non-nationals.

In the closing discussions of the final draft of the covenants in the Third Committee, an additional article was introduced on the subject of economic development. The representative of India offered it on behalf of his own and thirteen co-sponsoring nations. It stated,

> Nothing in the present Covenant shall be interpreted as impairing the inherent right of all peoples to enjoy and utilize fully and freely their natural wealth and resources.[11]

He argued that the rights described in the Economic, Social, and Cultural Rights Covenant "presupposed the existence of a certain level of economic and social development in order that those rights be freely realized."[12] The objections of the U.S. representative, Patricia Harris, focused on a somewhat technical issue of placement and the claim that the provisions of Article 1 might be considered modified by this addition to the implementation articles. Harris expressed U.S. support for the "principle expressed in Article 25 . . . [but] found the adoption of that article objectionable on procedural grounds."[13] Harris's concern was not shared in the committee, and the United States was one of four countries voting against the article.[14] The same article[15] was adopted as Article 47 of the Civil and Political Rights Covenant, with the United States being one of two countries voting against it.[16]

The U.S. executive, in transmitting the covenants, linked these two provisions of the Economic, Social, and Cultural Rights Covenant and recommended one declaration to address both.

> The United States declares that nothing in the Covenant derogates from the equal obligation of all States to fulfill their responsibilities under international law. The United States understands that under the Covenant everyone has the right to own property alone as well as in association with others, and that no one shall be arbitrarily deprived of his property.[17]

The letter of transmittal states that the United States does not approve of discrimination by developing nations against non-nationals and that actions against their property must be taken in accord with international legal standards. The letter goes on to state these standards as applied and interpreted by the United States: "Under international law, any taking of private property must be nondiscriminatory and for a public purpose, and must be accompanied by prompt, adequate, and effective compensation."[18] This declaration is clearly political, using the human rights treaty to reassert the traditional U.S. interpretation of the international law of expropriation and the right to private property. These issues are both covered by Article 5, paragraph 2, and the declarations have no legal justification.

Adapting the Civil and Political Rights Covenant

Although the original expectation was that the Western democracies would find the Civil and Political Rights Covenant the easier of the Human Rights Covenants to ratify, because it is essentially a document that establishes clear legal obligation in an area in which the United States prides itself, the United States may ironically find itself in the position of attaching more reservations to this treaty than to that on economic, social, and cultural rights. The legal obligations apply to current government practice; the covenant's operable section provides a list of rights to which individuals are now entitled rather than a list of hopes for future achievements. However, the subject of this treaty is one with which most Americans are more at ease—which is to say, protection from government is part of the American legal ideal, while services guaranteed by government have yet to attain full legitimacy in this country.

We have seen the major arguments that have persisted over time in regard to this treaty. One continuing idea is that citizens of the United States do not need this covenant and that by ratifying it we may even be giving up, eroding, our basic freedoms. There are at least three reasons why this critique is invalid. First, as will be seen below, the covenant broadens and expands some rights; there are significant additional protections for the individual that were not sufficiently recognized by the framers of the Constitution. Second, through the attachment of one reservation discussed below, Americans can be assured that there will be no diminution of their rights.[19] Third, philosophically as well as practically, this covenant raises the significance of the individual, focuses on the individual as the locus of rights, and lays a foundation for individual claims against the state. Instruments like this one affirm the rights of individuals apart from their association with any particular unit of the present political structure known as the nation-state system.

Capital Punishment

The right to life is defined in Article 6. The Carter administration primarily focused on the provisions on capital punishment. The members of the Human Rights Commission agreed on the need for an article on this subject. One minority view was that no one should be deprived of life under any circumstances. Those who held this view reasoned that since the right to life was the most basic, any mention of situations under which it could be suspended would appear to condone the taking of life. The objection to their position was that elimination of capital punishment was unrealistic and contrary to the domestic legal system of most states.

A compromise was eventually formulated, providing that capital punishment should be imposed (1) only for the most serious crimes, (2) as sentence of a competent court, and (3) in accordance with the law and not contrary to the Universal Declaration or the Genocide Convention. Provision was made for seeking pardon or commutation of the sentence. There was also general agreement on a provision to exempt pregnant women from execution.

During the commission sessions, U.S. representatives made several suggestions. First, the U.S. delegation proposed the addition of "arbitrarily" to the initial paragraph: "No one shall be deprived of his life." Second, it offered a revised paragraph 3:

> In countries where capital punishment exists, sentence of death may be imposed only as a penalty for the most serious crimes pursuant to the sentence of a competent court and in accordance with law.[20]

The United States also supported the provision for amnesty, pardon, and commutation of sentence.[21]

The final draft accepted by the commission read:

> 1. No one shall be arbitrarily deprived of his life. Everyone's right to life shall be protected by law.
> 2. In countries where capital punishment exists, sentence of death may be imposed only as a penalty for the most serious crimes pursuant to the sentence of a competent court and in accordance with law not contrary to the principles of the Universal Declaration of Human Rights or the Convention on the Prevention and Punishment of the Crime of Genocide.
> 3. Anyone sentenced to death shall have the right to seek pardon or commutation of the sentence. Amnesty, pardon or commutation of the sentence of death may be granted in all cases.
> 4. Sentence of death shall not be carried out on a pregnant woman.

When the draft article came to the Third Committee, the most important point of contention was in regard to the proposal by Colombia and Uruguay to replace Article 6 with:

> Every human being has the inherent right to life. The death penalty shall not be imposed on any person.[22]

Those in favor of this proposal argued that the covenant should stress the right to life, not the taking of it. They felt that abolition of the death penalty was in keeping with contemporary trends to reduce or eliminate crimes punishable by death and to stress rehabilitation as the aim of the prison system. They pointed out that innocent people might possibly be convicted and that there was no evidence the death penalty played any deterrent role. Those opposed felt that the amendment was too idealistic, and many representatives, even those who supported abolition of capital punishment, stated their objections to this provision on the grounds that it would become an obstacle to ratification. The U.S. delegation took the position that "persuasion, education and example would have more satisfactory results than formal undertakings, which would lead to some countries imposing their social and moral standards on others," and held that the article should be kept simple, the term "arbitrarily" should be used, and any list of limitations should be avoided.[23] In the final draft from the Third Committee two major additions were made: an exemption from capital punishment for persons under eighteen years of age and a prohibition of the use of treaty provisions to delay abolition of capital punishment.

The Carter administration's recommendations appear most ridiculous in reserving on Article 6, paragraphs 2, 4, and 5, which read:

2. In countries which have not abolished the death penalty, sentence of death may be imposed only for the most serious crimes in accordance with law in force at the time of the commission of the crime and not contrary to the provisions of the present Covenant and to the Convention on the Prevention and Punishment of the Crime of Genocide. This penalty can only be carried out pursuant to a final judgement rendered by a competent court.

4. Anyone sentenced to death shall have the right to seek pardon or commutation of the sentence. Amnesty, pardon or commutation of the sentence of death may be granted in all cases.

5. Sentence of death shall not be imposed for crimes committed by persons below eighteen years of age and shall not be carried out on pregnant women.

The letter of transmittal recommends the following reservation:

The United States reserves the right to impose capital punishment on any person duly convicted under existing or future laws permitting the imposition of capital punishment.[24]

There is no suggestion in the transmittal letter that these paragraphs are in conflict with the Constitution, only that U.S. law "is not entirely in accord with these standards."[25] The United States is, then, reserving the right to deny access to requests for pardon and to impose capital punishment for nonserious crimes. By refusing even to consider any possible change in U.S. law, the administration has put itself in the unenviable position of insisting on the right to execute children and pregnant women.

Liberty and Security of Person

Article 9 of the Covenant on Civil and Political Rights simply sets forth the right to liberty and security of person. There was no real argument over the need for this article; nor was there disagreement that it would require some restrictions. Again the debate developed over specific versus general limitation, with the list of limitations growing long and being rebutted with the argument of the impossibility of its being exhaustive. Both the United States and the Soviet Union argued for a general limitation, stressing the fact that a long list of limits tended to make the exceptions appear more important than the right.[26] The only difficulty with this article for the United States was the provision in paragraph 5 that stated,

> Anyone who has been the victim of unlawful arrest or deprivation of liberty shall have an enforceable right to compensation.

The U.S. representative argued that

> the liability imposed by the existing language was so sweeping and absolute as to put every law enforcement officer in the position of performing his duty at the peril of being penalized for any mistake, without any distinction being made as to whether it was accidental or wilful. . . .
>
> In the United States delegation's view, it was not necessary for the covenant to go into the details of liabilities and domestic remedies for the infringement or violation of rights under the several articles of the covenant. The United States delegation thought it unnecessary and in some way unwarranted to compel different legal systems to accept the peculiarities of others in the assessment of compensation.[27]

When it became clear that this paragraph was not going to be dropped, the United States withdrew[28] its proposal to delete the paragraph and suggested another text:

Every person who has been the victim of unlawful arrest or detention shall have a right of action for compensation.[29]

The argument given was that

it was necessary to draw a distinction, and to hold officials ac-
countable for malicious or grossly negligent conduct but not for
unfortunate accidents or mistakes in judgment. To do otherwise
might discourage them from performing their duties with the
necessary zeal. . . .
   In the United States the rule of liability in the cases of unlawful
arrest were not nearly so onerous as paragraph (5) proposed.
That paragraph should be drafted as to be acceptable to various
legal systems. That was the reason for the United States amendment, under which the individual would be enabled to seek redress in court and to receive compensation if he had been the
victim of unlawful arrest effected by persons acting in a wanton
fashion.[30]

The U.S. proposal was rejected 6-4, with 3 abstentions.[31]

The U.S. representative did not speak out on Article 9 during the
discussion in the Third Committee. The United Kingdom introduced
an amendment that would not have substantially altered its content,
changing "deprivation of liberty" to "detention."[32] This amendment
was adopted.[33] Harris voted for the article, which passed easily, 70-0,
with 3 abstentions. The relevant part of the adopted text read,

5. Anyone who has been the victim of unlawful arrest or detention shall have an enforceable right to compensation.

The administration also found Article 15, paragraph 1, to be in
conflict with current U.S. law. Article 15 prohibited punishment for an
act not constituting a crime at the time of commission; it also prohibited harsher penalties than those existing at the time a crime was
committed. The article had been drafted in the commission with little
controversy. Interestingly, the U.S. representative had supported the
entire article and had defended the particular sentence that the Carter
administration later found unacceptable.

Her delegation accepted article 14 [later 15] in its original form, for
that article prohibited both the punishment of a person for an act
or an omission which did not constitute an offense at the time
when it was committed, and the application of penalties heavier

than those provided by law at the time when the offense was committed. . . .

In the United States of America, however, it was thought that every accused person should have the advantage of subsequent legislative amendment which would result in a lighter sentence.[34]

The Third Committee did not alter the Commission draft and the United States voted for paragraph one, and for the article as a whole.[35]

The Carter administration's recommended reservation covers both Article 9, paragraph 5, and Article 15, paragraph 1:

The United States does not adhere to paragraph (5) of Article 9 or to the third clause of paragraph (1) of Article 15.[36]

There is good reason to believe that this reservation is completely unnecessary. In regard to Article 9, paragraph 5, it is unnecessary because the right to compensation for unlawful arrest has been established at the state and federal levels.[37] In the case of Article 15, paragraph 1, Christopher himself admits in the letter of transmittal that "this right is often granted in practice in the United States, but it is not required by law."[38]

Treatment of Accused and Convicted

A further provision of the Covenant on Civil and Political Rights with which the Carter administration was not entirely comfortable appears in Article 10. During the debate in the Human Rights Commission, there was little trouble over the basic provisions of this article. There was unanimous acceptance of the idea that people deprived of their liberty should nonetheless be treated with humanity. Although some question arose as to the practical difficulties of separating accused and convicted persons, provision was made that the former should have treatment appropriate to their status as unconvicted prisoners. Separation alone, it was felt, would not make it clear enough that they were not to be subject to the harsher conditions of those already convicted. Later the Third Committee adopted an amendment put forward by the Netherlands, adding the qualification "save in exceptional circumstances"[39] to provide some leeway for states unable to meet the separation requirement fully.

Although the Third Committee generally agreed with the draft as submitted by the commission, the delegate from Ceylon raised the issue of juvenile offenders and their special needs. Ceylon proposed the following:

Juveniles charged with delinquency shall be segregated from all other adult detainees and convicted persons and shall be subject, while detained, to separate treatment appropriate to their age and legal status and shall be brought as speedily as possible for judicial examination and adjudication.[40]

A discussion ensued of the pros and cons of providing for (1) separate detention of juveniles and (2) speedy adjudication of their cases. The U.S. representative spoke against these amendments, as being too detailed for inclusion in the treaty.[41] The provision was tightened and simplified and was adopted overwhelmingly.[42] The article as a whole was adopted by a vote of 67-0-2.[43] The final form of the Article 10 provisions that the Carter administration found objectionable were in paragraph 2,

a) Accused persons shall, save in exceptional circumstances, be segregated from convicted persons and shall be subject to separate treatment appropriate to their status as unconvicted persons.
b) Accused juvenile persons shall be separated from adults and brought as speedily as possible for adjudication.

and in paragraph 3,

The penitentiary system shall comprise treatment of prisoners the essential aim of which shall be their reformation and social rehabilitation. Juvenile offenders shall be segregated from adults and be accorded treatment appropriate to their age and legal status.

These provisions are not in conflict with U.S. law, but they may not yet be fully implemented throughout the legal system. The administration suggested an attachment stating,

The United States considers the rights enumerated in paragraphs (2) and (3) of Article 10 as goals to be achieved progressively rather than through immediate implementation. In explanation, the letter of submittal does not cite any conflict in law, but only "practice and policy."[44]

Even the suggested understanding obligates the United States to implement these provisions.

Fair Trial

Article 14 of the Civil and Political Rights Covenant sets out the legal standards for the conduct of trials. Fair trial might seem to some to be the bulwark of the American rights system and therefore superior to any system of protections that might be devised by an international organization. The letter of transmittal in fact states that "It is possible to read all the requirements contained in Article 14 as consistent with United States law, policy and practice."[45] The administration's decision *not* to so read them is inexplicable except in the context of the reservations game.

Article 14 was not especially controversial in the commission or Third Committee. The United States supported the commission draft and did not vote against the article or any of the individual paragraphs, all of which were voted upon separately.[46]

First, the administration expressed concern over several sections of paragraph 3, reading as follows:

In the determination of any criminal charge against him, everyone shall be entitled to the following minimum guarantees, in full equality: . . .
b) To have adequate time and facilities for the preparation of his defence and to communicate with counsel of his own choosing. . . .
d) To be tried in his presence, and to defend himself in person or through legal assistance of his own choosing; to be informed, if he does not have legal assistance, of this right; and to have legal assistance assigned to him, in any case where the interests of justice so require, and without payment by him in any such case if he does not have sufficient means to pay for it;
e) To examine, or have examined, the witnesses against him and to obtain the attendance and examination of witnesses on his behalf under the same conditions as witnesses against him.

The executive has recommended attaching an understanding that

subparagraphs 3 (b) and (d) of Article 14 do not require the provision of court-appointed counsel when the defendant is financially able to retain counsel or for petty offenses for which imprisonment will not be imposed. The United States further understands that paragraph (3) (e) does not forbid requiring an indigent defendant to make a showing that the witness is necessary for his attendance to be compelled by the court.[47]

Given that the administration felt that U.S. law was already in compliance, monumental efforts at second guessing the opposition or displaying knowledge of legal niceties appears to be at work here. For example, the letter of transmittal actually cites the titles from the U.S. Code that would cover Article 14, paragraph 6, which reads:

When a person has by a final decision been convicted of criminal offense and when subsequently his conviction has been reversed or he has been pardoned on the ground that a new or newly discovered fact shows conclusively that there has been a miscarriage of justice, the person who has suffered punishment as a result of such conviction shall be compensated according to law, unless it is proved that the non-disclosure of the unknown fact in time is wholly or partly attributable to him.

Even so, the recommendation is made that an understanding be attached to the effect that "the United States considers that provisions of United States law currently in force constitute compliance with paragraph (6)."[48] Is this not what the administration is saying, in fact, about the entire treaty, with the exception of those parts that have attachments?

Attachments to Provisions Found in Both Covenants

The Carter administration believed that three issues common to the two covenants required attention.

Limitations on the First Amendment

Each covenant contains a provision that the Carter administration and many others have interpreted as conflicting with the First Amendment to the United States Constitution. Although the Universal Declaration's Article 19 on freedom of expression reflects U.S. law and practice, a further provision on this subject, which the United States strongly opposed, was added to the Civil and Political Rights Covenant. The legislative history of this provision, Article 20, reveals active, if ultimately unsuccessful, efforts by the U.S. representative to have it deleted. The history also reveals that the origin and rationale for the inclusion of this article were neither Communist nor totalitarian, as has been suggested by opponents of the treaty.[49]

At the Human Rights Commission's earliest meeting in 1947 proposals were made to include in the covenant a provision prohibiting advocacy of racial hatred and war. The idea had been suggested for inclusion in the Universal Declaration by the Sub-Commission on Prevention of Discrimination and Protection of Minorities.[50] The proposal had been firmly rejected, yet there remained a clear preference on the part of numerous members for including such a provision in the covenant. The Chinese representative suggested that an amendment to the article on freedom of information could cover this topic.[51] Australia's representative proposed that this text be included as a new article, and the Chinese agreed to this proposal. The suggestion was adopted by the commission but then deleted by the Drafting Committee in 1949. However, the provision was again discussed at the fourth commission session; a text was offered by the Soviet Union, whose representative, A. P. Pavlov, made a strong plea on its behalf:

> Millions had perished because the propaganda of racial and national superiority, hatred and contempt, had not been stopped in time. Yet five years had hardly elapsed since the end of the war, and there were already signs of a revival of similar tendencies in various countries of the world.[52]

James Simsarian, a member of the U.S. delegation, echoed Eleanor Roosevelt's arguments opposing the article, when she had suggested that freedom of expression was more important than any protection that might be gained:

> The Supreme Court [of the United States] has held that the principle of democracy was better served by allowing individuals to create disputes and dissension than by suppressing their freedom of speech.[53]

Two texts were circulated to governments before the next session. One, from the Soviet Union, read,

> The propaganda in whatever form of fascist-Nazi views and the propaganda of racial and national superiority, hatred and contempt shall be prohibited by law.

And the other, from France, stated,

Any advocacy of national, racial or religious hostility that constitutes an incitement to violence or hatred shall be prohibited by
the law of the State.[54]

The United States' response to these proposals was to request omission of the article on the grounds that it would be open to abuse "and
might encourage the enactment of legislation limiting freedom of
speech and press."[55]

At the sixth session of the commission, Eleanor Roosevelt spoke
strongly, continuing her opposition to the article. First, she argued
that neither of the proposals fit into the format of the covenant since
they would result in limitations on the rights set forth on freedom of
information and the press. As she contended,

It would be extremely dangerous to encourage Governments to
issue prohibitions in that field, since any criticism of public or
religious authorities might all too easily be described as incitement to hatred and consequently prohibited. Article 21 [later
Article 20] was not merely unnecessary, it was also harmful.[56]

Second, she pointed out the severe shortcomings associated with the
vagueness of the wording:

It was difficult to draw a distinction between advocacy and incitement. It was equally difficult to differentiate between the various
shades of feeling ranging from hatred to ill-feeling and mere
dislike.[57]

She warned the commission against using such vague expressions as
"national hostility" and "religious hostility," which appeared in the
French text:

If the Commission were to adopt [these expressions], however
pure its intentions might be, it would only encourage Governments to punish all criticisms in the name of protections against
religious or national hostility.[58]

Third, she argued that the provision gave rise to limitations on fundamental rights and could be exploited by totalitarian regimes.[59] At this
sixth session the commission voted 7-4-3 to delete the article.[60]

Later, however, in 1953, the Sub-Commission on Prevention of Discrimination and Protection of Minorities introduced a form of the
article once again; it read:

Any advocacy of national, racial or religious hostility that constitutes an incitement to violence shall be prohibited by the law of the State.[61]

Poland offered another version:

Any advocacy of national or racial exclusiveness, hatred and contempt or religious hostility, particularly of such a nature as to constitute an incitement to violence, shall be prohibited by the law of the State.[62]

Platon Morosov, of the Soviet Union, repeated some of the same arguments that had been made earlier on behalf of the article. He rejected the notion that the provision might lead to restraints on free speech, which was strongly supported by the Soviet Union.

In point of fact, all national legislation, including that of the United Kingdom, forbade the propagation of certain ideas that were patently harmful to society. There were recognized limits to freedom of expression. As had been said by a judge in the United States of America, if someone in a theatre shouted "Fire!" and caused a panic, he would be held responsible for his action. . . . Similarly, everyone today was aware of the appalling consequences of Fascist propaganda. Everyone knew how Hitler's "Mein Kampf" had poisoned peoples' minds, and what the cost of the dissemination of those insidious ideas had been in terms of suffering borne by the freedom-loving peoples.[63]

The U.S. delegation expressed no opinion during this debate but cast a negative vote on the basis of a concern about possible government censorship.[64] The objection was to an amendment from Chile that inserted "hatred and" after "that constitutes an incitement to." The U.S. representative explained after the vote that "the Chilean amendment, . . . by admitting the possibility of government censorship, might lead to the destruction of certain fundamental freedoms."[65] The article was adopted with 11 countries in favor (including France, India, Chile, and the Soviet Union) and 3 against (the United Kingdom, the United States, and Australia), with 3 abstentions (Sweden, Belgium, and China).[66]

The Third Committee discussed the problem of propaganda at the 1961 session, following its vote on Article 19. The work of the committee was reorganized to allow this related issue to be discussed in sequence, and when the article under discussion was adopted, an affirmative vote determined that it would be renumbered and placed after Article 19. The consensus was that the former article set the standards for the individual's right to freedom of expression and information and the latter provision established a limitation by prohibiting a particular form of expression, that of propaganda for racial hatred and war.

The U.S. position was one of continued opposition to the article. Although numerous amendments were suggested, none came from the United States. The U.S. representative expressed a general "sympathy with the spirit of the article," but urged deletion. The grounds given were the same as those presented in the commission:

> [The article] was open to abuse, and its retention in the draft Convention might encourage the Governments of totalitarian States to impose limitations on freedom of speech and of the Press, thus undermining the rights set forth in article 19. [The U.S.] Government had always maintained that it would be dangerous to permit such prohibitions, because any criticism of public or religious authorities could easily be described as "incitement to hatred," especially since the term did not lend itself to easy definition as a penal offence.[67]

The United States did express support for a four-power amendment that would have replaced Article 20 and would have limited the prohibition to one against incitement to violence; it read,

> Any propaganda for war and any advocacy of national, racial or religious hatred inciting to violence shall be prohibited by law.[68]

U.S. constitutional law would have allowed support for a provision against incitement to violence. Following passage of the Smith Act, which prohibited advocacy of the overthrow of the government by violence, the Supreme Court heard a case[69] in which the outcome was a reversal of conviction based on the charge to the jury. The Court drew a distinction between advocacy of ideas and advocacy of taking specific active steps aimed at the overthrow of the government. Thus, the United States could support a provision prohibiting incitement to violence but would not be on firm constitutional ground supporting an article on incitement to hostility, hatred, or discrimination. All of the latter are, as was indicated during the debates, vague terms and are not supported by the Court's interpretations of incitement in the Smith Act.[70] The proposed amendment was withdrawn, and a sixteen-power joint amendment replaced it; the text that was adopted as Article 20 read:

1. Any propaganda for war shall be prohibited by law.
2. Any advocacy of national, racial, or religious hatred that constitutes incitement to discrimination, hostility or violence shall be prohibited by law.

The vote was strongly in favor, and supporters included nations from a broad range of political and economic systems.[71] Thus, the United States, despite strong efforts to delete the article, was unsuccessful. Commission and committee members were not persuaded of the dangers perceived and presented by the U.S. representatives.

This article does give rise to legitimate concerns about restrictions on freedom of expression since there is the possibility of conflict with the First Amendment to the United States Constitution. The Carter administration recommended, however, an unnecessarily broad reservation, which extends beyond constitutionality to include "laws and practice." The recommended reservation reads:

The Constitution of the United States and Article 19 of this Covenant contain provisions for the protection of individual rights, including the right of free speech, and nothing in this Covenant shall be deemed to require or to authorize legislation or other action by the United States which would restrict the right of free speech protected by the Constitution, laws, and practice of the United States.[72]

This reservation also covers Article 5, paragraph 1, of both covenants, which states,

Nothing in the present Covenant may be interpreted as implying for any State, group or person any right to engage in any *activity* or to perform *any act* aimed at the destruction of any of the rights or freedoms recognized herein, or at their limitation to a greater extent than is provided for in the present Covenant [emphasis added].

The recommended reservation is unnecessarily broad, extending beyond constitutionality to include "laws and practice." In fact, David Weissbrodt, a legal scholar who is an authority on the Carter administration attachments, has suggested that the reservation may have the effect of reducing the rights of U.S. citizens.[73]

The drafting histories provided in Chapter 3 speak to the strong influence the U.S. representatives had on the final form of the Human Rights Covenants. The article just discussed, which has been interpreted as limiting freedom of expression, is a lonely example of overwhelming opposition to the U.S. position leading to a constitutional problem.

Federal-State Clause

One critical constitutional issue raised by the acceptance of international obligations by a federal system is its impact on the subunits of which the system is composed. In some nations, the constitution requires that treaty provisions be translated into national legislation in order to be incorporated into the domestic legal system. According to the United States Constitution, however, treaties are the law of the land and, as such, are binding on the states.

U.S. representatives were active in the Human Rights Commission, proposing and supporting the inclusion of a federal-state article. Eleanor Roosevelt explicated the U.S. view and reiterated the need for this provision in spite of a variety of critical arguments in opposition. She argued,

> In order to make it possible for federal States to adhere to the Covenant, an article based on the principles laid down should be included. . . . The federal government of the United States was ready to subscribe to the obligations contained in the Covenant on any matters within its competence, but it could not do more than bring any obligations within the competence of the appropriate authorities in the forty-eight states to the attention of those authorities, with favorable recommendation, at the earliest possible moment.[74]

Those opposed to such an article argued that the clause would have the effect of establishing higher levels of obligation on unitary states than on federal ones. They also pointed to the subject of this particular treaty, referring to its "exalted nature."[75] A clause recognizing diminished responsibility for federal states would, they also argued, contradict the very fundamental nature of the subject of the treaty and undermine the objective of making it universal in application.

In 1954, once the United States decided not to ratify the covenants, the U.S. representatives withdrew as co-sponsor of a federal-state clause.[76] Australia and India urged adoption of this text[77] without the

United States. The same arguments against this article were repeated: that the rights set forth in the covenants should be universally applied and that an inequality of obligation would be created by such a provision. In the end, a draft article proposed by the Soviet Union[78] was adopted 8-7, with 3 abstentions. This article stated simply,

> The provisions of the present Covenant shall extend to all parts of federal States without any limitation or exceptions.

The U.S. representatives did nothing to address the federal-state issue during the Third Committee sessions. The text adopted was the same as that drafted by the commission. It appears as Article 28 in the Economic, Social, and Cultural Rights Covenant[79] and Article 50 of the Civil and Political Rights Covenant.[80]

The Carter administration proposed almost the exact same reservation for both covenants. The Economic, Social, and Cultural Rights Covenant is written in terms of goals and objectives, with subsequent legislation to be enacted to fulfill the obligations accepted. The difficulty of bounded authority and separate jurisdiction in areas requiring new law can be settled by Congress and state legislators as the statutes are enacted. Thus, there is no need for the proposed reservation, which stipulates:

> The United States shall progressively implement all the provisions of the Covenant over whose subject matter the Federal Government exercises legislative and judicial jurisdiction; with respect to the provisions over whose subject matter constituent units exercise jurisdiction, the Federal Government shall take appropriate measures, to the end that the competent authorities of the constituent units may take appropriate measures for the fulfillment of this Covenant.[81]

The reservation recommended for the Civil and Political Rights Covenant is the same as above except the word "progressively" is not included. This covenant states immediate obligations. If any state laws are at variance with the treaty, without a reservation, action by the states could place the United States in violation of its treaty obligations. If these rights are fundamental, however, the federal government should be in a position to assure their implementation throughout the country. As we have seen, many of those who are especially jealous of states' rights are also continuing guardians of domestic jurisdiction. The federal-state reservation has no doubt been proposed in order to provide reassurance of the maintenance of the traditional domains of authority that aroused so much controversy during the 1950s. Such a reservation is highly undesirable, given the content of the treaty, and the United States ought to be willing to take responsibility for the enforcement of these rights throughout our nation.

Non-Self-Executing Declaration

The opposition, as we have seen, often claimed that human rights treaties were dangerous because they would be self-executing. Since the Constitution provides that treaty provisions may be cited by the courts, even in the absence of implementing legislation, the issue of the covenants' being put to just such use was frequently raised. Ultimately, the question of whether or not any particular provision is self-executing is in fact a matter for the courts.

One purpose of the Bricker Amendment was to remove this issue permanently from the courts' jurisdiction by requiring that all treaties be treated as non-self-executing. The Carter administration accepted this same strategy by recommending the following declaration:

> The United States declares that the provisions of Articles 1 through 27 of this Covenant [i.e., the Civil and Political Rights Covenant; Articles 1–15 for the Economic, Social, and Cultural Rights Covenant] are not self-executing.[82]

This declaration would, in effect, eliminate the latitude of the courts in determining whether or not specific provisions might be cited on their own. Individuals and groups along the full range of the political spectrum would be foreclosed from one of the important avenues open to them for framing and advancing their concerns. In addition, crucial forums for the interpretation and application of any treaty— the domestic courts—would also be significantly restricted. These two reservations are unnecessary and undesirable. They reflect a nationalistic sense of superiority and a refusal to consider the possibility that change may potentially bring improvement rather than deterioration.

Conclusion

One major effect of the opposition to human rights treaties in the 1950s was the "legalization" of the ratification debate. The prominent position of the ABA and its members as the key expert witnesses against the treaties cast the discussion in legal terms. Proponents, attempting to gain acceptance for the treaties, designed legally correct attachments, which they claimed met the opposition's objections. Yet in adopting the legal framework, they yielded major ground, implying that the opposition's stated arguments were legitimate and nonpolitical. The effect of this concession was to cast future debates in legal terms, with the designing of ever more elaborate and detailed attachments becoming the routine method of addressing actual and potential opposition.

A further effect of this legalism was the marginalization of political arguments that were at the heart of the original opposition movement and that continue to dominate the current debate. A review of the attachments recommended for the Human Rights Covenants by the Carter administration and the drafting histories of the provisions they address provide important insights into Senate opposition to human rights treaties. With one exception, the attachments are unnecessary; the provisions for which they were proposed do not compromise or constrain the constitutionally protected rights of U.S. citizens. The case study presented here also reveals that U.S. representatives succeeded in achieving a codification of rights very much in the Western tradition, whereas the representatives of the Soviet Union were rarely successful when offering draft articles and amendments.

More generally, the case study exposes some fundamental assumptions that guide executive and legislative consideration of human rights treaties. One assumption is an ethnocentric notion not simply of the superiority of the U.S. system but even of its perfection. The United States could, as many other ratifying states have, accept the obligation to bring its legal system into compliance with the treaty. There is no constitutional or other legal bar to this option. The letter of transmittal only refers to "practice and policy," not to law. It could be argued that the United States should take this route. First, because the treaty is a statement of fundamental rights, and altering the intent of the treaty for the United States on a unilateral basis would diminish the significance of our ratification and still leave the treaty inapplicable as between the United States and any state that finds the reservations or understandings unacceptable. The attachments would also create rights for any other ratifying state in any future dispute involving the United States. Second, attachments like these highlight U.S. reluctance to accept international human rights standards and contradict any claim the nation might have to leadership in global human rights development and implementation. U.S. government officials in both the legislative and executive branches appear to believe that under no circumstances could an international formulation of human rights hold the potential for any improvement in the human rights of U.S. citizens. The 1950s fear of change, the belief that any possible change would definitely be for the worse, resulted in the practice of rejecting any conceivable interpretation of any treaty provision that might be at odds with U.S. law. A further and related assumption is that no political objective, however strong, could outweigh the need to resist any possible legal alteration, however small, however unlikely. Knowledge of these assumptions enables us to understand otherwise incomprehensible reservations such as the need to reserve the right to execute pregnant women.

Finally, the case study corroborates a conclusion arrived at in previous chapters, that the early debates firmly established human rights as inherently suspect and controversial. Remembering that the Carter administration attachments were designed by those who supported the treaties, in order to make them more acceptable to those who did not, one can see the assumption of controversy and opposition that is the legacy of the 1950s.

SEVEN

Current Situation and Future Prospects

It was completely predictable, because President Carter is surrounded by one-worlders, . . . that he would quickly and quietly move to urge the Senate to ratify two dangerous UN Covenants. . . . Both sound innocuous on their face but they are the cutting edge of the efforts of our enemies to thrust world courts, the United Nations and other "outside forces" into our everyday life and restructure our constitutional system. . . . We need the Bricker Amendment now as never before. Patriotic groups must rally behind this cause. The preservation of American sovereignty, once never in doubt, once never questioned, is now imperiled. We must rally the American people to defeat these dangerous Carter-backed covenants which would move the U.N. one step closer to world domination.
—Representative John Ashbrook, *Congressional Record*, 1978

At the opening of every congressional session while he was in the House of Representatives, Representative John Ashbrook (R.-Ohio) introduced the Bricker Amendment, citing as his reason the dangers posed to the American system by the United Nations Covenants on Human Rights. He argued that these treaties would diminish basic rights, promote world government, involve us in foreign courts, threaten our form of government, enhance Communist influence, infringe on our domestic jurisdiction, and increase our international entanglements. Representative Ashbrook appeared to share Senator Bricker's vision of the destruction to be wrought upon the United States by the U.N. covenants. He also shared the senator's belief that a constitutional amendment was the ideal method of preventing this catastrophe.

Although active support of the Bricker Amendment as a means of addressing the threats posed by human rights treaties is clearly limited, the arguments against human rights treaties developed in the 1950s, which crystallized during the debate over the Bricker Amendment, continue to influence contemporary congressional deliberations. This chapter offers additional data in support of this view.[1] The data are drawn from two investigations undertaken to evaluate the ongoing impact of the 1950s legacy: first, the 1953 hearings on the Bricker Amendment were compared with roughly comparable contemporary hearings on four human rights treaties in 1979; second, congressional staff members were interviewed in an attempt to assess the importance of the Bricker legacy from their perspective. After considering these data, insights gained from the interviews with congressional staff and the typology of arguments used throughout the book are applied here to the final debates over the Genocide Convention in 1985 and 1986. The chapter concludes with a consideration of whether or not the acceptance of the Genocide Convention signals a change in Senate opposition to human rights treaties.

Stability of Arguments over Time

To further investigate the persistence of the 1950s arguments against human rights treaties, two sets of congressional hearings were selected for content analysis. As already noted in Chapter 4, the Bricker hearings in 1953 represent the best source of arguments against human rights treaties from the 1950s. For more contemporary arguments, the single best source is the record of hearings held in 1979, concerning four human rights treaties that were sent to the Senate by President Carter in 1978.

Carter had signed the American Convention on Human Rights on 1 June 1977 and the two U.N. covenants on 5 October 1977. He sent these three treaties and the Convention on the Elimination of All Forms of Racial Discrimination, signed on 22 September 1966, to the Senate on 23 February 1978. Carter had made human rights a leading issue in his presidential campaign and a major foreign policy consideration after his election. He appears to have been motivated by a personal moral commitment, a desire to distance himself from the political realism of the Nixon-Kissinger years, and a hope of restoring to the United States an international moral leadership he believed had been lost during the Vietnam War. He was also responding to (1) congressional leadership that had been endeavoring to add human rights considerations to U.S. foreign policy and (2) the generally high place accorded human rights on the agenda of international organizations.[2]

Content analysis of the 1979 hearings, which included testimony from members of Congress as well as other witnesses, was limited to the testimony of those witnesses who either supported the Bricker Amendment in the 1953 hearings or opposed any of the treaties discussed at the 1979 hearings. The content of the testimony of each of

Table 2. Analysis of Arguments Made against Human Rights Treaties
(Based on Senate Hearings in 1953 and 1979)

	1953		1979	
Argument	Percentage	Rank	Percentage	Rank
Diminish basic rights	21.4	1	32.7	1
Violate states' rights	16.8	2	23.4	2
Promote world government	13.6	3	6.5	4
Enhance Soviet/ Communist influence	11.2	4	4.7	8
Subject citizens to trial abroad	10.6	5	0.9	10
Threaten the U.S. form of government	7.8	6	11.2	3
Infringe on domestic jurisdiction	6.5	7	5.6	6
Increase international entanglements	5.1	8	0.9	10
Create self-executing obligations	4.9	9	2.8	9
Other	2.1	10	4.8	7
New arguments in 1979	—	—	6.5	4
Total	100.0		100.0	
	(*n* = 387)		(*n* = 107)	

the witnesses was analyzed according to the typology of arguments
presented in Chapter 4. The major lines of arguments, and minor
variations on those arguments, are presented in Appendix B. All
specific references to one or more human rights treaties were examined, and each new appearance of an argument was assigned to the
proper category.[3] Hearings were coded independently by two investi-
gators, and inconsistent codings were analyzed further. Results of the
analysis are presented in Table 2, which provides figures that indicate,

of the total number of arguments made in the hearings, the percentage of times each individual argument appeared.

The results shown in the table reveal the consistency of arguments made in opposition to human rights treaties, along with some interesting variations over time. Perhaps the clearest indication of consistency is that 93.5 percent of the arguments appearing in the 1979 hearings were essentially unchanged from 1953. In addition, the relative frequency of arguments did not change significantly. The two principal arguments in both periods—that the treaties would diminish basic rights and violate states' rights—held the same rankings and together accounted for a substantial proportion of the total arguments (38.2 percent in 1953 and 56.1 percent in 1979). The only arguments that declined dramatically in frequency were that the treaties would subject U.S. citizens to trial abroad and that they would increase international entanglements. The remaining arguments from 1953 were all evident in the 1979 hearings, with their relative frequencies not significantly altered.

The two arguments that appeared for the first time during the 1979 hearings reflected changes in the political and economic environment. The first new argument was a response to the increased number of uncompensated expropriations of U.S. assets abroad and the apparent effort by developing countries to legitimize them. This argument attacks the covenant provision on permanent sovereignty over natural resources. As seen in Chapter 6, the United States argued throughout the drafting of the treaties that the wording might be interpreted as allowing expropriation of foreign investment without prompt and adequate compensation. Senator Jesse Helms was especially incensed about this provision, which he argued "would for the first time legitimize the unlawful expropriation without compensation or arbitrary seizure of Americans' property overseas."[4]

The second new argument arose from domestic opposition to the women's movement, particularly the Equal Rights Amendment. Phyllis Schlafly was vehement in her contention that the treaties would deprive American women of important protections. For example, she argued that the Covenant on Civil and Political Rights would obligate the federal government to "register and conscript women for military service" whenever men were registered and conscripted. She also linked the destruction of women's rights to the loss of states' rights:

> This covenant would change the marriage laws of most of the fifty states by imposing "equality of rights" as between the spouses

during marriage. . . . The Covenant would also take away the rights of state legislatures in the fifty states to enact and retain the marriage laws desired by the people of each state and devised in a process of democratic decision-making.[5]

Factors Inhibiting Action

A second avenue for exploring contemporary arguments against human rights treaties is to assess the current opinions of members of the Senate Foreign Relations Committee. Interviews were conducted with the primary foreign policy staff members of ten of the sixteen committee members in the Ninety-eighth Congress. Respondents were guaranteed anonymity. All unattributed quotations in this section are from these interviews. Interviews ranged in duration from forty to ninety minutes and were conducted in January 1984.[6]

At the time of the interviews, congressional action on human rights treaties appeared to be extremely unlikely. While still formally pending before the Senate Foreign Relations Committee, the treaties were not on the congressional agenda. Supporters of the treaties did not appear to be planning any action to stimulate congressional consideration. They saw little political benefit to be gained in advocating the treaties and feared the potential political controversy should the latent opposition to the treaties once again became vocal. Supporters were convinced that "if they brought [the treaties] up, they would be filibustered, and there would be efforts to amend them."

One clear finding is that, whatever the influence of the Bricker Amendment, that influence does not often come from direct knowledge of the Bricker debate. Few of the staff members interviewed were even familiar with the specifics of the debate in the 1950s. Instead, the legacy lies in the near-universal perception that human rights treaties are inherently controversial. As one respondent expressed it, what is "important is the perception of a given treaty. . . . Everything gets categorized." Anything associated with human rights is viewed as "not immediate, apparently controversial, so we can push it aside." Another staff member indicated that "it was the Bricker Amendment controversy, and the incredible knock-down-drag-out fight that Eisenhower had in fighting that off, that I think formed a lot of the basic background."

What would it take to overcome this legacy? Respondents were

Table 3. Rankings of Factors Inhibiting Passage of Human Rights
Treaties (Based on Interviews with Senate Staff, 1984)

| | Staff Members | | |
Factor	Republican ($n = 7$)	Democratic ($n = 3$)	All ($n = 10$)
Support of administration	1.9[a]	2.0	1.9
Internal Senate politics	2.3	3.0	2.5
Public opinion	3.6	1.3	2.9
Content of treaties	3.3	4.7	3.7
Current international situation	4.0	4.0	4.0

[a] Figures are the average ranking given to this factor by each category of
staff.

asked to rank five factors according to their importance in explaining
the current situation of the human rights treaties. According to the
figures in Table 3, the most important factor was the position of the
president. Respondents, particularly Republican respondents, perceived that the lack of interest on the part of the Reagan administration was the most important factor in explaining why the Senate had
no plans to consider, much less approve, the treaties. Presidential
support was viewed as an essential ingredient for passage: "the administration has to be mobilized for the Congress to be mobilized";
"the President would have to be behind them"; "a strong presidency
to twist arms is the only way for [human rights] treaties to get
through."

Respondents often referred to the Carter administration, which did
sign three human rights treaties and formally supported their passage
in the Senate. The Carter administration's support of the human
rights treaties, however, eventually became secondary to the support
of other treaties: "the President only has so many cards to play, and
Carter was sidetracked by Panama Canal and SALT II." In any case, a
decision to take an active role in advocating human rights treaties is a
difficult one to make, in light of the perceived meager political benefits. Advocating the treaties would be "politically costly" without tangible rewards: "the essential element [inhibiting passage] is a lack of

political constituency. . . . People cannot see a direct link between the treaties and their overall interest."

Debate over the Genocide Convention in 1984, which occurred subsequent to the completion of the interviews, certainly supports this view of the role of the executive branch in promoting consideration of human rights treaties. President Reagan had been the first president since Truman, who signed the treaty, not to support ratification publicly.[7] His unexpected endorsement of the Genocide Convention during a campaign speech before B'nai Brith calculated to appeal to the Jewish community, which had consistently supported the treaty, resulted in almost immediate Senate consideration. Approval of the treaty by the Senate Foreign Relations Committee came a few weeks later, despite universal pessimism on the part of Senate staff earlier that year.

A second general conclusion supported by Table 3 is that the actual content of the treaties is not viewed as the primary determinant of the current situation. Perception is important, not content. In general, staff members had not read any of the treaties and were unfamiliar with their content and objectives. They were, on the other hand, very clear about the expected response of opponents within and beyond the Senate. Reactions to the treaties were based on the perceived controversy surrounding them, the absence of a large and powerful supporting constituency, and the lack of active presidential support— not on the provisions of the documents. Where there was great controversy and the prospect of little tangible return, proponents of the treaties generally preferred to remain inactive rather than commit scarce resources of time, favors, and energy.

The Genocide Convention: Once More with Feeling

The conclusions drawn from the staff interviews were borne out by the subsequent executive and legislative action on the Genocide Convention. In the euphoria following Senate approval of the Genocide Convention, it is important to remember that this far from radical treaty took forty years to win ratification by the United States. The Senate approved the treaty on 19 February 1986; the House passed the implementing legislation on 25 April 1988, and the Senate on 14 October of the same year. This legislation was officially designated the

Proxmire Act as a way of honoring William Proxmire (D.-Wis.), the retiring senator who had made daily speeches on the floor of the Senate in support of the treaty. The act was signed by the president on 4 November 1988, and the instrument of ratification was deposited with the United Nations on 25 November.[8] Hearings on the convention were held in 1950, 1970, 1971, 1977, 1981, 1984, and 1985. It was reported out of committee favorably in 1970, 1971, 1973, 1976, 1984, and 1985. Two cloture motions failed in 1974, and a unanimous consent request to add the treaty to the agenda in the last days of the session in 1985 failed due to an objection by Senator Jesse Helms.[9] The blocking was a repeat of events in 1984; at that time the blocked Senate proceeded to vote 87-2 to consider the treaty "expeditiously" in 1985.[10] The House also passed H.R. 166[11] expressing the sense of the House that the United States should ratify the Genocide Convention.

One important change affecting consideration of the Genocide Convention was the decision by the American Bar Association in 1976 to support U.S. ratification of the treaty. At the midyear meeting that year, the association's House of Delegates approved a resolution proposed by the Section on International and Comparative Law recommending ratification of the Genocide Convention with four attachments.[12] The organization had already approved the Supplementary Slavery Convention in 1967 (see Chapter 5). Subsequent ABA recommendations called for ratification, again with reservations, of the Convention on the Elimination of All Forms of Racial Discrimination (1976), the American Convention on Human Rights (1979), and the U.N.-sponsored Covenants on Human Rights (1979). ABA members were very active in support of ratification of the Genocide Convention and worked extensively with other supporting groups and with the Senate Judiciary and Foreign Relations committees in pursuit of ratification.[13]

Conservative groups responded vigorously to the prospect of ratification. Right-wing publications ran stories, such as one pointing out how terrorists and radicals would be protected by the treaty.[14] And when the convention was approved, eight debilitating attachments were necessary in order to make the treaty acceptable to the necessary two-thirds majority in the Senate. One of these provisos required the passage of implementing legislation *before* the instrument of ratification could be deposited. Until this legislation was adopted on 4 November 1988, the United States could not officially submit the instrument of ratification, which was done on 25 November. In crucial ways, the ratification tells us more about Senate consideration of human rights treaties than the previous reviews and nonacceptance.

A notable feature of the final debates on Senate approval of the Genocide Convention was the quality of déjà vu. Senator Christopher Dodd (D.-Conn.) observed during the 1986 floor debate,

> The arguments that are raised against the Genocide Convention . . . are not new. They were raised and answered 30 years ago. They have been reiterated and rebutted ever since. Reading the record on the issue is frustrating—it is like listening to a dialog in which at least one of the parties is deaf.[15]

Throughout the hearings in the 1980s, the 1970 statement of former senator Sam Ervin was read into the record, a statement in which the senator opposed the convention because it would diminish rights, violate states' rights, place the United States under international review, especially before the International Court of Justice, and subject Americans to trials abroad. The 1985 hearings also included the introduction of a letter from Ervin in which he repeated his long-standing opposition and urged continued rejection of the treaty for the same reasons he had outlined in 1970. In his 1970 statement, Ervin described the treaty in 1950s terms:

> During the 1940's activists connected with the United Nations engaged in a strenuous effort to establish by treaties laws to supersede domestic laws of nations throughout the earth. The Genocide Convention represents one of these efforts.[16]

He also explained the history of the Senate consideration of the treaty and the wisdom of the Senate Foreign Relations Committee in not recommending approval in its 1950 report:

> Since this report was made, the Senate Foreign Relations Committee and the Senate itself by inaction have refused to ratify this convention. . . . In contrast to this attitude represented by this inaction during the preceding 20 years, the Senate Foreign Relations Committee has apparently revived the question of ratification . . . notwithstanding the fact that there has been no change of circumstances which would make what was unwise in 1950 wise in 1970.[17]

Senator Helms consistently cited Ervin's opposition as the impetus for his own negative position. When ultimately voting against the treaty, he described his vote as a symbolic gesture in tribute to his former colleague from North Carolina.

> So with the voice of Sam Ervin still ringing in my ears, still plead-ing that Senators should vote against the Genocide Convention, I must say that . . . I yet cannot vote in favor of the resolution of ratification.[18]

The language of Helms in his discussion of ratification reveals the continued "crusade" mentality of the opposition and the ideological fervor that still surrounded the issue of human rights treaties. Even with the eight provisos that edited out any possible domestic or inter-national ramifications for the United States, a type of political repug-nance remained and kept the staunchest opposition torchbearers from voting in favor of ratification. During the 1980s the major arguments from the 1950s reappeared in different voices but with little other change.

Diminish Basic Rights

A long-standing argument against the treaty was the threat it alleg-edly posed to basic constitutionally defined rights. In particular, oppo-nents claimed that First Amendment rights were endangered by the treaty's "loose" definition of genocide so that even racial slurs and jokes might be construed as genocidal acts.[19] During the 1985 and 1986 hearings, loss of First Amendment rights was a major concern. For example, Trisha Katson, legislative director of Liberty Lobby, out-lined a long list of statements and publications that, she argued, could be illegal under the Genocide Convention definition of "mental harm," thus abridging American First Amendment protections.[20]

One Helms proviso[21] was designed to address the concern that ratification would diminish the rights of Americans. The commentary to this proviso (number 2) reasserts the supremacy of the Constitution with high praise for the superiority of the U.S. legal system. By this proviso, Helms asserted,

> we would put the international community on notice that we regard our system as a superior protection of human rights than any other system in the world.[22]

Specifically referring to the First Amendment, the commentary extolled the uniqueness of U.S. rights and insisted on the need to prevent the Genocide Convention from being used as a basis for "foreclosing Constitutional rights."[23]

Violate States' Rights

A second persistent threat that opponents felt the Genocide Convention posed was its effect on states' rights. In the 1950s this argument was developed as a defense of racial segregation and state jurisdiction over acts of racial violence. Fears were expressed that the federal government would, through the Genocide Convention, legitimize intervention in race riots, lynchings, and other violence against blacks. Sam Ervin expressed the legal basis for these fears in his 1970 statement. At that time he said that "the provisions of the Genocide Convention would immediately supersede all State laws, and practices inconsistent with them."[24] During questioning, he indicated his belief that the United States Supreme Court would interpret the treaty as the law of the land and as self-executing:

> Of course, this is in a field that involves racial questions just like the genocide treaty involves racial questions. If the Court can envision such an ordinance dealing with racial questions, that it can uphold, then the Court can certainly uphold similar legislation enacted by Congress under treaty, or the treaty itself, which is the supreme law of the land.[25]

In his new 1985 statement Ervin did not discuss race, but he continued to express a grave fear that power would be lost from the states and transferred to the federal government.

> If the Senate should ratify the Genocide Treaty, the duty and the power to prosecute and punish criminal homicide, assaults and batteries, and kidnappings . . . would be initially transferred from the states which have always had such duty and power in respect to such crimes to the federal government.[26]

Phyllis Schlafly, speaking for Eagle Forum, although not directly addressing the states' rights issue, evoked the 1950s fear of such use of the Genocide Convention in noting accusations that would be valid, in her opinion, if made against the United States under the treaty: "Individual American citizens are accused of genocide because of actions involving discrimination against minority groups, school busing, or

State legislative action limiting welfare benefits."[27] Schlafly also reiterated her version of the Ervin argument in criticizing Article 5 of the treaty: "This would transfer a large area of criminal law from the States to the Federal Government and cause widespread confusion."[28]

Although the states' rights argument was less frequently cited at the 1985 and 1986 discussions, it continued to be important and was fully presented through the Helms-Ervin testimony and statements. The commentary to the third Helms proviso also suggests this line of thinking in criticizing Article 2, when it complains, "It could be interpreted to mean a psychological or social disorientation of a more general sort, as referred to in the U.S. Supreme Court's decision in *Brown v. Board of Education*."[29]

Promote World Government

The Genocide Convention, as the first postwar human rights treaty, appeared to anti-internationalists as a major step toward the subjection of the United States to world government. A clear example of the extreme form of this position was seen in testimony during the 1985 hearings. Iris Shidler of the American Independent Party chastised the senators in her statement.

> Some of you forgot your patriotism and your purpose when you signed the Declaration of Interdependence at Independence Hall in 1976, relinquishing the sovereignty of the United States to a one-world government.
>
> For 36 years the patriots of this Nation held opposition to the Genocide Convention, and for 36 years and more one-worlders have been diligently at the task of ratifying the Genocide Convention.[30]

Trisha Katson expressed similar concerns:

> As we believe that the internationist [*sic*] forces working together fully intend to set up machinery someday to institute real international law with machinery to enable the World Court to enforce its rulings, as part of an eventual "global government," we, quite frankly, view any senators—who are sworn to obey their oath to uphold the United States Constitution—who vote for the GC, and it is ratified, of being guilty of sedition.[31]

Senator Helms's 1986 condemnation of the treaty, while not going this far, does echo the 1950s accusation that an international legal agreement like the Genocide Convention was designed to erode U.S. sovereignty and supplant U.S. jurisdiction with that of an international body, in this case the World Court.

> My chief objective with regard to the Genocide Convention has been to see that the independent sovereignty of the United States is protected from interference by an international regime of law. . . . We all know that even with these protections [the provisos], ratification of the convention means that we submit in an entirely new way to a regime of international law. We enter into a direct relationship with a system that is hostile to our national interests, and even to our sovereignty.[32]

In fact, Helms called his set of provisos the "sovereignty package," a label used by other concurring senators during the floor debate. Senator Orrin Hatch (R.-Utah) argued that acceptance of the reservations would ensure that "the convention will never again pose a threat to U.S. sovereignty and American liberties."[33] He went on to plead for ratification with the sovereignty package, because if the treaty resolution were defeated the treaty would "inevitably . . . rise again" and perhaps be ratified without the reservations he believed were essential to protect U.S. sovereignty.[34]

Specifically, the anti–world government argument took the form of attacks on the International Court of Justice, and the notion of its supremacy, as a threat to the sovereignty of the United States. Ervin had elaborated how this supremacy would be imposed under the Genocide Convention:

> The World Court would have plenary power to overrule or modify any ruling of the Supreme Court of the United States, or of any federal court, or of any state court interpreting the Convention; to nullify or alter any decision of the President, or any Governor, or any federal or state executive officer applying the provision[s] of the Convention; to nullify any act of Congress or any state legislature. . . . How can any Senator who entertains an intelligent love for his country vote to ratify an instrument which thus subordinates the United States and the fifty states to the World Court?[35]

Fears were particularly aroused by dissatisfaction with the decision of the International Court of Justice in the Nicaragua case, in which the

United States contended that the court did not have jurisdiction. The court heard the case and declared that the United States had violated Nicaraguan sovereignty, ordering the United States to pay reparations to Nicaragua. Phyllis Schlafly claimed,

> The Genocide Convention will put our national head in the noose of the World Court, which recently demonstrated its lack of respect for the law by grabbing jurisdiction over a case it had no legal right to take, and then ruling 15-1 against the United States.[36]

And Senator Helms was similarly concerned.

> The World Court confounded its U.S. supporters by doing exactly what Senator Ervin and many of his colleagues had always predicted they would—namely, that the World Court would exceed its mandate, and attempt to involve the United States in matters clearly outside the jurisdiction of the World Court.[37]

In thus citing the danger of the World Court, Helms was expressing the fears of many of his colleagues and also of many in the State Department and the Reagan administration, which had previously opposed a reservation to the court's jurisdiction.[38] The Helms proviso required U.S. consent before any dispute under the convention could be referred to the International Court of Justice. In explaining this reservation, the Helms commentary asserts,

> In the light of the recent decision of the International Court of Justice claiming jurisdiction over the Nicaraguan case in the absence of factual basis in customary international law, this condition is necessary to protect the national security of the United States.[39]

Enhance Soviet/Communist Influence

The 1950s opposition to the Genocide Convention often argued that the Soviet Union and its supporters at home and abroad designed and advocated the treaty in order to advance Soviet and Communist influence. The Soviets, it was claimed, achieved this objective through extensions of the authority of the United Nations, which they controlled. This line of thinking is reflected in the statement by A. Clifford Barker, chair of the John Birch Society, that appeared in the records of the 1985 hearings. It was his belief that "Senate approval of this [genocide] treaty would subordinate U.S. law to an international order under the Communist and Marxist-dominated United Nations."[40]

This belief is also professed in the testimony of Howard Phillips of the Conservative Caucus:

> Would any Senator wish to place himself at the mercy of the U.N. General Assembly, where the votes of the Soviet puppet regimes in Bulgaria, East Germany, or even Communist-dominated Afghanistan would carry the same weight and power and would indeed cancel out the vote of the 240 million people of the United States of America?
>
> There is absolutely no sound argument for making American citizens subject in any way to the World Court, the United Nations, or to any other international body heavily influenced and sometimes dominated by personnel from Communist dictatorships.[41]

Iris Shidler concurred. Worrying, as Frank Holman had thirty years earlier, that secret conspiracies were being launched, she believed that the American people were "unaware that the Constitution is being systematically amended into socialism."[42] The Genocide Convention was central to this plot.

> In 1948, the architects of the Genocide Convention designed it to supersede the Constitution of the United States and bring the people of this Nation under the rule of one-world government dominated by the Communist countries at the United Nations.[43]

During the 1986 floor debate, Senator Malcolm Wallop (R.-Wyo.) argued that the convention was designed as a political instrument for propaganda purposes. It would be used by the Soviet Union to "mock us before the World Court."[44] He labeled the convention "evil"[45] and claimed it would subject the United States to the United Nations, "which is run by the Soviet Union and its client states."[46]

Subject Citizens to Trial Abroad

A frequent argument against the Genocide Convention since the 1950s is that it would subject U.S. citizens to trials before foreign domestic and international tribunals. Senator Ervin, urging rejection of the treaty in 1985, spelled out one common form of this argument.

> How can any intelligent Senator who loves our country vote to
> ratify a Convention which sanctions the trial and punishment in
> the court of a foreign foe or in an internal [sic; international] penal
> tribunal of an American soldier whose only offense is that he
> killed or wounded an enemy of the United States while fighting
> for his country in a land beyond the seas.[47]

The same fear was expressed by Senator Steven Symms (R.-Idaho)
during the floor debate.

> [Article 1] envisions the possibility that American soldiers fight-
> ing in a foreign country could be tried for genocide under the
> Convention by the government of that country.[48]

Howard Phillips has argued that similar problems would be faced by
Americans outside the military.

> Would any Member of the Senate prefer to be subject to Byelorus-
> sian justice, Ugandan justice, Iranian justice, Vietnamese justice
> or even British justice, rather than American justice? If the answer
> is no, how then can they vote to place their constituents so at
> risk?[49]

Senator Strom Thurmond (R.-S.C.), during the floor debate, repeated
his continuing criticism of the treaty, based on this exact issue:

> I have always opposed provisions in the treaty which would
> allow U.S. citizens to be extradited, tried in the country where the
> so called act of genocide was committed, and punished under the
> laws of that country.[50]

Opponents who objected to U.S. acceptance of the jurisdiction of
the World Court often also objected to the proposed international
penal tribunal. This judicial body, envisioned in the treaty, has not yet
been established, and U.S. participation in its realization would require acceptance of another international agreement.[51] For Phyllis
Schlafly this issue was paramount.

> I think the big issue is, could Americans be called up before some
> international penal tribunal where, of course, we would not have
> any of those [Bill of Rights] guarantees. . . . No other country in
> the world would give us those rights, certainly no international
> tribunal.[52]

The Helms proviso is the same as the understanding proposed by the Foreign Relations Committee in 1976 and reaffirmed in 1984. It would allow the United States "to bring to trial before its own tribunals any of its nationals for acts committed outside [the] state."[53]

Threaten the U.S. Form of Government

At times, to hear opponents tell it, the entire republic of the United States appeared to be in danger from the Genocide Convention. In addition to internationalists and Communists specifically, sources not explicitly identified would put in motion evolutionary or revolutionary changes as a result of ratification. Senator Ervin, for example, in both 1970 and 1985 talked of "fundamental alteration" in the way the criminal justice system "has been administered since our country came into existence as a Free Republic."[54] And Howard Phillips saw the nation's entire governmental system at risk with ratification of the Genocide Convention:

> America's system of checks and balances, separation of powers and federalism have made us the freest people in the history of the world. Why place these at risk?[55]

Trisha Katson spoke of the "erosion of our constitutional form of government."[56]

Sometimes the object threatened is not only the U.S. legal system but also the traditional values of the country's majority. Phillips suggested as much in arguing that one cannot trust the decisions and interpretations of an international body or the promises of U.S. senators:

> Those promises will be a flimsy guarantee of American liberties in the future. It is really a question of by which law system do we wish to be governed? Do we wish to be governed in accordance with the Judeo-Christian system of American liberty?[57]

Infringe on Domestic Jurisdiction

Senator Ervin enunciated this argument in his 1970 statement:

> The Genocide Convention goes a bow shot beyond the charter of the United Nations; it undertakes to regulate certain domestic affairs of the parties to it by converting what have always been domestic crimes into international crimes.[58]

And Trisha Katson also stated her belief that the treaty invades U.S. domestic jurisdiction because it would require specific implementing legislation. She cites the work of Robert Friedlander, who testified against the treaty: "He has researched the intent of our Founding Fathers and found that they never wanted treaties to dictate domestic legislation."[59]

Increase International Entanglements

During the decade following World War II there were many who felt that the United States should refrain from actions involving the country in affairs that might lead to another war. Many believed that the country would return to a position of self-sufficiency and independence. To them, any form of international agreement was a possible source of involvement in unjustifiable activity beyond our borders. Senator Helms explained the 1980s version of this reluctance when linking the convention to the United Nations.

> At this point in history, we should be seeking to disentangle the United States from this enemy of democracy and freedom. . . . I think that the United States should be moving away from entangling alliances, not moving toward more.[60]

Trisha Katson took a similar stance, decrying the series of alliances that the United States shaped after World War II, which have led to the stationing of American troops all over the world.

> The GC epitomizes the dangerous position our public servants have now placed America in. We would be far better off if we were to begin to disengage ourselves from some of these international entanglements and executive agreements [and] start concentrating on our own national interests.[61]

Create Self-Executing Obligations

As seen above, 1980s opponents of the treaty, like those of the 1950s, could catalog nefarious uses to which the convention might be put. These uses would be made easier and more immediately disturbing if the treaty were to be considered self-executing. Most of the opponents felt that at least some of the treaty provisions were self-executing and therefore would be binding upon ratification as the supreme law of the land, superseding prior legislation and available to be cited in the courts; Senator Ervin, in his 1970 statement, cited Orie Phillips to this effect.[62] A. Clifford Barker was also angered by this dimension of the treaty.

> Should the Senate ratify this Convention, its self-executing provisions would immediately supersede all state laws inconsistent with them. Also, those self-executing provisions would supersede all federal law, and prior treaty law which might also be inconsistent with them.[63]

The final Helms proviso was especially designed to deal with this perceived defect. It requires that implementing legislation be passed before the instrument of ratification may be submitted. Senator Hatch stressed the reason why this proviso was necessary:

> It . . . means that the Genocide Convention is not to be self-executing. That is a significant qualification, since the language of the Convention, despite State Department denials to the contrary, appears to create several self-executing articles. . . . It forestall[s] a later claim by the executive branch that certain provisions of the convention are self-executing in nature.[64]

Conclusion

Contemporary consideration of human rights treaties reveals the tremendous legacy of the 1950s. First, the treaties have effectively been excluded from the agenda of the United States Senate. Getting a human rights treaty on the agenda is considered by Senate staff to be a political risk, and it is not easily achieved. Interviews with staff members indicate that senators fear attacks from the opposition and assume that these attacks will succeed in preventing action by the Senate. The 1950s fears that led to the original attacks on human rights treaties are now echoed in the minds of 1980s senators and their staffs—fears not engendered by the substance of the treaties but rather by the cloud of controversy placed over them by the 1950s opposition.

The Reagan administration's sudden decision to support the Genocide Convention on the eve of the 1984 election admirably validates the views of Senate staff. The attitude within the Senate prior to this announcement was that there was no chance of Senate consideration of the Genocide Convention. After the announcement, the Senate began the procedures that two years later ended with the passage of a resolution of ratification.

Careful review of the arguments presented during the final consideration of the Genocide Convention clearly reveals the legacy of the 1950s. The typology of arguments used throughout this book retains its utility in analyzing the last Senate debates over the Genocide Convention. These debates corroborate for the 1980s the conclusion drawn from content analysis of hearings in the 1950s and 1970s: that the arguments against human rights treaties developed in the early 1950s have survived the decades with little modification.

The evidence and analysis presented in this study have shown that opposition to human rights treaties in the United States Senate arose with the first consideration of such treaties and has continued to exercise a residual effect on contemporary consideration of the treaties as well. During the 1950s, internal and external forces coalesced to create an environment unfavorable for consideration of human rights treaties. Even an instrument as widely supported and symbolically appealing as the Genocide Convention was successfully attacked and discredited. In the forefront of this attack was a special committee of the American Bar Association.

Led by former ABA president Frank Holman, the Special Committee on Peace and Law Through United Nations organized an education campaign that presented the Genocide Convention and other human rights treaties as destructive of the American system. They focused on fears of fundamental change: diminution of states' rights through dismantling of the structures of segregation and discrimination, loss of U.S. sovereignty through gains by world government proponents, and enhanced Communist influence and control through the spread of socialist ideas and programs at home and abroad. Opposition to the Genocide Convention was expanded to include all human rights treaties. "Government by treaty" became a code phrase used by treaty opponents to insinuate the existence of a United Nations campaign, inspired by world government proponents and the

Soviet Union, aimed at fundamentally altering the U.S. domestic system.

Although the Genocide Convention was the initial treaty to be considered, the Human Rights Covenants framed by the United Nations proved to be the bane of the opposition forces. These two treaties recognized a host of general human rights obligations. The United States was active in pressing the need for and in actually formulating these treaties, and U.S. representatives were very successful during the drafting process in deflecting the challenge posed by numerous Soviet recommendations and amendments. Ultimately, the United States secured two favorably designed treaties. One codified civil and political rights in traditional Western form and established immediately binding obligations for their implementation. The other codified economic and social rights, stressing the language of "progressive achievement." In spite of this success, the covenants were perceived by some opponents as so dangerous that only an amendment to the Constitution would restore security to the American system.

Under the guidance of Senator John Bricker, a strategy for this amendment evolved, eventually attracting a very large following— falling only one vote short, in fact, of the two-thirds majority necessary to pass the first stage of the amending process. During the debate within and beyond the United States Senate, the rudimentary arguments against the Genocide Convention and the covenants were extended and refined; the effort to pass the Bricker Amendment saw arguments against human rights treaties elaborated in their fullest form and given national attention. Because of the strong historical support of the United States for human rights treaties, and the leading role this country played in drafting them, many had assumed that the question before the Senate would be, Why not ratify the treaties? The hearings on the Bricker Amendment effectively turned that question around. Proponents of the treaties were put on the defensive, having to respond to a host of legal and political criticisms. By the end of the hearings, these arguments and the aura of controversy surrounding them had crystallized into a set of objections that, judging from analysis of the stability of arguments over time, appeared essentially unchanged in 1979 Senate hearings and were still being presented in the 1986 debate on the Genocide Convention.

The Eisenhower administration promised to refrain from signing or ratifying human rights treaties in an effort to satisfy and deflate the Bricker Amendment movement, but the promise ended when the administration left office. The Kennedy administration forwarded three human rights treaties to the Senate, including one that the Eisenhower administration had specifically named in its rejection of human rights treaties. Over the next sixteen years the Senate discussed and finally passed two of these treaties. Both were discussed not as human rights treaties but as specific, narrowly defined agreements that would have no effect on U.S. domestic law. Both were passed in connection with the celebration of specific U.N. commemorative years as symbolic gestures of U.S. participation. Neither caught the attention of vocal opposition interest groups, like the ABA, and neither was actively opposed by conservatives in the Senate. Even though these treaties contain provisions that, in other treaties, allegedly raise serious "legal" questions, these two treaties were adopted without reservations.

Reservations have been a key component of human rights treaties from the earliest consideration of the Genocide Convention. Taking the superiority of U.S. domestic human rights law as the starting point, reservations and other attachments became the strategy for resisting change by adapting international agreements to U.S. law. Any provision that might be interpreted as requiring a change in U.S. law would be neutralized by a U.S. addendum. One excellent case of this strategy in action is the set of attachments to the Human Rights Covenants suggested by the Carter administration. Other than one reservation conflicting with constitutional protection of free speech, the package of attachments makes a mockery of the international human rights consensus reflected in these treaties. Jesse Helms's provisos adopted with Senate passage of the Genocide Convention reflect a similar unwillingness to join the international human rights community on truly international terms. The use of a legal framework to constrain the discussion of political issues masks the nature of the opposition to human rights treaties and results in legal prescriptions that undermine the best instrument the United States has available for the peaceful forging of an international consensus reflective of many of its own values.

What is the significance of continued nonratification of human rights treaties by the United States? In part, the significance is clearly symbolic. The United States has prided itself on leadership in human rights, and refusal to ratify international definitions of these rights gives the appearance of either ethnocentrism or indifference. U.S. criticism of other governments for alleged violations of human rights is undermined by nonratification of human rights treaties. The United States has put itself in the position of implying either that the violating government is bound by U.S. standards or that the government is bound by an international standard applicable to foreign governments but not to the United States.

Beyond symbolism, there is also substantive significance to the United States' refusal to ratify, or to accept without debilitating reservations, these treaties to which so many other nations have subscribed. The United States, as one of the most powerful states in the present international system, undermines the international human rights movement by failing to become a party to these treaties. U.S. ratification would signal support for international human rights specifically and international law generally. As a status quo power, the United States has much to gain from fostering the maintenance of international law and reinforcing the Western civil and political rights tradition that is codified in most human rights treaties.

By not becoming a party to these treaties, the United States is also prevented from participation in the human rights bodies established by the treaties. These bodies, in addition to monitoring the human rights practices of states, engage in an ongoing interpretation of the meaning and implications of the treaties' terms. The United States is missing an important opportunity to foster its own concepts of human rights and human rights law and to contribute its expertise to the developing debate on international human rights theory and practice.

Finally, failure to ratify these treaties vitiates an important perspective and standard for the reexamination of our own human rights law and practice. Treaties become a part of the law of the land and are available to be cited in public debate as well as in the courts. One of the chief purposes of human rights law is to provide a guideline for behavior and a critique of governmental practice. Human rights treaties could be an important source for domestic human rights groups along the full range of the political spectrum in their efforts to advance the implementation of human rights within the United States. This particular use of the treaties would be most fruitful if the treaties were to be accepted without unnecessary reservations or understandings and as self-executing whenever possible. Ratification of the treaties in this manner would enhance the ability of domestic groups to cite the treaties' provisions in examining U.S. law and practice.

Old shibboleths persist in the corridors of the United States Senate. The arguments of the 1950s fostered the perception that human rights treaties were controversial and potentially dangerous. And, as fears once raised are not easily laid to rest, these long-standing arguments have not been readily overcome. The recent experience of the ABA provides a good case in point. Although very successful throughout the 1950s in dramatizing what it perceived to be the dangers of the treaties, the ABA in the mid-1970s reversed its position on all of the human rights treaties covered in this study and recommended Senate approval with reservations. Yet the treaties still have not received sustained Senate attention. The ABA has, in fact, been engaged in a very active campaign in support of the treaties, working diligently to persuade the Senate that the treaties should be ratified. The task has been, and will continue to be, extremely difficult. The resistance to change within the Senate is a further legacy of the negative campaign of the ABA's Committee on Peace and Law, which provided the underpinning for decades of opposition.

Arguments against human rights treaties endure today despite deep and widespread changes in U.S. domestic law on human rights and the ascendancy of human rights in regional and international forums. Continued U.S. inaction on human rights treaties confuses most of our citizens (when they learn of it) and many of our allies. Yet ratification remains unlikely. The personal campaign of Senator Bricker to "bury" human rights treaties continued as late as 1971, when he wrote to the Senate Foreign Relations Committee during its hearings on the Genocide Convention: "I do not want to live to see the day that the Constitution of the United States and the Bill of Rights becomes a mere scrap of paper, and this treaty, if ratified, would be the beginning of such a process."[1] The legacy of the opposition from the 1950s and the movement for the Bricker Amendment is continued opposition to human rights treaties, continued neglect of them by the United States Senate, and continued evidence of the success of Senator Bricker's burial tactics.

Major Versions of the Bricker Amendment (Operative Paragraphs)

S.J. 130, February 1952[1]

Section 1. No treaty or executive agreement shall be made respecting the rights of citizens of the United States protected by this Constitution, or abridging or prohibiting the free exercise thereof.

Section 2. No treaty or executive agreement shall vest in any international organization or in any foreign power any of the legislative, executive, or judicial powers vested by this Constitution in the Congress, the President, and in the courts of the United States, respectively.

Section 3. No treaty or executive agreement shall alter or abridge the laws of the United States or the Constitution or laws of the several States unless, and then only to the extent that, Congress shall so provide by act or joint resolution.

Section 4. Executive agreements shall not be made in lieu of treaties.

Executive agreements shall, if not sooner terminated, expire automatically 1 year after the end of the term of office for which the President making the agreement shall have been elected, but the Congress may, at the request of any President, extend for the duration of the term of such President the life of any such agreement made or extended during the next preceding presidential term.

The President shall publish all executive agreements except that those which in his judgment require secrecy shall be submitted to appropriate committees of the Congress in lieu of publication.

S.J. 1, January 1953[2]

Section 1. A provision of a treaty which denies or abridges any right enumerated in this Constitution shall not be of any force or effect.

Section 2. No treaty shall authorize or permit any foreign power or any international organization to supervise, control, or adjudicate rights of citizens of the United States within the United States enumerated in this Constitution or any other matter essentially within the domestic jurisdiction of the United States.

Section 3. A treaty shall become effective as internal law in the United States only through the enactment of appropriate legislation by the Congress.

Section 4. All executive or other agreements between the President and any international organization, foreign power, or official thereof, shall be made only in the manner and to the extent to be prescribed by law. Such agreements shall be subject to the limitations imposed on treaties, or the making of treaties by this article.

S.J. 43, February 1953[3]

Section 1. A provision of a treaty which conflicts with any provision of this Constitution shall not be of any force or effect. A treaty shall become effective as internal law in the United States only through legislation which would be valid in the absence of treaty. Executive agreements shall be subject to regulation by the Congress and to the limitations imposed on treaties by this article.

Judiciary Committee Version, June 1953[4]

Section 1. A provision of a treaty which conflicts with this Constitution shall not be of any force or effect.

Section 2. A treaty shall become effective as internal law in the United States only through legislation which would be valid in the absence of treaty.

Section 3. Congress shall have power to regulate all executive and other agreements with any foreign power or international organization. All such agreements shall by subject to the limitation imposed on treaties by this article.

Knowland Version, February 1954[5]

A provision of a treaty or other international agreement which conflicts with this Constitution shall not be of any force or effect.

Clause 2 of Article VI of the Constitution of the United States is hereby amended by adding at the end thereof the following: "Notwithstanding the foregoing provisions of this clause, no treaty made after the establishment of this Constitution shall be the supreme law of the land unless made in pursuance of this Constitution."

George Substitute Amendment, February 1954[6]

A provision of a treaty or other international agreement which conflicts with this Constitution shall not be of any force or effect.

An international agreement other than a treaty shall become effective as internal law in the United States only by an act of the Congress.

Typology of Arguments against U.S. Ratification of Human Rights Treaties

1. *Diminish basic rights.* Human rights treaties reflect a lower standard than is currently guaranteed; they will take away U.S. rights and protections.

    1a. Endanger the Bill of Rights.

    1b. Constitute an attack on the concept of inalienable rights.

    1c. Deprive U.S. citizens of freedom of assembly.

    1d. Deprive U.S. citizens of freedom of religion.

    1e. Deprive U.S. citizens of freedom of the press.

    1f. Deprive U.S. citizens of freedom of speech.

    1g. Deprive U.S. citizens of the right of private property.

    1h. Deprive U.S. citizens of the right to private medical care and to operate private medical practice.

2. *Violate states' rights.* Human rights treaties violate constitutional protection of states' rights. They will give the federal government powers meant to be retained by the states.

    2a. Land ownership by aliens may be allowed.

    2b. Professional medical and bar practice by aliens may be allowed.

    2c. There is no federal-state provision in the treaties.

    2d. Racial matters.

    2e. Other states' rights.

3. *Promote world government.* Human rights treaties are being used to move toward world government.

    3a. Open us up to criticism in international forums.

    3b. Require us to impose international standards, which would constitute an erosion of sovereignty.

    3c. Subordinate us to foreign powers.

4. *Enhance Soviet/Communist influence.* Human rights treaties foster communism, soviet policies, and socialist rights.

    4a. Human rights treaties are a part of the Communist effort to take over the world.

4b. Specific mention of the Soviet Union.

4c. Contain socialist rights, including economic, social, and cultural rights.

4d. Obligate governments to provide private sector services as public sector rights (food, shelter, clothing).

4e. Challenge the free enterprise system (right to strike, form trade unions).

4f. Anti-ILO.

5. *Subject citizens to trial abroad.*

    5a. Deprive U.S. citizens of right to trial by jury.

    5b. Anti–international criminal court.

6. *Threaten the U.S. form of government.* Human rights treaties will erode fundamental governmental powers.

    6a. The Founding Fathers would not approve.

    6b. Increase power of the president at the expense of Congress.

    6c. Result in loss of control over immigration.

    6d. Give the president new power to seize property.

7. *Infringe on domestic jurisdiction.* Human rights treaties contain subjects that infringe on domestic matters.

8. *Increase international entanglements:* Human rights treaties are a creation of the United Nations, which is a suspect organization, and will draw us into matters that should not concern us.

    8a. Anti-United Nations.

    8b. Neo-isolationist.

9. *Create self-executing obligations.* Treaties are self-executing.

    9a. There is no non-self-executing provision in the treaties.

    9b. Other states can ratify without the treaties becoming domestic law; the United States cannot.

10. *Other.*

    10a. Human rights treaties will undermine the ability of the United Nations to do its major job of security.

    10b. Human rights treaties contain only the rights we already have and provide no additional protections for U.S. citizens.

    10c. Experts say that human rights treaties should not be ratified.

11. *New arguments in 1979.*

    11a. Legitimate expropriation of U.S. property abroad.

    11b. Diminish the rights of U.S. women.

Attachments Proposed by the Senate Foreign Relations Committee for the Genocide Convention, 1950 and 1971

1950[1]

Understandings

1. The United States understands and construes that article IX shall be understood in the traditional sense of responsibility to another state for injuries sustained by nationals of the complaining state in violation of principles of international law and shall not be understood as meaning that a state can [be] held liable in damages for injuries inflicted by its own nationals.

2. The United States government understands and construes the crime of genocide, which it undertakes to punish in accordance with this convention, to mean the commission of any of the acts enumerated in article II of the convention with the intent to destroy an entire national, ethnical, racial or religious group within the territory of the United States in such a manner as to affect a substantial portion of the group concerned:

> That the United States Government understands and construes the words "mental harm" appearing in article II of this convention to mean permanent physical injury to mental faculties.

3. The United States Government understands and construes the words "complicity in genocide" appearing in article II of this convention to mean participation before and after the fact and aiding and abetting in the commission of the crime of genocide.

Declaration

In giving its advice and consent to the ratification of the Convention on the Prevention and Punishment of the Crime of Genocide, the

Senate of the United States of America does so considering this to be an exercise of the authority of the Federal Government to define and punish offenses against the law of nations, expressly conferred by article I section 8 clause 10 of the United States Constitution, and, consequently, the traditional jurisdiction of the several States of the Union with regard to crime is in no way abridged.

1971[2]

Understandings

1. That the United States Government understands and construes the words "intent to destroy, in whole or in part, a national, ethnical, racial or religious group, as such" appearing in article II to mean the intent to destroy a national, ethnical, racial, or religious group by the acts specified in article II in such manner as to affect a substantial part of groups concerned.

2. That the United States Government understands and construes the words "mental harm" appearing in article II(b) of this convention to mean permanent impairment of mental faculties.

3. That the United States Government understands and construes article VI of the convention in accordance with the agreed language of the report of the Legal Committee of the United Nations General Assembly that nothing in article VI shall affect the right of any state to bring to trial before its own tribunals any of its nationals for acts committed outside the state.

Declaration

1. That the United States Government declares that it will not deposit its instrument of ratification until after the implementing legislation referred to in article V has been enacted.

ABA Proposed Reservations to the Genocide Convention[1]

Be It Resolved, that the American Bar Association favors the accession of the United States to the United Nations Convention on the Prevention and Punishment of the Crime of Genocide with the following Understandings and Declaration which have been approved by the Senate Committee on Foreign Relations:

1. That the U.S. Government understands and construes the words "intent to destroy, in whole or in part, a national, ethnical, racial or religious group as such" appearing in article II to mean the intent to destroy a national, ethnical, racial or religious group by the acts specified in article II in such manner as to affect a substantial part of the group concerned.

2. That the U.S. Government understands and construes the words "mental harm" appearing in article II(b) of this Convention to mean permanent impairment of mental faculties.

3. That the U.S. Government understands and construes article VI of the Convention in accordance with the agreed language of the Report of the Legal Committee of the United Nations General Assembly that nothing in article VI shall affect the right of any state to bring to trial before its own tribunals any of its nationals for acts committed outside the state.

4. That the U.S. Government declares that it will not deposit its instrument of ratification until after the implementing legislation referred to in article V has been enacted.

Lugar-Helms Provisos, 1985[1]

The Senate's advice and consent is subject to the following reservations:

1. That with reference to Article IX of the Convention, before any dispute to which the United States is a party may be submitted to the jurisdiction of the International Court of Justice under this article, the specific consent of the United States is required in each case.

2. That nothing in the Convention requires or authorizes legislation or other action by the United States of America prohibited by the Constitution of the United States as interpreted by the United States.

The Senate's advice and consent is subject to the following understandings, which shall apply to the obligations of the United States under this Convention:

1. That the term "intent to destroy, in whole or in part, a national, ethical [sic], racial, or religious group as such" appearing in Article II means the specific intent to destroy, in whole or in substantial part, a national, ethnical, racial, or religious group as such by the acts specified in Article II.

2. That the term "mental harm" in Article II(b) means permanent impairment of mental faculties through drugs, torture, or similar techniques.

3. That the pledge to grant extradition in accordance with a state's laws and treaties in force found in Article VII extends only to acts which are criminal under the laws of both the requesting and the requested state and nothing in Article VI affects the rights of any state to bring to trial before its own tribunals any of its nationals for acts committed outside a state.

4. That acts in the course of armed conflicts committed without the specific intent required by Article II are not sufficient to constitute genocide as defined by this Convention.

5. That with regard to the reference to an international penal tribunal in Article VI of the Convention, the United States declares that it reserves the right to effect its participation in any such tribunal by a treaty entered into specifically for that purpose with the advice and consent of the Senate.

The Senate's advice and consent is subject to the following declaration:

That the President will not deposit the instrument of ratification until after the implementing legislation referred to in Article V has been enacted.

NOTES

Abbreviations

ABAJ	*American Bar Association Journal*
RABA	*Reports of the American Bar Association*
U.N.Doc.	United Nations Document
U.N.Eco.Soc.	United Nations Economic and Social Council
U.N.G.A.	United Nations General Assembly

Chapter One

1. President's Committee on Civil Rights, *To Secure These Rights*, pp. 20–47.

2. Official Truman administration statement, as quoted in Berman, *Politics of Civil Rights*, p. 232. For an authoritative discussion of the use of international human rights norms in U.S. civil rights litigation see Lockwood, "The United Nations Charter and Civil Rights Litigation."

3. Freeland, *Truman Doctrine*, p. 9.

4. Ibid., p. 11.

5. Robert Griffith, "American Politics and the Origins of McCarthyism," p. 10.

6. Buckley, "The Party and the Deep Blue Sea," pp. 392–93.

7. Ibid.

8. Lora, "A View from the Right," p. 69.

9. Harry Truman, *Public Papers of the Presidents: Harry S. Truman, 1948*, p. 122, as quoted in Berman, *Politics of Civil Rights*, p. 5.

10. Cushman, "Our Civil Rights," p. 12.

11. "Senate Group," *Christian Century*, 20 September 1950, p. 1091.

12. Mathews, "Civil Liberties Upside Down," pp. 38–43.

13. Holman, *Life and Career*, p. 384.

14. Ibid., p. 383.

15. *National Cyclopaedia*, vol. H, pp. 58–59.

16. Holman, "Treaty Law-Making: A Blank Check," p. 788.

17. Holman, *1956*, p. 4.

18. Ibid., pp. 7–8.

19. Holman, "Greatest Threat," p. 984.

20. Ibid., p. 985.

21. Holman, "Comments on Mr. Moskowitz's Reply," p. 290.

22. Holman, "Treaty Law-Making: A Blank Check," p. 788.

23. Holman, *Life and Career*, p. 570, and similar story, p. 538.

24. Holman, "Treaty Law-Making: A Blank Check," p. 787.

25. Ibid.

26. Holman, " 'World Government' No Answer," p. 719.

27. Holman, *Life and Career*, p. 571.

28. Ibid., p. 398.

29. Holman, "Greatest Threat," p. 981.

30. Holman, "Treaty Law-Making," p. 395.

31. Holman, *1956*, p. 5.

32. Schmidhauser and Berg, "The ABA and the Human Rights Conventions," pp. 362–410. See also "Treaty Power," p. 233.

33. Ornstein et al., *Vital Statistics*, p. 21.

34. *Congressional Record*, 82d Cong., 2d sess., 1952, 98, pt. 1:910.

35. "New Special Committee," *ABAJ* 30 (May 1944): 274.

36. Originally the name was the Special Committee to Report on Proposals for the Organization of the Nations for Peace and Law; the name was changed in November 1946 to the Special Committee for Peace and Justice Through United Nations. "The United Nations," *ABAJ* 32 (December 1946): 873. In 1947 the Board of Governors changed the name to Special Committee on Peace and Law Through the United Nations. "Reports of the Board of Governors," *RABA* 72 (1947): 394. All later ABA reports and publications omit "the" before "United Nations" when referring to the special committee.

37. Orie Phillips, who also became an outspoken critic of the treaties was an original member of the committee as well. The names of members appointed are listed in "New Special Committee," *ABAJ* 30 (May 1944): 274.

38. "Proceedings of the House of Delegates—1944," *ABAJ* 30 (April 1944): 236.

39. Ibid.

40. "Covenant on Human Rights," *ABAJ* 34 (April 1948): 277.

41. Ibid., p. 278.

42. "House of Delegates Proceedings—1948," *RABA* 73 (1948): 359–61.

43. These members were Ransom, Holman, Finch, Phillips, and Rix. "Covenant on Human Rights," *ABAJ* 34 (April 1948): 278.

44. "Declaration on Human Rights," *ABAJ* 34 (October 1948): 883.

45. Ibid.

46. "Report of the Special Committee—1948," *RABA* 73 (1948): 288.

47. Although there were and are claims that the Universal Declaration, as the draft was later entitled, provided an authoritative interpretation of the charter provisions on human rights, it was not expected to be immediately binding. The covenant, on the other hand, was designed to implement the Universal Declaration through a binding treaty.

48. "Report of the Special Committee—1948," *RABA* 73 (1948): 424.

49. "House of Delegates Proceedings—1948," *RABA* 73 (1948): 102.

50. "House of Delegates Proceedings—1948," *RABA* 73 (1948): 101.

51. "Highlights," *ABAJ* 34 (October 1948): 861.

52. "First Regional Conference," *ABAJ* 35 (March 1949): 204.

53. "House of Delegates Proceedings—1949," *RABA* 74 (1949): 145.

54. Ibid., p. 147.

55. Ibid., p. 150.

56. Holman, *Life and Career*, p. 403.

57. A 1943 resolution of the association provided "that it is the sense of this meeting that membership in the American Bar Association is not dependent upon race, creed, or color." "Special Membership Committee Report—1949," *RABA* 74 (1949): 315.

58. *New York Times*, 11 December 1949.

59. Ibid., 5 September 1949.

60. Ibid., 6 September 1949.

61. Ibid., 11 December 1949.

62. "Report of the Special Committee on Membership—1952," *RABA* 77 (1952): 316.

63. Ibid., p. 317.

64. *New York Times*, 24 February 1956.

65. "House of Delegates Proceedings—1950," *RABA* 75 (1950): 430.

66. Ibid., p. 415.

67. "Report of the Committee on Constitutional Aspects of International Agreements," *RABA* 75 (1950): 35.

68. Ibid., p. 34.

69. "Report of the Special Committee—1950," *RABA* 75 (1950): 305.

70. The resolution suggested that the constitutional amendment provide that (1) all treaties would be non-self-executing, (2) legislation implementing treaties could not authorize what the Constitution forbids, and (3) no treaty could alter the Bill of Rights or states' rights. "Report of the Section on International and Comparative Law—1950," *RABA* 75 (1950): 117–18, 286–329.

71. Ibid., p. 118.

72. Ibid., pp. 118–20.

73. *New York Times*, 15 October 1950.

74. Ibid.

75. Ibid., 16 October 1950.

76. Holman, *Life and Career*, pp. 389–93.

77. Ibid., p. 392.

78. Subcommittee of the Senate Committee on Foreign Relations, *Genocide Convention Hearings* (1950), pp. 154–56.

79. *Congressional Record*, 82d Cong., 1st sess., 1951, 97, pt. 9:11361.

80. No hearings were held, and it died with that session of Congress.

81. "House of Delegates Proceedings—1951," *RABA* 76 (1951): 548.

82. Holman, *Life and Career*, p. 519.

83. "House of Delegates Proceedings—1951," *RABA* 76 (1951): 136–37.

84. *Congressional Record*, 82d Cong., 2d sess., 1952, 98, pt. 1:907–14.

85. Ibid., p. 910.

86. This interpretation is supported by the committee report, which described the resolution as promoting human rights through an ILO-type system "and not by legally binding multipartite treaties." This language is not in the resolution itself but was cited in the report. It was quoted in connection with the consideration of the draft covenant. "Report of the Committee on Peace and Law—1952," *RABA* 77 (1952): 525.

87. Ibid., p. 512.

88. Ibid., p. 510.

89. "House of Delegates Proceedings—1952," *RABA* 76 (1952): 43.

90. Ibid., pp. 448–49.

91. Finch, speaking for the committee argued that such a tribunal would violate the principle of territoriality of crime—that the trial take place where the crime occurred—and also the Sixth Amendment of the Constitution, which guarantees speedy, public, and impartial trial in the jurisdiction where the crime was committed. Ibid., p. 449.

92. Ibid., pp. 433–34.

93. Ibid., p. 249.

94. Ibid., pp. 122–23.

95. Ibid.

96. Ibid., p. 124.

97. S.J. 130, introduced during the Eighty-second Congress, expired with that Congress. The amendment, S.J. Res. 1, was co-sponsored by sixty-two senators. It was referred to the Senate Judiciary Committee. *Congressional Record*, 83d Cong., 1st sess., 1953, 99, pt. 1:160.

98. "Report of the Standing Committee on Peace and Law—1953," *RABA* 78 (1953): 412.

99. Ibid., p. 416.

100. Ibid.

101. Ibid., p. 387.

102. See Appendix A for the text of the resolution.

103. "Bricker Treaty Amendment," p. 254.

104. Dulles, "Challenge of Our Time," p. 1062.

105. Ibid., p. 144; see also "Report of the Standing Committee on Peace and Law Through United Nations—1954," *RABA* 79 (1954): 540.

106. "Report of the Standing Committee on Peace and Law Through United Nations—1954," *RABA* 79 (1954): 255.

107. Ibid., p. 146.

108. Ibid., p. 148.

109. The major versions are presented in Appendix A.

110. "Bricker Treaty Amendment," p. 255.

111. Ibid.

112. S.J. Res. 181, *Congressional Record*, 83d Cong., 2d sess., 100, pt. 10:13456.

113. Ibid.

114. "Report of the Standing Committee on Peace and Law Through United Nations—1954," *RABA* 79 (1954): 265.

115. Senate, *Treaties and Executive Agreements* (1953), pp. 2–15.

Chapter Two

1. "House of Delegates Proceedings—1949," *RABA* 74 (1949): 145.

2. At the time of these hearings the United Nations Human Rights Commission had only one covenant before it, one which contained civil and political rights as well as economic, social, and cultural rights. It was only later

that provisions in regard to different types of rights were divided between two separate treaties.

3. Finch addressing the annual meeting of the American Society of International Law, 29 April 1949. Cited in "Report of the Special Committee—1949," *RABA* 74 (1949): 336.

4. Department of State, *Questions and Answers*, title page.

5. Subcommittee of the Senate Committee on Foreign Relations, *Genocide Convention Hearings* (1950), pp. 207–8.

6. Ibid., p. 308.

7. Senate Foreign Relations Committee, *Executive Sessions* III, p. 382.

8. Holman, "Comments," *ABAJ* 35 (March 1949): 202.

9. Letter to the editor, *ABAJ* 35 (July 1949): 604–5.

10. See the discussion of the drafting of the covenants in Chapter 3.

11. Subcommittee of the Senate Committee on Foreign Relations, *Genocide Convention Hearings* (1950), p. 159.

12. "Congress Takes a Careful Look." Also Subcommittee of the Senate Committee on Foreign Relations, *Genocide Convention Hearings* (1950), pp. 208, 220, 294, 300.

13. Subcommittee of the Senate Committee on Foreign Relations, *Genocide Convention Hearings* (1950), p. 159.

14. "Congress Takes a Careful Look," p. 312.

15. See Chapter 1.

16. Schweppe citing ABA committee report, Subcommittee of the Senate Committee on Foreign Relations, *Genocide Convention Hearings* (1950), p. 169.

17. Ibid., p. 305.

18. Ibid., p. 169.

19. Ibid., p. 304.

20. "Congress Takes a Careful Look," p. 312.

21. Senate Committee on Foreign Relations, *Executive Sessions* II, p. 399.

22. Ibid., p. 384.

23. In 1950, the United States and its allies dominated the organization.

24. Subcommittee of the Senate Committee on Foreign Relations, *Genocide Convention Hearings* (1950), p. 219.

25. Rix, "Human Rights and International Law," p. 551.

26. Subcommittee of the Senate Committee on Foreign Relations, *Genocide Convention Hearings* (1950), pp. 293, 294.

27. Senate Committee on Foreign Relations, *Executive Sessions* II, p. 379.

28. Subcommittee of the Senate Committee on Foreign Relations, *Genocide Convention Hearings* (1950), p. 169. Schweppe makes the same point on p. 198, and Phillips makes the same point in "Congress Takes a Careful Look," p. 314.

29. Subcommittee of the Senate Committee on Foreign Relations, *Genocide Convention Hearings* (1950), pp. 306, 308.

30. "Congress Takes a Careful Look," p. 312.

31. Senate Committee on Foreign Relations, *Executive Sessions* IV, p. 461.

32. Ibid.

33. Subcommittee of the Senate Committee on Foreign Relations, *Genocide Convention Hearings* (1950), p. 158.

34. Ibid., p. 162.
35. Ibid., p. 230.
36. Ibid., p. 208.
37. "Congress Takes a Careful Look," p. 318.
38. Leander Perez, district attorney of Louisiana, Subcommittee of the Senate Committee on Foreign Relations, *Genocide Convention Hearings* (1950), p. 222.
39. Judge Florence Allen, as cited in the ABA committee report submitted to the hearings record. Subcommittee of the Senate Committee on Foreign Relations, *Genocide Convention Hearings* (1950), p. 160.
40. Ibid., p. 219. The same point was made by Barger, ibid., p. 308.
41. Submitted to the hearings record, ibid., p. 168.
42. Ibid., p. 230.
43. Ibid., p. 220.
44. Ibid., p. 168.
45. Ibid.
46. Ibid., p. 162.
47. Senate Committee on Foreign Relations, *Executive Sessions* III, p. 381.
48. Subcommittee of the Senate Committee on Foreign Relations, *Genocide Convention Hearings* (1950), p. 224.
49. Ibid., p. 162.
50. Ibid., p. 217.
51. Ibid., pp. 199–200.
52. Ibid., p. 217.
53. Ibid., p. 208.
54. Ibid., p. 305–6.
55. Senate Committee on Foreign Relations, *Executive Sessions* II, p. 384.
56. Subcommittee of the Senate Committee on Foreign Relations, *Genocide Convention Hearings* (1950), p. 168.
57. Ibid., p. 201.
58. Senate Committee on Foreign Relations, *Executive Sessions* II, p. 391.
59. Subcommittee of the Senate Committee on Foreign Relations, *Genocide Convention Hearings* (1950), p. 131.
60. Ibid., pp. 203–5.
61. Department of State, *Questions and Answers*, title page.
62. Ibid., p. 4.
63. Subcommittee of the Senate Committee on Foreign Relations, *Genocide Convention Hearings* (1950), p. 51.
64. One understanding was recommended in the report of the acting secretary of state sent with the message of transmittal by President Truman when submitting the treaty to the Senate. Department of State, "Report of the Acting Secretary of State." See Appendixes C–E for the texts of various sets of recommended reservations to the Genocide Convention. For a full discussion of the history and analysis of reservations see the works of Lawrence LeBlanc listed in the Bibliography.
65. Senate Committee on Foreign Relations, *Executive Sessions* II, p. 803.
66. Ibid.
67. Ibid., p. 805.

68. Ibid., p. 804.
69. Ibid.
70. "Congress Takes a Careful Look," p. 291.
71. Ibid.

Chapter Three

1. Bricker, *Congressional Record*, 81st Cong., 1st sess., 1951, 97, pt. 6:8254–63. See Appendix A for the various forms of the Bricker Amendment. The text of the Senate resolution (S. Res. 177) read: (1) "The draft International Covenant on Human Rights . . . would, if ratified as a treaty, prejudice those rights of the American people which are now protected by the Bill of Rights of the Constitution of the United States." (2) "The President of the United States should advise the United Nations that the proposed Covenant on Human Rights is not acceptable to the United States." (3) "The President of the United States should instruct United States representatives at the United Nations to withdraw from further negotiations with respect to the Covenant on Human Rights, and all other covenants, treaties and conventions which seek to prescribe restrictions on the liberty which, if passed by the Congress as domestic legislation, would be unconstitutional."

2. U.N. Charter, Article 68.

3. United Nations, *Action in the Field of Human Rights*, p. 8.

4. A third possibility, that of amending the charter to include a statement of basic rights, was never discussed with any great seriousness in the commission. Humphrey, *Human Rights*, p. 26.

5. Malik was the commission's rapporteur and Chang was its vice chair.

6. Ramcharan, *Human Rights*, p. 23, and Humphrey, *Human Rights*, p. 29.

7. Humphrey, *Human Rights*, p. 32.

8. Ramcharan, *Human Rights*, p. 26.

9. For example, the Soviet Union tried to get a provision on the right to self-determination included in the draft declaration but was strongly defeated in this effort, even though less than a decade later the General Assembly voted to include an article on this subject in both covenants. Humphrey, *Human Rights*, p. 66.

10. U.N.Doc. E/CN.4/SR 206, p. 12.

11. U.N.Doc. A/777.

12. Ramcharan, *Human Rights*, p. 26, and Humphrey, *Human Rights*, p. 63.

13. U.N.Doc. A/CN.3/SR 225.

14. U.N.Doc. A/784.

15. U.N.Doc. A/785/Rev. 2.

16. Humphrey, *Human Rights*, p. 72.

17. U.N.G.A.O.R., 3d sess., 10 December 1948, p. 910.

18. Ramcharan, *Human Rights*, p. 37; Henkin, *International Bill of Rights*, p. 9; Humphrey, *Human Rights*, pp. 65, 76; Secretary General in U.N.Doc.

A/CN.4/245, p. 196; Pechota, "Covenant on Civil and Political Rights," p. 34; McDougal, Lasswell, and Chen, *Human Rights and World Public Order*, p. 258–59, 272–74, 317–18, 324–30. For a discussion of the continuing controversy over the legal status of the Universal Declaration see Sohn and Buergenthal, *International Protection of Human Rights*, pp. 945–46, and Sieghart, *International Law of Human Rights*, p. 53.

19. Humphrey, *Human Rights*, p. 64.

20. White, "Tomorrow One May Be Guilty of Genocide," p. 229: "There would still be room for reluctance on our part if our federal Bill of Rights was copied exactly."

21. *New York Times*, 18 November 1948.

22. Ibid.

23. Ibid., 1 February 1949.

24. Ibid.

25. Ibid.

26. Ibid.

27. Fleming, "Danger to America," p. 858.

28. Ibid., p. 817. A similar argument was made in Reynolds and Lucas, "Wake Up America," p. 941, and in Patton and Lucas, "Bill of Rights," p. 1237.

29. Fleming, "Danger to America," p. 858.

30. Ibid., p. 798.

31. Ibid., p. 857.

32. On the original ad hoc commission Roosevelt was selected by the Economic and Social Council to serve in an independent capacity, not as an official representative of the United States. Even here, however, she followed the leadership of the State Department. Hendrick (assistant to the chief of the International Affairs Division at the Department of State), as quoted in Lash, *Eleanor*, p. 56.

33. Holman, "An 'International Bill of Rights,' " p. 985.

34. Reynolds and Lucas, "United Nations," p. 191.

35. Bricker, "Blueprint for Tyranny," p. 266. Also argued in a letter from Judge Claude McCullock to Frank Holman, cited in Holman, *Life and Career*, p. 507.

36. Lash, *Eleanor*, pp. 62, 64, 79.

37. Mower, *The United States, the United Nations, and Human Rights*, p. 48.

38. Hendrick, as quoted in Lash, *Eleanor*, p. 56.

39. Ibid., p. 66.

40. Ibid., p. 74.

41. Ibid., pp. 74, 76, and Mower, *The United States, the United Nations, and Human Rights*, p. 67.

42. *New York Times*, 14 September 1948. The two other Anglo-Saxon members were Colonel William Hodgson of Australia and Lord Dukeston of the United Kingdom.

43. Eleanor Roosevelt, as quoted in Lash, *Eleanor*, p. 71.

44. Ibid.

45. Ibid., p. 72.

46. Letter dated 2 February 1949, cited in Lash, *Eleanor*, pp. 79–80.

47. Ibid., pp. 65, 66, and also in Mower, *The United States, the United Nations, and Human Rights*, p. 48.

48. Lash, *Eleanor*, p. 221.

49. Fleming, "Danger to America," p. 794.

50. Ibid., p. 796.

51. Holman, "Treaty Law-Making: A Blank Check," p. 707. He gives the impression here that the Soviets had more members than the United States, when clearly the majority of the commission at that time was more sympathetic to Western rights traditions.

52. Fleming, "Danger to America," p. 860.

53. Ibid., p. 859.

54. Some of the arguments in regard to the drafting of the covenants presented in this chapter were made previously in Hevener, "Drafting the Human Rights Covenants."

55. U.N.Doc. E/800/Annex B, p. 1.

56. U.N.Eco.Soc. Resolution 303 C (XI) and 303 I (XI).

57. U.N.G.A. Resolution 421 (V).

58. Ibid.

59. U.N.Doc. E/CN.4/SR 236, p. 5.

60. U.N.Doc. E/CN.4/SR 248, p. 13.

61. U.N.Doc. E/CN.4/SR 248.

62. U.N.Doc. E/CN.4/619/Rev. 1.

63. U.N.Doc. E/CN.4/SR 248, p. 8.

64. This proposal was defeated by a 5-12-1 vote. U.N.Doc. E/CN.4/SR 248, p. 26.

65. The Soviet representative stated "that the Covenant must be a unified whole, and that economic, social and cultural rights must not be relegated to a position of secondary importance, dragged in for reason of, 'force majeure.'" U.N.Doc. E/CN.4/SR 248, p. 12.

66. U.N.Doc. E/CN.4/SR 203, p. 4.

67. Ibid.

68. This proposal was defeated 8-8-2. U.N.Doc. E/CN.4/SR 234.

69. U.N.Eco.Soc. Resolution 384 (XIII).

70. U.N.G.A. Resolution 543 (VI).

71. U.N.Doc. E/CN.4/SR 275, p. 6.

72. U.N.Doc. E/CN.4/SR 273, p. 6. The Soviet Union did ultimately vote for this article when a paragraph it wanted on nondiscrimination was included. The representative did, however, register his disagreement with paragraph 1. U.N.Doc. E/CN.4/SR 275, p. 7.

73. U.N.Doc. E/CN.4/SR 331, p. 12.

74. U.N.Doc. E/CN.4/SR 248, p. 12.

75. U.N.Doc. E/CN.4/SR 390, p. 20.

76. *New York Times*, 18 September 1948.

77. Holman, "Comments on Mr. Moskowitz's Reply," p. 361. The covenant was also criticized on this ground in Patton and Lucas, "Covenant of Human Rights," p. 662, and Holman, "An 'International Bill of Rights,'" p. 986.

78. U.N.Doc. E/CN.4/599.

79. U.N.Doc. E/CN.4/SR 230, p. 22.

80. U.N.Doc. E/CN.4/614.

81. Ibid.

82. The representative of Uruguay made a further proposal which added a provision for required compensation. U.N.Doc. E/CN.4/603.

83. U.N.Doc. E/CN.4/L 313, p. 2.

84. U.N.Doc. E/CN.4/SR 231, p. 17.

85. U.N.Doc. E/CN.4/L 66 and Rev. 1.

86. U.N.Doc. E/2256, paragraph 146.

87. The subcommission draft read: "(1) The States Parties to this Covenant undertake to respect the right of everyone to own property alone as well as in association with others. This right shall be subject to such limitations and restrictions as are imposed by law in the public interest and in the interest of social progress in the country concerned. (2) No one shall be deprived of his property without due process of law. Expropriation may take place only for considerations of public necessity or utility as defined by law and subject to such compensation as may be prescribed." U.N.Doc. E/CN.4/L 321.

88. U.N.Doc. E/CN.4/SR 413, pp. 4, 5.

89. U.N.Doc. E/CN.4/SR 417, p. 9.

90. The notion that the language of this proposal was not a purely Communist or Soviet design is supported by Humphrey, *Human Rights*, p. 44.

91. United Nations, *Conference on Freedom of Information*.

92. U.N.Doc. E/2573, Annex 1B.

93. The U.S.-proposed text read: "(1) Everyone shall have the right to freedom of expression without governmental interference: this right shall include freedom to hold opinions, to seek, receive and impart information and ideas, regardless of frontiers, either orally, in writing or in print, in the form of art, or by any other media. (2) This right shall be subject only to such limitations as are provided by law and necessary for the protection of national security, public order, safety, health or morals, or the rights, reputation or freedoms of other persons." U.N.Doc. E/CN.4/365, p. 49.

94. U.N.Doc. E/CN.4/SR 165, pp. 17, 18.

95. U.N.Doc. E/CN.4/SR 162, p. 13.

96. U.N.Doc. E/CN.4/365, p. 45.

97. U.N.Doc. E/CN.4/SR 165, p. 14.

98. U.N.Doc. E/CN.4/432.

99. U.N.Doc. E/CN.4/SR 162, p. 10.

100. Ibid., p. 12.

101. U.N.Doc. E/CN.4/SR 162, p. 5.

102. Ibid.

103. U.N.Doc. E/CN.4/SR 163, p. 8.

104. U.N.Doc. E/CN.4/SR 162, p. 5.

105. U.N.Doc. E/CN.4/SR 165, p. 12.

106. U.N.Doc. E/2573, Annex 1B.

107. U.N.Doc. A/C.3/L 921.

108. U.N.Doc. E/CN.4/SR 1074, p. 58.

109. U.N.Doc. A/C.3/L 925.

110. U.N.Doc. E/CN.4/SR 1074, p. 73.

111. The article was adopted by a vote of 82 in favor and 1 opposed, with 7 abstentions. Paragraph 1, as drafted by the commission, was adopted unanimously. Paragraph 2 was adopted 88-0-1. Paragraph 3 was adopted 71-7-12. U.N.Doc. E/CN.4/SR 1077, p. 91.

112. The French translation "ordre public" was added in the final sentence. U.N.Doc. A/5000, p. 6.

113. U.N.G.A. Resolution 545 (VI).

114. She stated that the negative U.S. vote on this issue in the General Assembly reflected disapproval of "faulty drafting" and not of the content of the resolution. U.N.Doc. E/CN.4/SR 256, p. 13.

115. U.N.Doc. E/CN.4/L 21. The United States voted with a majority of the commission to accept the following text as paragraph 1: "All peoples and all nations shall have the right of self-determination, namely, the right freely to determine their political, economic, social and cultural status."

116. U.N.Doc. E/CN.4/SR 256, p. 6, and U.N.Doc. E/CN.4/SR 361, p. 5. In particular, they cited Articles 1, 55, 73b, and 76b. The latter two, of course, refer to "self-government" and "independence" and are found in the section of the charter which deals with non-self-governing territories and their administration.

117. U.N.Doc. E/CN.4/SR 256, p. 6.

118. Ibid.

119. Ibid., p. 12.

120. Ibid., p. 6.

121. Ibid.

122. Ibid.

123. U.N.Doc. E/CN.4/L 24.

124. U.N.Doc. E/CN.4/SR 260, p. 6.

125. Ibid., p. 7.

126. Ibid., p. 8.

127. Ibid., pp. 8–9.

128. Ibid., p. 9.

129. Countries voting for the article were Chile, Egypt, India, Lebanon, Pakistan, Poland, Ukrainian SSR, USSR, Uruguay, and Yugoslavia. Ibid., p. 5.

130. U.N.Doc. E/CN.4/SR 259, p. 5.

131. Subsequently, the Third Committee brought about the inclusion of references to international economic cooperation and international law which should have removed any legal difficulty for U.S. acceptance. U.N.Doc. A/3077, pp. 35–36.

132. During the final stages of the commission drafting process, an additional article dealing specifically with propaganda for racial hatred was added to the draft. This provision is discussed in Chapter 6.

Chapter Four

1. Of the major foreign policy writers who treat the Bricker Amendment, the following view it primarily as an attempt to curb the use of executive agreements: Pusey, *Eisenhower the President*, p. 231; Stupak, *American Foreign*

Policy, p. 112; Deconde, *History of American Foreign Policy*, p. 778; Kegley and Wittkopf, *American Foreign Policy*, p. 416; Rehm, "Making Foreign Policy through International Agreement," p. 128; and Spanier, "Congress and the Presidency," p. xix. Other writers link the Bricker Amendment to congressional nostalgia for lost power (Murphy, *Congress and the Court*, p. 258), an attempt to restrict presidential freedom to commit U.S. troops overseas (Spanier and Uslaner, *How American Foreign Policy Is Made*, p. 81), and a neo-isolationist movement to curtail U.S. internationalism (Gerson, *J. F. Dulles*, pp. 118–22).

2. Steve Garrett, "Foreign Policy and the American Constitution," pp. 187–220.

3. Subcommittee of the Senate Committee on the Judiciary, *Treaties and Executive Agreements* (1953), pp. 2–3.

4. Department of State, *Foreign Relations of the United States*, pp. 1781–82, 1790–91, 1798, 1809–16, 1843.

5. Ibid., pp. 1782, 1798, 1817–19, 1821.

6. Bricker, as quoted in "Bricker Treaty Amendment," p. 254.

7. Subcommittee of the Senate Committee on the Judiciary, *Treaties and Executive Agreements* (1953), p. 11.

8. Bricker, "Making Treaties," p. 137.

9. *Geofroy v. Riggs*, 133 U.S. 266 (1889).

10. Ibid.

11. *Missouri v. Holland*, 252 U.S. 433 (1919).

12. At the time of these hearings there was still a single Covenant on Human Rights.

13. Subcommittee of the Senate Committee on the Judiciary, *Treaties and Executive Agreements* (1953), p. 6.

14. Ibid., p. 825.

15. *Missouri v. Holland*, 252 U.S. 432 (1919).

16. Bricker, "Making Treaties," p. 136.

17. Henkin, "Treaty Makers and Law Makers," pp. 910–11.

18. Subcommittee of the Senate Committee on the Judiciary, *Treaties and Executive Agreements* (1953), p. 9.

19. Ibid., p. 12.

20. Ibid., p. 7.

21. Ibid., pp. 7–8.

22. An attachment to the ratification resolution for the Genocide Convention eventually passed by the U.S. Senate required exactly this step: that implementing legislation be enacted by Congress *before* the treaty would be officially ratified by the United States.

23. Subcommittee of the Senate Committee on the Judiciary, *Treaties and Executive Agreements* (1953), pp. 7–8.

24. *U.S. v. Pink*, 315 U.S. 230 (1942).

25. Subcommittee of the Senate Committee on the Judiciary, *Treaties and Executive Agreements* (1953), p. 9.

26. Ibid., p. 10.

27. *Congressional Record*, 82d Cong., 2d sess., 1952, 97:11361.

28. Ibid., 98, pt. 1:907–14.

29. Ibid., p. 908.

30. S.J. Res. 130 was introduced and expired during the Eighty-second Congress.

31. As cited in Bricker and Webb, "Bricker Amendment," p. 531.

32. Subcommittee of the Senate Committee on the Judiciary, *Treaties and Executive Agreements* (1953), p. 825.

33. Ibid.

34. "Bricker Treaty Amendment," p. 255.

35. Ibid.

36. The George version received the required two-thirds majority, but the resolution to refer the amendment to the states fell one vote short of the two-thirds required.

37. Subcommittee of the Senate Committee on the Judiciary, *Treaties and Executive Agreements* (1953).

38. *Congressional Record*, 82d Cong., 2d sess., 1952, 98, pt. 1:910.

39. Subcommittee of the Senate Committee on the Judiciary, *Treaties and Executive Agreements* (1953), p. 158. It was suggested that Senator Bricker was in thrall to the ABA and that the special committee members and Holman kept him from reaching a compromise with the Eisenhower administration. Department of State, *Foreign Relations of the United States*, p. 1830.

40. Subcommittee of the Senate Committee on the Judiciary, *Treaties and Executive Agreements* (1953), p. 3.

41. Ibid., p. 158.

42. Ibid., p. 59.

43. Ibid., p. 143.

44. Ibid., p. 116.

45. Ibid., pp. 115–16.

46. Ibid., p. 145.

47. Ibid., p. 116.

48. Ibid., p. 119.

49. Ibid., pp. 100, 120–23, 1107, 1131, 1132.

50. Ibid., p. 105.

51. Ibid., p. 143.

52. Ibid., p. 1108.

53. Ibid., p. 115.

54. Ibid., p. 168.

55. Ibid., pp. 143–44.

56. Ibid., p. 47.

57. Ibid., p. 144.

58. Ibid., pp. 1109–10.

59. Ibid., p. 136.

60. Ibid., p. 155.

61. Ibid., p. 112.

62. Ibid., p. 133.

63. Ibid., p. 115.

64. Ibid., p. 1123.

65. Ibid., p. 1148.

66. Ibid., pp. 273–74.

67. Ibid., p. 565.
68. Ibid., p. 142.
69. Ibid., p. 176.

Chapter Five

1. Interview with Morella Hanson, staff member and historian of the Senate Foreign Relations Committee from 1947 to 1977, on 13 March 1985.

2. Senate Committee on Foreign Relations, *Human Rights Conventions, Part I*, p. 1.

3. The U.S. government voted in favor; the U.S. employers' delegate abstained on the basis of the form of the instrument. Department of State, "Background Statement," p. 7.

4. The General Assembly in 1946 adopted resolution 56(I), recommending that states adopt legislation, in pursuit of the objectives stated in Article I of the United Nations Charter, which would give women equal political rights with men. The Universal Declaration of Human Rights (1948) includes a provision on this subject in Article 21.

5. See Hevener, *International Law and the Status of Women*, p. 112.

6. U.N.G.A. Resolution 640 (VII), 20 December 1952.

7. Senate Committee on Foreign Relations, *Women's Political Rights Conventions*, p. 2.

8. Department of State, "Report of the Secretary of State," p. 3.

9. Ambassador Goldberg speaking for the president, Senate Committee on Foreign Relations, *Human Rights Conventions, Part I*, p. 29.

10. Department of State, *Bulletin*, 28:30. Roosevelt stated: "A question does arise, however, as to whether the term 'public office' is intended to include military service. My delegation believes it is not so intended. Almost all countries make some distinctions in the kinds of military duty they regard as suitable for women. The most usual distinction, and a natural and proper one, is that women are not used as combat troops and are not appointed to certain posts which might involve the direction of combat operations. Our attitude towards article 3 is, therefore, based on the understanding that it does not include military service."

11. Subcommittee of the Senate Committee on Foreign Relations, *Genocide Convention Hearings* (1950), p. 221.

12. Ibid., p. 825.

13. Interview with Morella Hanson, 13 March 1985.

14. "Report of the Standing Committee on Peace and Law—1967," *RABA* 92 (1967): 519.

15. Ibid.

16. Ibid., p. 521.

17. "Report of the Section on International and Comparative Law—1967," *RABA* 92 (1967): 341.

18. Senate Committee on Foreign Relations, *Executive Sessions*, 6 April 1967, p. 56.

19. Ibid.

20. Senate Committee on Foreign Relations, *Executive Sessions*, 8 June 1967, pp. 45–57.

21. Senate Committee on Foreign Relations, *Executive Sessions*, 6 April 1967, pp. 3–4.

22. Senate Committee on Foreign Relations, *Human Rights Conventions, Part II*, p. 4.

23. See Chapter 3.

24. Senate Committee on Foreign Relations, *Human Rights Conventions, Part II*, p. 39.

25. Ibid., p. 76.

26. Ibid., p. 123.

27. Ibid., p. 2.

28. Letter from the legal advisor, U.S. Department of State, cited in ibid., p. 6.

29. Ibid., pp. 81–82.

30. Ibid., pp. 50, 106–7.

31. Senate Committee on Foreign Relations, *Human Rights Conventions, Part I*, p. 45.

32. Senate Committee on Foreign Relations, *Human Rights Conventions, Part II*, p. 123.

33. Senate Committee on Foreign Relations, *Human Rights Conventions, Part I*, p. 44.

34. Senate Committee on Foreign Relations, *Human Rights Conventions, Part II*, p. 77.

35. Ibid.

36. Ibid., pp. 43, 49.

37. Ibid., p. 8.

38. Ibid., p. 101.

39. Ibid., p. 7.

40. Ibid.

41. Ibid., p. 39.

42. Ibid.

43. Ibid., p. 41.

44. Ibid., p. 4.

45. Ibid., p. 37.

46. Ibid., p. 101.

47. Ibid., pp. 101–2.

48. Some of the many instances appear in ibid., pp. 7, 37, 76, 78, 101.

49. Ibid., p. 37.

50. Ibid., p. 72.

51. Ibid., pp. 102–3.

52. Ibid., p. 97.

53. Ibid., p. 21.

54. Ibid., p. 35.

55. Ibid., p. 103.

56. Ibid., p. 70.
57. Ibid., p. 100.
58. Ibid., p. 125.
59. Ibid., p. 70.
60. Ibid., p. 76.
61. Ibid.
62. Ibid.
63. Ibid., p. 101.
64. Ibid., p. 75.
65. Ibid., p. 78.
66. Ibid., pp. 4, 33, 78.
67. Ibid., p. 73.
68. Ibid., p. 78.
69. Senate Committee on Foreign Relations, *Executive Sessions*, 6 April 1967, pp. 5–7, and similar position, p. 44.
70. Ibid., p. 6.
71. Senate Committee on Foreign Relations, *Human Rights Conventions, Part II*, p. 47.
72. Ibid., pp. 23, 24.
73. Senate Committee on Foreign Relations, *Human Rights Conventions, Part I*, pp. 48, 18, and *Human Rights Conventions, Part II*, pp. 61, 65, 82, 101, 102. Also Senate Foreign Relations Committee, *Executive Sessions*, 11 October 1967, pp. 4–5.
74. Senate Committee on Foreign Relations, *Women's Political Rights Conventions*, p. 7; *Congressional Record*, 94th Cong., 1st sess., 1975, 121:40904, 40906–10.
75. A resolution of ratification was also unanimously passed at the same time, accepting the Inter-American Convention on Granting of Political Rights to Women. This convention was adopted at the Ninth International Conference of American States on 2 May 1948 and submitted to the United States Senate in 1949. This treaty contains the same basic provisions as the U.N. Convention on the Political Rights of Women and was never discussed by the Senate until the day the resolution of ratification was passed. *Congressional Record*, 94th Cong., 2d sess., 1976, 122, pt. 1:679–80.
76. Congressional staff interview, January 1984.

Chapter Six

1. See Chapter 2 and Appendixes C, D, and E. The Genocide Convention reservations as finally passed were significantly increased from these considered by the ABA in the 1950s and recommended by the ABA in 1976.
2. For a critical analysis of the attachments see Weissbrodt, "United States Ratification of the Human Rights Covenants"; Rodley, "On the Necessity of United States Ratification"; Henkin, "Covenant on Civil and Political Rights"; and Skelton, "United States Approach to Ratification."
3. *Reid v. Covert*, 354 U.S. 1 (1957).

4. Interview with staff, Office of Legal Advisor, Department of State, 6 October 1977.

5. Department of State, "Letter of Submittal," p. xi.

6. One may note, however, that the covenant would provide a fertile source for certain domestic groups, for example those working to establish unions in the South, as a statement of U.S. goals and direction.

7. Department of State, "Letter of Submittal," p. ix.

8. Ibid.

9. U.N.Doc. A/C.3/L 1027.

10. U.N.Doc. A/C.3/L 1027/Rev. 3 and 4 were generally unsuccessful.

11. U.N.Doc. A/C.3/L 1357.

12. U.N.Doc. A/C.3/SR 1404, p. 155.

13. U.N.Doc. A/C.3/SR 1406, p. 165.

14. The article was adopted 75-4, with 20 abstentions. U.N.Doc. A/6546, p. 17.

15. U.N.Doc. A/C.3/L 138 and Add. 1 and 2.

16. The vote was 50 in favor and 2 against, with 17 abstentions. U.N.Doc. A/6546, p. 57.

17. Department of State, "Letter of Submittal," p. ix.

18. Ibid.

19. Also see Article 5, paragraph 2, of both treaties.

20. U.N.Doc. E/CN.4/365, p. 22.

21. Ibid.

22. U.N.Doc. A/C.3/L 644.

23. U.N.Doc. A/C.3/SR 812, p. 250.

24. Department of State, "Letter of Submittal," p. xii.

25. Ibid.

26. U.N.Doc. A/CN.3/SR 95, pp. 9, 10.

27. U.N.Doc. A/CN.3/SR 147, p. 17.

28. U.N.Doc. E/CN.3/SR 148, p. 7.

29. U.N.Doc. E/CN.4/394.

30. U.N.Doc. E/CN.4/SR 148, p. 3.

31. Ibid., p. 7.

32. U.N.Doc. A/C.3/L 686.

33. The vote was 30-27, with 14 abstentions.

34. U.N.Doc. E/CN.3/SR 159.

35. U.N.Doc. A/4625, pp. 4, 5.

36. Department of State, "Letter of Submittal," p. xii.

37. Weissbrodt, "United States Ratification of the Human Rights Covenants," p. 75.

38. Department of State, "Letter of Submittal," p. xii.

39. U.N.Doc. A/C.3/L 691/Rev. 1. The amendment was adopted 27-25, with 2 abstentions.

40. U.N.Doc. A/C.3/L 691/Rev. 1.

41. U.N.Doc. A/C.3/SR 868.

42. The vote was 67-0, with 2 abstentions. U.N.Doc. A/3824, p. 12.

43. Ibid.

44. Department of State, "Letter of Submittal," p. xii.

45. Ibid., p. xiii.

46. Most of the paragraphs were not voted on by roll call, but there were no negative votes on any paragraph or on the article as a whole. There were some abstentions. U.N.Doc. A/4299, pp. 13–14.

47. Department of State, "Letter of Submittal," p. xiii.

48. Ibid. Similarly, the administration recommended an understanding relevant to paragraph 7 prohibiting double jeopardy: "The United States understands that the prohibition on double jeopardy contained in paragraph (7) is applicable only when the judgment of acquittal has been rendered by a court of the same governmental unit, whether the Federal Government or a constituent unit, which is seeking a new trial for the same cause."

49. See Chapter 3.

50. U.N.Doc. E/CN.4/SR 34, p. 9.

51. U.N.Doc. E/CN.4/SR, p. 11.

52. U.N.Doc. E/CN.4/SR 123, p. 4.

53. Ibid., p. 5.

54. U.N.Doc. E/CN.4/356, p. 57.

55. U.N.Doc. E/CN.4/265, p. 57.

56. U.N.Doc. E/CN.4/SR 174, p. 57.

57. Ibid., p. 7.

58. Ibid.

59. Ibid.

60. U.N.Doc. E/CN.4/SR 175, p. 6.

61. U.N.Doc. E/2256, p. 54.

62. U.N.Doc. E/CN.4/SR 377, p. 4.

63. Ibid., pp. 10–11.

64. U.N.Doc. E/CN.4/SR 379, p. 14.

65. Ibid.

66. Ibid., p. 13.

67. U.N.Doc. E/CN.4/SR 1078, p. 93.

68. The amendment was proposed by Lebanon, the Philippines, Saudi Arabia, and Thailand. U.N.Doc. A/C.3/L 932.

69. *Yates v. U.S.*, 354 U.S. 298 (1957).

70. Also see *Scales v. U.S.*, 367 U.S. 203 (1961).

71. The vote was as follows: paragraph 1, 53-21 (United States against), with 9 abstentions; paragraph 2, 50-18 (United States against), with 15 abstentions; the article as a whole, 52-19 (United States against), with 12 abstentions. U.N.Doc. A/6546, p. 15.

72. Department of State, "Letter of Submittal," pp. x, xi–xii, and the same statement for the Economic, Social, and Cultural Rights Covenant with "of the International Covenant on Civil and Political Rights" added to the first sentence of Article 19.

73. Weissbrodt, "United States Ratification of the Human Rights Covenants," p. 63. Weissbrodt suggests that the proposed reservation might be interpreted to justify "laws and practice" less protective than Article 19. Examples of such practices include police surveillance of peaceful demonstrators and denial of visas to unpopular speakers.

74. U.N.Doc. A/Conf. 2/21, pp. 16–17.

75. Ibid., pp. 12–21.
76. U.N.Doc. E/CN.4/SR 437, p. 11.
77. U.N.Doc. E/2447, Annex II, Section B(III).
78. U.N.Doc. E/CN.4/L 340/Corr. 1.
79. Adopted 72-0-3. U.N.Doc. A/6546, p. 22.
80. The final articles of the Civil and Political Rights Covenant were adopted unanimously as a package. U.N.Doc. A/6546, p. 58.
81. Department of State, "Letter of Submittal," p. x.
82. Ibid., pp. xi, xiv.

Chapter Seven

1. These data were first presented in an article co-authored with David Whiteman: Kaufman and Whiteman, "Opposition to Human Rights Treaties."
2. Hevener, "Introduction," *Dynamics of Human Rights,* pp. 1–2. See also Falk, "Ideological Patterns," pp. 34–35, 49–50.
3. For similar efforts see Holsti, *Content Analysis,* and del Sesto, "Nuclear Reactor Safety."
4. Senate Committee on Foreign Relations, *International Human Rights Treaties,* p. 8.
5. Ibid., pp. 105, 108.
6. Congressional staff interviews, January 1984.
7. Eisenhower had supported the treaty prior to the Bricker Amendment campaign. See Chapter 2. No president, however, had actively engaged in efforts to gain a ratification resolution from the Senate.
8. The legislation from the House was H.R. 4243, from the Senate S. 1851.
9. *Congressional Quarterly Almanac,* 1985, p. 2595.
10. Ibid.
11. *Congressional Record,* 99th Cong., 1st sess., 1985, 131:3382–87.
12. "Report of the Section on International Law," *RABA* 101 (1976): 237–38, 301–3.
13. Interviews with ABA members, 1983, 1984, and 1985, and with Senate staff, 1984 and 1985.
14. *Washington Alert,* January 1985, p. 3.
15. *Congressional Record,* 99th Cong., 2d sess., 1986, 132:1373.
16. Ervin speaking against the Genocide Convention at the 1970 hearings, cited in *Congressional Record,* 99th Cong., 2d sess., 1986, 132:1263.
17. Ibid.
18. Ibid.
19. See Chapter 2. This point was also made and rejected by Senator William Proxmire, who quoted William Rehnquist. *Congressional Record,* 99th Cong., 2d sess., 1986, 132:1260.
20. Senate Committee on Foreign Relations, *Crime of Genocide: Hearing,* pp. 121–23.

21. See Appendix E for the text of the eight provisos.

22. Senate Committee on Foreign Relations, *Crime of Genocide: Hearing*, p. 16.

23. Ibid., p. 15.

24. Senate Committee on Foreign Relations, *Genocide Convention Hearings* (1970), p. 196.

25. Ibid., p. 203.

26. Senate Committee on Foreign Relations, *Crime of Genocide: Hearing*, p. 161.

27. Ibid., p. 103.

28. Ibid., p. 105.

29. Ibid., p. 16.

30. Ibid., p. 113.

31. Ibid., p. 131.

32. *Congressional Record*, 99th Cong., 2d sess., 1986, 132:1261, 1262.

33. Ibid., p. 1275.

34. Ibid.

35. Senate Committee on Foreign Relations, *Crime of Genocide: Hearing*, p. 164.

36. Ibid., p. 102.

37. *Congressional Record*, 100th Cong., 1st sess., 1987, 133:1261.

38. Testimony citing the need for a reservation limiting the jurisdiction of the International Court of Justice as recorded in Senate Committee on Foreign Relations, *Crime of Genocide: Hearing*, includes that of Senator Richard Lugar (R.-Ind.) (pp. 2, 5); Abrams, Robinson, and Tarr of the Department of State (pp. 9, 10, 12); and Grover Rees, 56, 60.

39. Senate Committee on Foreign Relations, *Crime of Genocide: Hearing*, p. 18.

40. Ibid., p. 205.

41. Ibid., pp. 106, 107.

42. Ibid., p. 112.

43. Ibid., p. 113.

44. *Congressional Record*, 99th Cong., 2d sess., 1986, 132:1367.

45. Ibid.

46. Ibid., p. 1379.

47. Senate Committee on Foreign Relations, *Crime of Genocide: Hearing*, p. 163.

48. *Congressional Record*, 99th Cong., 2d sess., 1986, 132:1287.

49. Senate Committee on Foreign Relations, *Crime of Genocide: Hearing*, p. 106.

50. *Congressional Record*, 99th Cong., 2d sess., 1986, 132:1363.

51. Some opponents argued that this acceptance might bypass the Senate, taking the form of an executive agreement, but it is difficult to imagine the Senate allowing such a controversial decision to be removed from its jurisdiction.

52. Senate Committee on Foreign Relations, *Crime of Genocide: Hearing*, p. 108.

53. Ibid., p. 18.

54. Senate Committee on Foreign Relations, *Genocide Convention Hearings* (1970), p. 200. Senate Committee on Foreign Relations, *Crime of Genocide: Hearing*, pp. 150, 163.

55. Ibid., p. 106.

56. Ibid., p. 129.

57. Ibid., p. 110.

58. Senate Committee on Foreign Relations, *Genocide Convention Hearings* (1970), p. 206. Senate Committee on Foreign Relations, *Crime of Genocide: Hearing*, p. 153.

59. Ibid., p. 118.

60. *Congressional Record*, 99th Cong., 2d sess., 1986, 132:1262. Similar remarks on p. 1369.

61. Senate Committee on Foreign Relations, *Crime of Genocide: Hearing*, p. 130.

62. Senate Foreign Relations Committee, *Genocide Convention Hearings* (1970), p. 208. Senate Committee on Foreign Relations, *Crime of Genocide: Hearing*, p. 153.

63. Ibid., pp. 204–5.

64. *Congressional Record*, 99th Cong., 2d sess., 1986, 132:1275.

Conclusion

1. U.S. Congress, Subcommittee of the Senate Committee on Foreign Relations, *Genocide Convention Hearings* (1971), pp. 137–39.

Appendix A

1. *Congressional Record*, 82d Cong., 2d sess., 1952, 98, pt. 1:908.

2. *Congressional Record*, 83d Cong., 1st sess., 1953, 99, pt. 1:160.

3. *Congressional Quarterly Almanac* 9 (1953): 234.

4. *Congressional Quarterly Almanac* 10 (1954): 255.

5. Ibid.

6. Ibid.

Appendix C

1. Senate Committee on Foreign Relations, *Confidential Committee Print No. 3*, 2:803.

2. Senate Committee on Foreign Relations, *Crime of Genocide* (1971), pp. 1, 2.

Appendix D

1. Adopted by the ABA House of Delegates, February 1976. American Bar Association, *International Human Rights Treaties*, pp. 21–22.

Appendix E

1. Senate Committee on Foreign Relations, *Genocide Convention: Report*, pp. 18, 19, 21, 23, 25, 26. Senator Richard Lugar, chair of the Senate Foreign Relations Committee at this time, joined Helms in sponsoring the provisos. *Congressional Record*, 99th Cong., 2d sess., 1986, 132:1370.

United States Government Documents

U.S. Congress. *Congressional Quarterly Almanac.* Various issues, 1950–89.
———. *Congressional Record.* Various volumes, 1945–89.
———. Congressional Research Service. *A Background Report on the United Nations Convention on the Prevention and Punishment of the Crime of Genocide.* Prepared by Ann Marjorie Brown. 23 July 1970, with addendum, 29 April 1976.
U.S. Congress. Senate. Committee on Foreign Relations. *Confidential Committee Print No. 3. International Convention on the Prevention and Punishment of the Crime of Genocide, May 1950. Executive Sessions.* (Historical Series) 81st Cong., 1st and 2d sess., 1949–50. Made public July 1976. pp. 797–805.
———. *Crime of Genocide: Hearing on the Convention on the Prevention and Punishment of the Crime of Genocide.* 99th Cong., 1st sess., 5 March 1985.
———. *Executive Sessions of the Senate Foreign Relations Committee* (Historical Series) II. 81st Cong., 1st and 2d sess., 1949–50. Made public August 1976.
———. *Executive Sessions of the Senate Foreign Relations Committee* (Historical Series) III. 82d Cong., 1st sess., 1951. Made Public August 1976.
———. *Executive Sessions of the Senate Foreign Relations Committee* (Historical Series) IV. 82d Cong., 2d sess., 1952. Made public October 1976.
———. *Executive Sessions of the Senate Foreign Relations Committee.* 90th Cong., 1st sess., 6 April, 8 June, 22 August, and 11 October 1967. Made public August 1985.
———. *Genocide Convention: Hearing on Executive O. 81st Congress, 1st Session—The Convention on the Prevention and Punishment of the Crime of Genocide.* 97th Cong., 1st sess., 3 December 1981.
———. *Genocide Convention: Hearing on Executive O. 81st Congress, 1st Session—The Convention on the Prevention and Punishment of the Crime of Genocide.* 98th Cong., 2d sess., 12 September 1984.
———. *Genocide Convention: Hearings before a Subcommittee of the Committee on Foreign Relations.* 91st Cong., 2d sess., 24, 27 April and 22 May 1970.
———. *Genocide Convention: Hearings on the International Convention on the Prevention and Punishment of the Crime of Genocide.* 95th Cong., 1st sess., 24, 26 May 1977.
———. *Genocide Convention: Report on the International Convention on the Prevention and Punishment of the Crime of Genocide.* 81st Cong., 1st sess., 18 July 1985.
———. *Human Rights Conventions: Hearings before a Subcommittee of the Committee on Foreign Relations. Part I.* 90th Cong., 1st sess., 23 February and 8 March 1967.

———. *Human Rights Conventions: Hearing before the Committee on Foreign Relations. Part II.* 90th Cong., 1st sess., 13 September 1967.

———. *International Convention on the Prevention and Punishment of the Crime of Genocide. Report of the Committee on Foreign Relations.* 81st Cong., 1st sess., 24 September 1984.

———. *International Convention on the Prevention and Punishment of the Crime of Genocide.* 92d Cong., 1st sess., 4 May 1971.

———. *International Convention on the Prevention and Punishment of the Crime of Genocide.* 94th Cong., 2d sess., 29 April 1976.

———. *International Human Rights Treaties: Hearing before the Committee on Foreign Relations.* 96th Cong., 1st sess., 14, 15, 16, 19 November 1979.

———. *Women's Political Rights Conventions. Report of the Committee on Foreign Relations.* 94th Cong., 1st sess., 18 December 1975.

U.S. Congress. Senate. Subcommittee of the Committee on Foreign Relations. *Genocide Convention: Hearing on Executive O., 81st Congress, 1st Session—The Convention on the Prevention and Punishment of the Crime of Genocide.* 92d Cong., 1st sess., 10 March 1971.

———. *The Genocide Convention. Hearings on Executive O.—The International Convention on the Prevention and Punishment of the Crime of Genocide.* 81st Cong., 2d sess., 23, 24, 25 January and 9 February 1950.

U.S. Congress. Senate. Subcommittee of the Committee on the Judiciary. *Constitutional Issues Relating to the Proposed Genocide Convention: Hearing before the Subcommittee on the Constitution of the Committee on the Judiciary.* 99th Cong., 1st sess., 26 February 1985.

———. *Treaties and Executive Agreements: Hearings on S.J. Res. 130—Proposing an Amendment to the Constitution of the United States Relative to the Making of Treaties and Executive Agreements.* 82d Cong., 2d sess., 21, 22, 27, 28 May and 9 June 1952.

———. *Treaties and Executive Agreements: Hearings on S.J. Res. 1 and S.J. Res. 43—Proposing an Amendment to the Constitution of the United States Relative to the Making of Treaties and Executive Agreements.* 83d Cong., 1st sess., 18, 19, 25 February, 4, 10, 16, 27, 31 March, and 6, 7, 8, 9, 10, 11 April 1953.

U.S. Department of State. "Background Statement Regarding the Development of Convention No. 105." In *Message from the President of the United States Transmitting the Convention Concerning the Abolition of Forced Labor (Convention No. 105), Adopted by the International Labor Conference at the 40th Session, Geneva, June 25, 1957.*

———. *Bulletin.* Various issues, 1944–89.

———. *Foreign Relations of the United States: 1952–1954.* Vol. 1, pt. 2. Washington, 1983.

———. "Letter of Submittal." In *Message from the United States Transmitting Four Treaties Pertaining to Human Rights,* 23 February 1978, pp. v–xv.

———. "Letter of Transmittal." In *Message from the President of the United States Transmitting Four Treaties Pertaining to Human Rights,* 23 February 1978, pp. iii–iv.

———. *Message from the President of the United States, Transmitting A Certified Copy of the Convention on the Prevention and Punishment of the Crime of Genocide.* 16 June 1949.

_____. *Message from the President of the United States Transmitting Four Treaties Pertaining to Human Rights*. 23 February 1978.

_____. *Message from the President of the United States Transmitting the Convention Concerning the Abolition of Forced Labor (Convention No. 105), Adopted by the International Labor Conference at the 40th Session, Geneva, June 25, 1957*.

_____. *Message from the President of the United States Transmitting the Convention on the Political Rights of Women, Signed at New York, March 31, 1953*. 22 July 1963.

_____. "Report of the Acting Secretary of State." In *Message of the President of the United States Transmitting a Certified Copy of the Convention on the Prevention and Punishment of the Crime of Genocide*. 16 July 1949.

_____. "Report of the Secretary of State." In *Message from the President of the United States Transmitting the Convention on the Political Rights of Women, Signed at New York, March 31, 1953*. 22 July 1963.

_____. *United States Participation in the United Nations, 1948*. Washington, 1949.

_____. Office of Public Affairs. *Questions and Answers on the U.N. Charter, Genocide Convention, and Proposed Covenant on Human Rights*. Washington, June 1952.

U.S. President's Committee on Civil Rights. *To Secure These Rights*. Washington, 1947.

United Nations Documents

United Nations. *Conference on Freedom of Information: Final Act*. Geneva, Switzerland, 23 March, 21 April 1948.

United Nations. *Multilateral Treaties Deposited with the Secretary General: Status as at 31 December 1988*. New York, 1988.

United Nations. *United Nations Action in the Field of Human Rights*. New York, 1980.

United Nations. *The United Nations and Human Rights*. New York, 1973.

United Nations. *Yearbook on Human Rights*. Various volumes, 1946/47–1978/79. New York, published biannually.

United Nations. Commission on Human Rights. U.N. Doc. E/CN.4, Summary Records (SR). Various volumes, 1946–78.

United Nations. Economic and Social Council. *Official Records*. Various volumes, 1946–80.

United Nations. General Assembly. *Official Records*. Various volumes, 1946–80.

Interviews

Interviews with Committee and Members staff of the U.S. Senate Committee on Foreign Relations and Committee on the Judiciary, 1984–85.

Interviews with members of the American Bar Association, 1983–86.

Newspapers and Periodicals

American Bar Association Journal, 1944–85.
Christian Century, 1950–56.
Christian Science Monitor, 1950–88.
Daily Worker, 1950–56.
Daughters of the American Revolution Magazine, 1950–56.
The Freeman, 1950–56.
International Lawyer, 1967–79.
Life, 1945–58.
Los Angeles Times, 1950–89.
New York Times, 1944–89.
Reports of the American Bar Association, 1944–80.
Saturday Evening Post, 1945–56.
Washington Alert, 1985.

Books and Articles

Allen, Florence D. *The Treaty as an Instrument of Legislation*. New York: Macmillan, 1952.

Alston, Philip. "The U.N.'s Specialized Agencies and Implementation of the International Covenant on Economic, Social and Cultural Rights." *Columbia Journal of Transnational Law* 18 (1979): 79–118.

American Bar Association. *International Human Rights Treaties, the Rule of Law, and the United States—A Time of Decision* (Washington, D.C.: American Bar Association, 1978).

Asher, Robert E., et al. *The U.N. and Promotion of the General Welfare*. Washington, D.C.: Brookings Institution, 1957.

Auerbach, Jerold. *Unequal Justice: Lawyers and Social Change in Modern America*. New York: Oxford University Press, 1976.

Avery, W. P., and D. P. Forsythe. "Human Rights, National Security, and the U.S. Senate." *International Studies Quarterly* 23 (June 1979): 303–20.

Backus, Dana C. "Preserve the Treaty-Making Powers." *Foreign Policy Bulletin* 32 (15 May 1953): 4, 6.

Ballew, Joseph H. "Assault on American Sovereignty." *The Freeman* 2 (24 March 1952): 397–400.

Barley, Mary F. "Do Americans Want the Genocide Convention Ratified?" *Daughters of the American Revolution Magazine* 85 (April 1951): 289–90.

Barrett, W. "Human Rights and American Foreign Policy—A Symposium." *Commentary* 72 (1981): 25–63.

Berman, William C. *The Politics of Civil Rights in the Truman Administration*. Columbus: Ohio State University Press, 1970.

Bigman, Stanley K. "The 'New Internationalism' Under Attack." *Public Opinion Quarterly* 14 (Summer 1950): 235–61.

Bishop, William W. *International Law Cases and Materials*. Boston: Little, Brown, 1962.

Bitker, Bruno. "Application of the United Nations Universal Declaration of Human Rights Within the United States." *DePaul Law Review* 21 (Winter 1971): 337–75.

_____. "The Constitutionality of International Agreements on Human Rights." *Santa Clara Lawyer* 12 (1972): 279–93.

_____. "Remarks on U.S. Policy of Ratification of the International Human Rights Conventions." *Human Rights Journal* 11 (1969): 657.

_____. "The United States and International Codification of Human Rights: A Case of Split Personality." In *The Dynamics of Human Rights in U.S. Foreign Policy*, edited by Natalie Kaufman Hevener, pp. 77–100. New Brunswick, N.J.: Transaction Books, 1981.

Bleicher, Samuel. "The Legal Significance of Re-Citation of General Assembly Resolutions." *American Journal of International Law* 63 (July 1969): 444.

Borchard, Edwin. "Shall the Executive Agreement Replace the Treaty?" *Yale Law Review* 53 (1944): 664–83.

_____. "Treaties and Executive Agreements: A Reply." *Yale Law Review* 54 (1945): 616–64.

Bradshaw, Mary. "Congress and Foreign Policy since 1900." *Annals of the American Academy* 289 (September 1953): 40–48.

Bricker, John W. "The Application of Constitutional Restraints to the Treaty-Making Power." *Daughters of the American Revolution Magazine* 88 (March 1954): 233–34, 264.

_____. "Making Treaties and Other International Agreements." *Annals of the American Academy* 289 (September 1953): 134–44.

_____. "Safeguarding the Treaty Power." *Federal Bar Journal* 13 (December 1952): 77–98.

_____. "UN Blueprint for Tyranny." *The Freeman* 2 (28 January 1952): 265–68.

Bricker, John W., and Charles H. Webb. "The Bricker Amendment: Treaty Law vs. Domestic Constitutional Law." *Notre Dame Lawyer* 29 (August 1954): 529–50.

"The Bricker Amendment." *Michigan State Bar Journal* 34 (1955): 20–37.

"Bricker Treaty Amendment Debate." *Congressional Quarterly Almanac* 10 (1954): 254–62.

Brown, Ben, Jr. "Congress and the Department of State." *Annals of the American Academy* 289 (September 1953): 100–107.

Brownlie, Ian. *Basic Documents on Human Rights*. Oxford: Clarendon Press, 1971.

Buckley, William F., Jr. "The Party and the Deep Blue Sea." *Commonweal* 55 (25 January 1952): 391–93.

Buergenthal, Thomas, ed. *Human Rights, International Law and the Helsinki Accord*. Montclair, N.J.: Allanheld, Osmun, 1978.

Bunyon, Bryant, and Robert H. Jones. "The U.S. and the 1948 Genocide Convention." *Harvard International Law Journal* 16 (Summer 1975): 683–704.

Carlston, Kenneth S. "The Genocide Convention: A Problem for the American Lawyer." *American Bar Association Journal* 36 (March 1950): 206–9.

Carroll, Mitchell B. "Further Action on United Nations Charter." *American Bar Association Journal* 31 (September 1945): 457–58.

———. "State Department and the Bar Discuss World Organization." *American Bar Association Journal* 31 (March 1945): 124–25.

Cater, Douglass. "Congress and the President." *The Reporter* 8–9 (May 12, 1953): 15–16.

Chafee, Zechariah, Jr. "Stop Being Terrified of Treaties: Stop Being Scared of the Constitution." *American Bar Association Journal* 38 (September 1952): 731–34.

Christenson, Gordon A. "The Uses of Human Rights Norms to Inform Constitutional Interpretation." *Houston Journal of International Law* 4 (Autumn 1981): 39–57.

Clinchy, Russel J. "Danger to Our Rights Seen." *New York Times*, 9 April 1952.

Commission to Study the Organization of Peace. *The United Nations and Human Rights: Eighteenth Report of the Commission to Study the Organization of Peace*. Dobbs Ferry, N.Y.: Oceana, 1968.

"Congress Takes a Careful Look at the UN's Genocide Treaty." *Congressional Digest* 29 (December 1950): 291–320.

"Curbing the Treaty Power." *Congressional Digest* 31 (November 1952): 257–88.

Cushman, Robert. *Leading Constitutional Decisions*. New York: Appleton-Century-Crofts, 1966.

———. "Our Civil Rights Become a World Issue." *New York Times Magazine*, 11 January 1948, 12, 22–24.

Dalfiume, Richard. *Desegregation of the U.S. Armed Forces: Fighting on Two Fronts, 1939–1953*. Columbia: University of Missouri Press, 1969.

D'Amato, Anthony. "The Concept of Human Rights in International Law." *Columbia Law Journal* 82 (1982): 1110–59.

Davies, Lawrence. "Bar Group Seeks Curb on President." *New York Times*, 16 September 1952.

Deconde, Alexander. *A History of American Foreign Policy*. New York: Charles Scribner's Sons, 1971.

Delbrueck, Jost. "International Protection of Human Rights and State Sovereignty." *Indiana Law Journal* 57 (1983): 567–78.

Del Sesto, Steven. "Nuclear Reactor Safety and the Role of the Congressman: A Content Analysis of Congressional Hearings." *Journal of Politics* 42 (1980): 227–41.

Deutsch, Eberhard P. "The Need for a Treaty Amendment: A Restatement and a Reply." *American Bar Association Journal* 38 (September 1952): 735–80.

Dewar, Helen. "Senate Ratifies Genocide Ban." *Washington Post*, 20 February 1986.

Divine, Robert A. *Since 1945: Politics and Diplomacy in Recent American History*. New York: John Wiley and Sons, 1975.

Dulles, John Foster. "The Challenge of Our Time: Peace with Justice." *American Bar Association Journal* 39 (December 1953): 1063–66.

Eckel, George. "U.S. Delay Urged on U.N. Rights Plan." *New York Times*, 1 February 1949.

Edwards, Richard, Jr. "Contribution of the Genocide Convention to the Development of International Law." *Ohio Northern University Law Review* 8 (1981): 300–328.

Fagen, Patricia Weiss. "The U.S. and International Human Rights 1946–1977." *Universal Human Rights* 2 (1980): 19–33.

Falk, Richard A. *Human Rights and State Sovereignty*. New York: Holmes & Meier, 1981.

———. "Ideological Patterns in the United States Human Rights Debate: 1945–1978." In *The Dynamics of Human Rights in U.S. Foreign Policy*, edited by Natalie Kaufman Hevener, pp. 29–51. New Brunswick, N.J.: Transaction Books, 1981.

Farer, Tom, ed. *Toward a Humanitarian Diplomacy: A Primer for Policy*. New York: New York University Press, 1980.

Farmer, Fyke. "Now—Is the Accepted Time." *American Bar Association Journal* 32 (May 1946): 267–71.

Feder, Don. "The Genocide Treaty: Empty Words and Dangerous Responsibilities." *Los Angeles Daily Journal*, 3 June 1985.

Felton, John. "Approval of Genocide Treaty Expected Soon." *Congressional Quarterly Almanac* 132 (7 September 1985): 1751.

Fensterwald, Bernard, Jr. "Trojan Horse or Don Quixote's Windmill?" *Federal Bar Journal* 13 (1953): 86.

Ferguson, C. C. "The United Nations Human Rights Covenants: Problems of Ratification and Implementation." *American Society of International Law Proceedings* 62 (1968): 83–96.

Finch, George. "Genocide Convention." *American Journal of International Law* 43 (October 1949): 732–38.

Fitzpatrick, William H. "Government by Treaty: What We Can Do About It." *New Orleans State*, 18 December 1950.

Fleming, William. "Danger to America: The Draft Covenant on Human Rights." *American Bar Association Journal* 37 (October, November 1951): 739–99, 816–60.

Forsythe, David P. *Human Rights and United States Foreign Policy*. Gainesville: University of Florida Press, 1988.

———. *Human Rights and World Politics*. Lincoln: University of Nebraska Press, 1983.

Freeland, Richard. *The Truman Doctrine and the Origins of McCarthyism*. New York: Alfred A. Knopf, 1972.

Friedlander, Robert H. "Should the U.S. Constitution's Treaty-Making Power Be Used as the Basis for Enactment of Domestic Legislation?: Implications of the Senate-Approved Genocide Convention." *Case Western Reserve Journal of International Law* 18 (Spring 1986): 267–76.

Friedman, Leon. *The Civil Rights Reader: Basic Documents of the Civil Rights Movement*. New York: Walker, 1986.

Gamble, John King. "Reservations to Multilateral Treaties: A Macroscopic View of State Practice." *American Journal of International Law* 74 (April 1980): 372–94.

Garrett, Garet. "Nullification by Treaty." *The Freeman* 3 (4 May 1953): 549–50.

Garrett, Steve. "Foreign Policy and the American Constitution: The Bricker

Amendment in Contemporary Perspective." *International Studies Quarterly* 16 (June 1972): 187–220.

Gerson, Louis. *J. F. Dulles*. Vol. 17 of *The American Secretaries of State and Their Diplomacy*, edited by Robert Ferrell (New York: Cooper Square Publishers, 1962).

Glennon, Michael J. "The Senate Role in Treaty Ratification." *American Journal of International Law* 77 (April 1983): 257–80.

Goebel, Dorothy. "Congress and Foreign Relations Before 1900." *Annals of the American Academy* 289 (September 1953): 22–39.

Goldberg, Arthur, and Richard Gardner. "Time to Act on the Genocide Convention." *American Bar Association Journal* 58 (February 1972): 141–45.

Graglia, Lino A. *Disaster by Decree: The Supreme Court Decisions on Race and the Schools*. Ithaca: Cornell University Press, 1976.

Green, James Frederick. *The United Nations and Human Rights*. Washington, D.C.: The Brookings Institution, 1956.

Gregory, Tappan. "International Legislation Without the Consent of Congress?" *American Bar Association Journal* 34 (August 1948): 698–700.

Griffith, Ernest. "The Place of Congress in Foreign Relations." *Annals of the American Academy* 289 (September 1953): 11–21.

Griffith, Robert. "American Politics and the Origins of 'McCarthyism.' " In *The Specter*, edited by Robert Griffith and Athan Theoharis, pp. 2–17. New York: New Viewpoints, 1974.

Gurewitsch, A. David. *Eleanor Roosevelt: Her Day*. New York: Quadrangle/New York Times, 1973.

Hackworth, Green H. "The International Court of Justice and the Codification of International Law." *American Bar Association Journal* 32 (February 1946): 81–86.

Haight, G. W. "Human Rights Covenants." *American Society of International Law Proceedings* (1968): 96–103.

———. "United Nations Affairs: International Covenants on Human Rights (1966)." *International Lawyer* 1 (1966–67): 475–89.

Hambro, Edvard. "Human Rights and States Rights." *American Bar Association Journal* 56 (April 1970): 360–63.

Hatch, Vernon. "The Treaty-Making Power: 'An Extraordinary Power Liable to Abuse.' " *American Bar Association Journal* 39 (September 1953): 808–11, 853–55.

Hatch, Vernon, George Finch, and Frank Ober. "The Treaty Power and the Constitution: The Case for Amendment." *American Bar Association Journal* 40 (March 1954): 207–10, 252–60.

Hazlitt, Henry. "Give the House a Treaty Vote." *The Freeman* 4 (5 April 1954): 479–81.

———. "Secretarial Somersault." *The Freeman* 4 (5 October 1953): 13–14.

Hendrick, James P. "An International Bill of Human Rights." *U.S. Department of State Bulletin* 18 (15 February 1948): 195–208.

———. "Progress Report on Human Rights." *U.S. Department of State Bulletin* 19 (8 August 1948): 159–72, 186.

Henkin, Louis. "The Constitution, Treaties and International Human Rights." *University of Pennsylvania Law Review* 116 (1965): 1012–32.

_____. "Constitutional Issues in Foreign Policy." *Journal of International Affairs* 23 (1969): 210–24.

_____. The Covenant on Civil and Political Rights." In *U.S. Ratification of the Human Rights Treaties: With or Without Reservations?*, edited by Richard B. Lillich, pp. 20–26. Charlottesville: University Press of Virginia, 1981.

_____. *Foreign Affairs and the Constitution.* New York: W. W. Norton, 1972.

_____. *The International Bill of Rights.* New York: Columbia University Press, 1981.

_____. "The Treaty Makers and the Law Makers: The Law of the Land and Foreign Relations." *University of Pennsylvania Law Review* 107 (May 1959): 903–36.

Heros, Alfred. *The Southerner and World Affairs.* Baton Rouge: Louisiana State University Press, 1965.

Hevener, Natalie Kaufman. "Drafting the Human Rights Covenants: An Exploration of the Relationship Between U.S. Participation and Non-Ratification." *World Affairs* 148 (Spring 1986): 233–44.

_____. *International Law and the Status of Women.* Boulder, Colo.: Westview Press, 1982.

_____, ed. *The Dynamics of Human Rights in U.S. Foreign Policy.* New Brunswick, N.J.: Transaction Books, 1981.

Hevener, Natalie Kaufman, and Steven Mosher. "General Principles of Law and the UN Covenant on Civil and Political Rights." *International and Comparative Law Quarterly* 27 (July 1978): 596–613.

Hill, Gladwin. "U.N. Rights Drafts Held Socialistic." *New York Times*, 18 September 1948.

Hinton, Harold C. "The Bricker Amendment." *Commonweal* 56 (15 August 1952): 458–60.

Hogan, Edward. "Limitations on the Secret Treaty Power." *Hastings Law Journal* 5 (Spring 1954): 118–32.

Holcombe, Arthur N. "The Covenant on Human Rights." *Law and Contemporary Problems* 14 (1949): 413–30.

Holloway, Kaye. *Modern Trends in Treaty Law: Constitutional Law, Reservations and the Three Modes of Legislation.* Dobbs Ferry, N.Y.: Oceana, 1967.

Holman, Frank E. "The Greatest Threat to American Freedom." *Daughters of the American Revolution Magazine* 47 (August 1953): 981–88, 1005.

_____. *History of the Bricker Amendment.* Seattle: Argus Press, 1955.

_____. "An 'International Bill of Rights': Proposals Have Dangerous Implications for U.S." *American Bar Association Journal* 34 (November 1984): 984–86, 1078–81.

_____. *The Life and Career of a Western Lawyer, 1886–1961.* Baltimore: Port City Press, 1963.

_____. "1949 Regional Conference Solicitous for American System of Rights." *American Bar Association Journal* 35 (March 1949): 203–4.

_____. *1956: The Year of Victory.* Seattle: Argus Press, 1955.

_____. "President Holman's Comments on Mr. Moskowitz's Reply." *American Bar Association Journal* 35 (April 1949): 288–90, 360–62.

_____. "The President's Page." *American Bar Association Journal* 35 (March 1949): 201–3.

_____. "Treaty Law-Making." *Washington Law Review and State Bar Journal* 25 (November 1950): 382–400.

_____. "Treaty Law-Making: A Blank Check for Writing a New Constitution." *American Bar Association Journal* 36 (September 1950): 707–10, 787–90.

_____. " 'World Government' No Answer to America's Desire for Peace." *American Bar Association Journal* 32 (October 1946): 642–44, 718–21.

Holsti, Ole. *Content Analysis for the Social Sciences and Humanities.* Menlo Park, Calif.: Addison-Wesley, 1969.

Hudson, Manley O. "The World Court: America's Declaration Accepting Jurisdiction." *American Bar Association Journal* 32 (December 1946): 832–36, 895–97.

_____. "World Court: Reservations to the Genocide Convention." *American Journal of International Law* 46 (1952): 1–8.

Hula, Erich. "International Law and the Protection of Human Rights." In *Law and Politics in the World Community,* edited by George Lipsky, pp. 162–90. Berkeley: University of California Press, 1953.

Humphrey, John P. *Human Rights and the United Nations: A Great Adventure.* New York: Transnational Publishers, 1984.

_____. "The U.N. and Human Rights." *Howard Law Journal* 11 (Spring 1965): 373–79.

Johnson, Lock, and James McCormick. "The Making of International Agreements: A Reappraisal of Congressional Investment." *Journal of Politics* 40 (May 1973): 468–78.

Kaufman, Natalie Hevener, and David Whiteman. "Opposition to Human Rights Treaties in the United States Senate: The Legacy of the Bricker Amendment." *Human Rights Quarterly* 10 (1988): 309–37.

Kefauver, Estes. "Executive-Congressional Liaison." *Annals of the American Academy* 289 (September 1953): 108–13.

Kegley, Charles W., Jr., and Eugene R. Wittkopf. *American Foreign Policy: Pattern and Process.* New York: St. Martin's Press, 1982.

Kluger, Richard. *Simple Justice: The History of Brown vs. Board of Education and Black America's Struggle for Equality.* New York: Alfred A. Knopf, 1976.

Koh, Jean Kyongun. "Reservations to Multilateral Treaties: How Legal Doctrine Reflects World Visions." *Harvard International Law Journal* 23 (Spring 1982): 71–116.

Kotschnig, Walter. "ECOSOC 1948: A Review and Forecast." *U.S. Department of State Bulletin* 20 (2 January 1949): 3–17.

Kuhn, A. K. "The Genocide Convention and States Rights." *American Journal of International Law* 43 (July 1949): 498–501.

Kushin, Phil. "The Genocide Convention: Unknown Treaty Incites Furor." *United States Press,* 5 March 1985.

Lash, Joseph. *Eleanor: The Years Alone.* New York: W. W. Norton, 1972.

LeBlanc, Lawrence J. "The ICJ, the Genocide Convention, and the United States." *Wisconsin International Law Journal* 6 (Fall 1987): 43–74.

_____. "The Intent to Destroy Groups in the Genocide Convention: The Proposed U.S. Understanding." *American Journal of International Law* 78 (April 1984): 369–85.

_____. "The United Nations Genocide Convention and Political Groups:

Should the United States Propose an Amendment?" *Yale Journal of International Law* 13 (Summer 1988): 268–95.

Lerche, Charles O., Jr. *The Uncertain South*. Chicago: Quadrangle Books, 1964.

Lillich, Richard B. "The Contributions of the United States to the Promotion and Protection of International Human Rights." In *The Dynamics of Human Rights in U.S. Foreign Policy*, edited by Natalie Kaufman Hevener, pp. 291–319. New Brunswick, N.J.: Transaction Books, 1981.

———. *U.S. Ratification of the Human Rights Treaties: With or Without Reservations?* Charlottesville: University Press of Virginia, 1981.

Lipsky, George, ed. *Law and Politics in the World Community*. Berkeley: University of California Press, 1953.

Lockwood, Bert B., Jr. "The United Nations Charter and United States Civil Rights Litigation: 1946–1955." *Iowa Law Review* 69 (May 1984): 901–49.

Lora, Ronald. "A View From the Right: Conservative Intellectuals, the Cold War, and McCarthy." In *The Spector*, edited by Robert Griffith and Athan Theoharis, pp. 40–71. New York: New Viewpoints, 1974.

Lord, Mrs. Oswald B. "Economic and Social Council's Work in Social Field." *U.S. Department of State Bulletin* 31 (27 December 1954): 1008–11.

———. "A New Approach to Human Rights." *U.S. Department of State Bulletin* 33 (15 August 1955): 277–82.

———. "New U.S. Action Program for Human Rights." *U.S. Department of State Bulletin* 29 (17 August 1953): 215–22.

———. "Principles Involved in Human Rights Covenants." *U.S. Department of State Bulletin* 31 (6 December 1954): 876–79.

McBride, Nicholas. "After 40 Years, U.S. Appears Ready to Ratify U.N. Genocide Treaty." *Christian Science Monitor*, 10 May 1988.

MacChesney, Brunson. "The Bricker Amendment: The Fallacies in the Case for the Amendment." *Notre Dame Lawyer* 29 (August 1954): 551–82.

———. "Should the United States Ratify the Covenants?: A Question of Merits, Not of Constitutional Law." *American Journal of International Law* 62 (October 1968): 912–17.

MacChesney, Brunson, Myres McDougal, Robert E. Matthews, Covey T. Oliver, and F. D. G. Ribbie. "The Treaty Power and the Constitution: The Case Against Amendment." *American Bar Association Journal* 40 (March 1954): 203–6, 248–52.

McDougal, Myres, and R. Arens. "Genocide Convention and the Constitution." *Vanderbilt Law Review* 3 (June 1950): 683–710.

McDougal, Myres, and Lung-Chu Chen. "Human Rights and Jurisprudence." *Hofstra Law Review* 9 (1981): 337–56.

McDougal, Myres, and Asher Lans. "Treaties and Congressional-Executive or Presidential Agreements: Interchangeable Instruments of National Policy." *Yale Law Journal* (March 1945): 181–351, 534–615.

McDougal, Myres, Harold D. Lasswell, and Lung-Chu Chen. *Human Rights and World Public Order*. New Haven: Yale University Press, 1980.

Mathews, J. B. "Civil Liberties Upside Down." *American Mercury* 72 (March–April 1953): 34–49.

Merin, K. D. *The Bricker Amendment: Limiting the Treaty Power by Constitutional*

Amendment. Congressional Research Service. Washington, D.C.: Library of Congress, 1978.

Molineu, Harold. "Carter and Human Rights: Administrative Impact of a Symbolic Policy." *Policy Studies Journal* 8 (1980): 879–83.

Morse, Wayne. "Significance of the Senate Action for International Justice Through Law." *American Bar Association Journal* 32 (November 1946): 776–79, 812–15.

Mower, Glenn. *The United States, the United Nations, and Human Rights: The Eleanor Roosevelt and Jimmy Carter Eras.* Westport, Conn.: Greenwood Press, 1979.

Murphy, Cornelius F., Jr. "Objections to Western Conceptions of Human Rights." *Hofstra Law Review* 9 (1981): 434–47.

Murphy, Walter F. *Congress and the Court.* Chicago: University of Chicago Press, 1962.

The National Cyclopaedia of American Biography. New York: James T. White, 1952.

Newberg, Paula. *The Politics of Human Rights.* New York: New York University Press, 1981.

Newman, Frank C., and Richard B. Lillich. *International Human Rights: Problems of Law and Policy.* Boston: Little, Brown, 1979.

Ober, Frank. "The Treaty-Making and Amending Powers: Do They Protect Our Fundamental Rights?" *American Bar Association Journal* 36 (September 1950): 715–19, 793–96.

Oliver, Covey T. "The Enforcement of Treaties by a Federal State." *Recueil de Cours* 141 (1974): 332–412.

———. "Getting the Senators to Accept the Reference of Treaties to Both Houses for Approval by Simple Majorities." *The American Journal of International Law* 74 (1980): 142–44.

———. "Problems of Cognition and Interpretation in Applying Norms of Customary International Law of Human Rights in United States Courts." *Houston Journal of International Law* 4 (Autumn 1981): 59–63.

———. "The Treaty Power and National Foreign Policy as Vehicles for the Enforcement of Human Rights in the United States." *Hofstra Law Review* 9 (1981): 411–32.

Ornstein, Norman J., Thomas E. Mann, Michael J. Malbin, and John F. Bibby. *Vital Statistics on Congress: 1982.* Washington, D.C.: American Enterprise Institute for Public Policy Research, 1982.

Patton, Marguerite, and Frances B. Lucas. "Bill of Rights." *Daughters of the American Revolution Magazine* 88 (December 1954): 1237–38.

———. "Covenant of Human Rights." *Daughters of the American Revolution Magazine* 88 (June 1954): 662.

———. "The Story of the Bricker Amendment." *Daughters of the American Revolution Magazine* 88 (September 1954): 936–38.

———. "The United Nations." *Daughters of the American Revolution Magazine* 87 (August 1953): 997–99.

Pearson, Theodore, and Dana Converse Backus. "Save the Peace Power: Don't Strait-Jacket Treaties." *American Bar Association Journal* 39 (September 1953): 804–8.

Pechota, Vratislav. "The Development of the Covenant on Civil and Political Rights." In *The International Bill of Rights*, edited by Louis Henkin, pp. 32–71. New York: Columbia University Press, 1981.

Philips, Draper W. "The Senate Must Recover Its Lost Powers in Treaty Making." *Saturday Evening Post* 223 (3 March 1951): 12.

Phillips, Orie L. "The Genocide Convention: Its Effect on Our Legal System." *American Bar Association Journal* 35 (August 1949): 623–25.

Phillips, Orie L., and Eberhard P. Deutsch. "Pitfalls of the Genocide Convention." *American Bar Association Journal* 56 (July 1970): 641–46.

Pusey, Merlo J. *Eisenhower the President*. New York: Macmillan, 1956.

Ramcharan, B. G., ed. *Human Rights: Thirty Years After the Declaration*. The Hague: Martinus Nijhoff, 1979.

Ransom, William. "United Nations Will Proceed with Declaration and Covenant on Human Rights." *American Bar Association Journal* 34 (December 1948): 1091.

Raymond, Jim. "Don't Ratify the Human Rights Conventions." *American Bar Association Journal* 54 (February 1968): 141.

Raymond, John. "Genocide: An Unconstitutional Human Rights Convention?" *Santa Clara Lawyer* 12 (1972): 294–318.

Rehm, John B. "Making Foreign Policy through International Agreement." In *The Constitution and the Conduct of Foreign Policy*, edited by Francis O. Wilcox and Richard A. Frank, pp. 126–38. New York: Praeger, 1976.

Reynolds, Katharine, and Frances Lucas. "International Criminal Court." *Daughters of the American Revolution Magazine* 87 (February 1953): 191–92.

――――. "International Criminal Jurisdiction." *Daughters of the American Revolution Magazine* 86 (January 1952): 31.

――――. "Let Us Be Thankful." *Daughters of the American Revolution Magazine* 84 (November 1950): 877.

――――. "Mid-Century Appraisal." *Daughters of the American Revolution Magazine* 87 (June 1953): 767–69.

――――. "A Proposed Constitutional Amendment." *Daughters of the American Revolution Magazine* 86 (May 1952): 609.

――――. "Threats to Americanism." *Daughters of the American Revolution Magazine* 86 (December 1952): 1299–1304.

――――. "United Nations." *Daughters of the American Revolution Magazine* 87 (February 1953): 191–92.

――――. "Wake Up America." *Daughters of the American Revolution Magazine* 84 (December 1950): 939–42.

――――. "We Take Our Stand." *Daughters of the American Revolution Magazine* 86 (June 1952): 733–37.

Rix, Carl B. "Human Rights and International Law: Effect of the Covenant Under Our Constitution." *American Bar Association Journal* 35 (July 1949): 551–54, 618–21.

Robertson, A. H., ed. *Human Rights in National and International Law*. Dobbs Ferry, N.Y.: Oceana, 1968.

――――. *Human Rights in the World*. Manchester: Manchester University Press, 1972.

Rodley, Nigel. "On the Necessity of United States Ratification of the International Human Rights Conventions." In *U.S. Ratification of the Human Rights Treaties: With or Without Reservations?*, edited by Richard B. Lillich, pp. 3–19. Charlottesville: University Press of Virginia, 1981.

Roosevelt, Eleanor. "Progress Toward Completion of Human Rights Covenant." *U.S. Department of State Bulletin* 26 (30 June 1952): 1024–28.

———. "Reply to Attack on U.S. Attitude Toward Human Rights Covenant." *U.S. Department of State Bulletin* 26 (14 January 1952): 59–61.

Rosenthal, Jay. "Legal and Political Considerations of the United States Ratification of the Genocide Convention." *Antioch Law Journal* 3 (Spring 1985): 111–44.

Rovere, Richard. "A Letter from Washington." *New Yorker* 25 (11 February 1950): 50–58.

Rovine, Arthur W. "Separation of Powers and International Executive Agreements." *Indiana Law Journal* 52 (Winter 1977): 397–431.

Rubin, Barry M., and Elizabeth P. Spiro. *Human Rights and U.S. Foreign Policy*. Boulder, Colo.: Westview Press, 1979.

Schiller, Barry M. "Life in a Symbolic Universe: Comments on the Genocide Convention and International Law." *Southwestern University Law Review* 4 (1977): 47–83.

Schlueter, Bernard. "Domestic Status of Human Rights Clauses of the United Nations Charter." *California Law Review* 61 (1973): 110–64.

Schmidhauser, John, and Larry Berg. "The ABA and the Human Rights Conventions: The Political Significance of Private Professional Associations." *Social Forces* 38 (1971): 362–410.

Schwelb, Egon. "Entry into Force of the International Covenants on Human Rights and the Optional Protocol to the International Covenant on Civil and Political Rights." *American Journal of International Law* 70 (July 1976): 511–19.

———. *Human Rights and the International Community*. Chicago: Quadrangle Books, 1964.

———. "The United Nations and Human Rights." *Howard Law Journal* 2 (Spring 1965): 356–73.

Sieghart, Paul. *The International Law of Human Rights*. Oxford: Clarendon Press, 1983.

Simsarian, James. "Economic, Social and Cultural Provisions in the Human Rights Covenant." *U.S. Department of State Bulletin* 24 (25 June 1951): 1003–14.

———. "Human Rights: Draft Covenant Revised at Fifth Session of Commission on Human Rights." *U.S. Department of State Bulletin* 21 (11 July 1949): 3–12.

———. "Proposed Human Rights Covenant." *U.S. Department of State Bulletin* 22 (12 June 1950): 945–54.

———. "United Nations Action on Human Rights in 1948." *U.S. Department of State Bulletin* 20 (2 January 1949): 18–23.

Sinclair, Ian. *The Vienna Convention on the Law of Treaties*. Manchester: Manchester University Press, 1984.

Skelton, James W. "United States Approach to Ratification of the International Covenants on Human Rights." *Houston Journal of International Law* 1 (Spring 1979): 103–25.

Sohn, Louis. "The Development of International Law: Drafting and Implementing an International Covenant on Human Rights." *American Bar Association Journal* 34 (March 1948): 200–201.

_____. "A Short History of United Nations Documents on Human Rights." In *The United Nations and Human Rights: Eighteenth Report of the Commission to Study the Organization of Peace*, by Commission to Study the Organization of Peace, pp. 39–186. Dobbs Ferry, N.Y.: Oceana, 1968.

Sohn, Louis, and Thomas Buergenthal. *International Protection of Human Rights*. New York: Bobbs-Merrill, 1973.

Spanier, John. "Congress and the Presidency: The Weakest Link in the Policy Process." In *Congress, the Presidency, and American Foreign Policy*, edited by John Spanier and Joseph Nogee, pp. ix–xxxii. New York: Pergamon Press, 1981.

Spanier, John, and Eric Uslaner. *How American Foreign Policy is Made*. New York: Praeger, 1975.

Stettinius, Edward. "United Nations Conference on International Organization: Provisions on Human Rights." *U.S. Department of State Bulletin* 12 (1945): 928–30.

Stover, Henry. "Genocide Treaty Dead for This Year: Major Victory for Populists over Internationalists." *The Spotlight* 10 (22 October 1984).

Stupak, Ronald J. *American Foreign Policy*. New York: Harper and Row, 1976.

Sutherland, Arthur. "The Bricker Amendment, Executive Agreements, and Imported Potatoes." *Harvard Law Review* 67 (1953–54): 281–92.

_____. "Restricting the Treaty Power." *Harvard Law Review* 65 (1951–52): 1305–38.

Swindler, William F. "The Politics of 'Advice and Consent.'" *American Bar Association Journal* 56 (July 1970): 533–42.

Tondel, Lyman M. "The Section on International Law: Its Work and Its Objectives." *American Bar Association Journal* 38 (November 1952): 928–31.

"Treaty Power (Bricker) Amendment." *Congressional Quarterly Almanac* 9 (1953): 233–37, 255–58.

Trussell, C. P. "Bar Group Accused by Carnegie Fund." *New York Times*, 15 October 1950.

Tuttle, James C. "Are the 'Human Rights' Conventions Really Objectionable?" *International Lawyer* 3 (1968–69): 385–96.

_____. "International Human Rights Law and Practice. The Role of the United Nations, the Private Sector, the Government, and Their Lawyers." *International Lawyer* 13 (Summer 1979): 572–74.

Van Dyke, Vernon. *Human Rights, the United States, and World Community*. New York: Oxford University Press, 1970.

Vogelgesang, Sandy. *American Dream, Global Nightmare: The Dilemma of U.S. Human Rights Policy*. New York: W. W. Norton, 1980.

Walz, Jay. "Narrower Limits on Treaties Urged." *New York Times*, 19 February 1953.

Weissbrodt, David. "United States Ratification of the Human Rights Covenants." *Minnesota Law Review* 63 (November 1978): 35–78.

Weston, Burns H. "U.S. Ratification of the International Covenant on Economic, Social and Cultural Rights: With or Without Qualifications?" In *U.S. Ratification of the Human Rights Treaties: With or Without Reservations?*, edited by Richard B. Lillich, pp. 27–28. Charlottesville: University Press of Virginia, 1981.

White, A. A. "Tomorrow One May Be Guilty of Genocide." *Texas Bar Journal* 12 (May 1949): 203–4, 225–29.

Whiteman, Marjorie. "Mrs. Franklin D. Roosevelt and the Human Rights Commission." *American Journal of International Law* 62 (1968): 918–21.

Whitton, J. B., and J. E. Fowler. "Bricker Amendment: Fallacies and Dangers." *American Journal of International Law* 48 (1954): 23–56.

Widener, Alice. "United Nations Bars Private Property as a Human Right." *Human Events*, 25 June 1977.

———. "The UN's Pink Sisters." *The Freeman* 3 (29 December 1952): 233–36.

Wright, Quincy. "National Courts and Human Rights: The Fujii Case." *American Journal of International Law* 45 (1951): 63–82.